AN ESSAY CONCERNING HUMANE UNDERSTANDING, VOLUME II

By John Locke

NATAL PUBLISHING LLC
ARS LONGA, VITA BREVIS

BOOK III
OF WORDS

CHAPTER I.

OF WORDS OR LANGUAGE IN GENERAL.

1. Man fitted to form articulated Sounds.
God, having designed man for a sociable creature, made him not only with an inclination, and under a necessity to have fellowship with those of his own kind, but furnished him also with language, which was to be the great instrument and common tie of society. Man, therefore, had by nature his organs so fashioned, as to be fit to frame articulate sounds, which we call words. But this was not enough to produce language; for parrots, and several other birds, will be taught to make articulate sounds distinct enough, which yet by no means are capable of language.

2. To use these sounds as Signs of Ideas.
Besides articulate sounds, therefore, it was further necessary that he should be able to use these sounds as signs of internal conceptions; and to make them stand as marks for the ideas within his own mind, whereby they might be made known to others, and the thoughts of men's minds be conveyed from one to another.

3. To make them general Signs.
But neither was this sufficient to make words so useful as they ought to be. It is not enough for the perfection of language, that sounds can be made signs of ideas, unless those signs can be so made use of as to comprehend several particular things: for the multiplication of words would have perplexed their use, had every particular thing need of a distinct name to be signified by. [To remedy this inconvenience, language had yet a further improvement in the use of GENERAL TERMS, whereby one word was made to mark a multitude of particular existences: which advantageous use of sounds was obtained only by the difference of the ideas they were made signs of: those names becoming general, which are made to stand for GENERAL IDEAS, and those remaining particular, where the IDEAS they are used for are PARTICULAR.]

4. To make them signify the absence of positive Ideas.
Besides these names which stand for ideas, there be other words which men make use of, not to signify any idea, but the want or absence of some ideas, simple or complex, or all ideas together; such as are NIHIL in Latin,

and in English, IGNORANCE and BARRENNESS. All which negative or privative words cannot be said properly to belong to, or signify no ideas: for then they would be perfectly insignificant sounds; but they relate to positive ideas, and signify their absence.

5. Words ultimately derived from such as signify sensible Ideas.

It may also lead us a little towards the original of all our notions and knowledge, if we remark how great a dependence our words have on common sensible ideas; and how those which are made use of to stand for actions and notions quite removed from sense, have their rise from thence, and from obvious sensible ideas are transferred to more abstruse significations, and made to stand for ideas that come not under the cognizance of our senses; v.g. to IMAGINE, APPREHEND, COMPREHEND, ADHERE, CONCEIVE, INSTIL, DISGUST, DISTURBANCE, TRANQUILLITY, &c., are all words taken from the operations of sensible things, and applied to certain modes of thinking. SPIRIT, in its primary signification, is breath; ANGEL, a messenger: and I doubt not but, if we could trace them to their sources, we should find, in all languages, the names which stand for things that fall not under our senses to have had their first rise from sensible ideas. By which we may give some kind of guess what kind of notions they were, and whence derived, which filled their minds who were the first beginners of languages, and how nature, even in the naming of things, unawares suggested to men the originals and principles of all their knowledge: whilst, to give names that might make known to others any operations they felt in themselves, or any other ideas that came not under their senses, they were fain to borrow words from ordinary known ideas of sensation, by that means to make others the more easily to conceive those operations they experimented in themselves, which made no outward sensible appearances; and then, when they had got known and agreed names to signify those internal operations of their own minds, they were sufficiently furnished to make known by words all their other ideas; since they could consist of nothing but either of outward sensible perceptions, or of the inward operations of their minds about them; we having, as has been proved, no ideas at all, but what originally come either from sensible objects without, or what we feel within ourselves, from the inward workings of our own spirits, of which we are conscious to ourselves within.

6. Distribution of subjects to be treated of.

But to understand better the use and force of Language, as subservient to instruction and knowledge, it will be convenient to consider:

First, TO WHAT IT IS THAT NAMES, IN THE USE OF LANGUAGE, ARE IMMEDIATELY
APPLIED.

Secondly, Since all (except proper) names are general, and so stand not particularly for this or that single thing, but for sorts and ranks of things, it will be necessary to consider, in the next place, what the sorts and kinds, or, if you rather like the Latin names, WHAT THE SPECIES AND GENERA OF THINGS ARE, WHEREIN THEY CONSIST, AND HOW THEY COME TO BE MADE. These being (as they ought) well looked into, we shall the better come to find the right use of words; the natural advantages and defects of language; and the remedies that ought to be used, to avoid the inconveniences of obscurity or uncertainty in the signification of words: without which it is impossible to discourse with any clearness or order concerning knowledge: which, being conversant about propositions, and those most commonly universal ones, has greater connexion with words than perhaps is suspected. These considerations, therefore, shall be the matter of the following chapters.

CHAPTER II.

OF THE SIGNIFICATION OF WORDS.

1. Words are sensible Signs, necessary for Communication of Ideas.
Man, though he have great variety of thoughts, and such from which others as well as himself might receive profit and delight; yet they are all within his own breast, invisible and hidden from others, nor can of themselves be made to appear. The comfort and advantage of society not being to be had without communication of thoughts, it was necessary that man should find out some external sensible signs, whereof those invisible ideas, which his thoughts are made up of, might be made known to others. For this purpose nothing was so fit, either for plenty or quickness, as those articulate sounds, which with so much ease and variety he found himself able to make. Thus we may conceive how WORDS, which were by nature so well adapted to that purpose, came to be made use of by men as the signs of their ideas; not by any natural connexion that there is between particular articulate sounds and certain ideas, for then there would be but one language amongst all men; but by a voluntary imposition, whereby such a word is made arbitrarily the mark of such an idea. The use, then, of words, is to be sensible marks of ideas; and the ideas they stand for are their proper and immediate signification.

2. Words, in their immediate Signification, are the sensible Signs of his Ideas who uses them.
The use men have of these marks being either to record their own thoughts, for the assistance of their own memory; or, as it were, to bring out their ideas, and lay them before the view of others: words, in their primary or immediate signification, stand for nothing but THE IDEAS IN THE MIND OF HIM THAT USES THEM, how imperfectly soever or carelessly those ideas are collected from the things which they are supposed to represent. When a man speaks to another, it is that he may be understood: and the end of speech is, that those sounds, as marks, may make known his ideas to the hearer. That then which words are the marks of are the ideas of the speaker: nor can any one apply them as marks, immediately, to anything else but the ideas that he himself hath: for this would be to make them signs of his own conceptions, and yet apply them to other ideas; which would be to make them signs and not signs of his ideas at the same time; and so in effect to have no signification at all. Words being voluntary signs, they cannot be voluntary signs imposed by him on things he knows not. That

would be to make them signs of nothing, sounds without signification. A man cannot make his words the signs either of qualities in things, or of conceptions in the mind of another, whereof he has none in his own. Till he has some ideas of his own, he cannot suppose them to correspond with the conceptions of another man; nor can he use any signs for them: for thus they would be the signs of he knows not what, which is in truth to be the signs of nothing. But when he represents to himself other men's ideas by some of his own, if he consent to give them the same names that other men do, it is still to his own ideas; to ideas that he has, and not to ideas that he has not.

3. Examples of this.

This is so necessary in the use of language, that in this respect the knowing and the ignorant, the learned and the unlearned, use the words they speak (with any meaning) all alike. They, in every man's mouth, stand for the ideas he has, and which he would express by them. A child having taken notice of nothing in the metal he hears called GOLD, but the bright shining yellow colour, he applies the word gold only to his own idea of that colour, and nothing else; and therefore calls the same colour in a peacock's tail gold. Another that hath better observed, adds to shining yellow great weight: and then the sound gold, when he uses it, stands for a complex idea of a shining yellow and a very weighty substance. Another adds to those qualities fusibility: and then the word gold signifies to him a body, bright, yellow, fusible, and very heavy. Another adds malleability. Each of these uses equally the word gold, when they have occasion to express the idea which they have applied it to: but it is evident that each can apply it only to his own idea; nor can he make it stand as a sign of such a complex idea as he has not.

4. Words are often secretly referred, First to the Ideas supposed to be in other men's minds.

But though words, as they are used by men, can properly and immediately signify nothing but the ideas that are in the mind of the speaker; yet they in their thoughts give them a secret reference to two other things.

First, THEY SUPPOSE THEIR WORDS TO BE MARKS OF THE IDEAS IN THE MINDS ALSO OF OTHER MEN, WITH WHOM THEY COMMUNICATE; for else they should talk in vain, and could not be understood, if the sounds they applied to one idea were such as by the hearer were applied to another, which is to speak two languages. But in this men stand not usually to examine, whether the idea they, and those they discourse with have in their minds be the same: but think it enough that they use the word, as they imagine, in the common acceptation of that language; in which they suppose that the idea they make it a sign of is precisely the same to which the understanding men of that country apply that name.

5. Secondly, to the Reality of Things.

Secondly, Because men would not be thought to talk barely of their own imagination, but of things as really they are; therefore they often suppose the WORDS TO STAND ALSO FOR THE REALITY OF THINGS. But this relating more particularly to substances and their names, as perhaps the former does to simple ideas and modes, we shall speak of these two different ways of applying words more at large, when we come to treat of the names of mixed modes and substances in particular: though give me leave here to say, that it is a perverting the use of words, and brings unavoidable obscurity and confusion into their signification, whenever we make them stand for anything but those ideas we have in our own minds.

6. Words by Use readily excite Ideas of their objects.

Concerning words, also, it is further to be considered:

First, that they being immediately the signs of men's ideas, and by that means the instruments whereby men communicate their conceptions, and express to one another those thoughts and imaginations they have within their own breasts; there comes, by constant use, to be such a connexion between certain sounds and the ideas they stand for, that the names heard, almost as readily excite certain ideas as if the objects themselves, which are apt to produce them, did actually affect the senses. Which is manifestly so in all obvious sensible qualities, and in all substances that frequently and familiarly occur to us.

7. Words are often used without Signification, and Why.

Secondly, That though the proper and immediate signification of words are ideas in the mind of the speaker, yet, because by familiar use from our cradles, we come to learn certain articulate sounds very perfectly, and have them readily on our tongues, and always at hand in our memories, but yet are not always careful to examine or settle their significations perfectly; it often happens that men, even when they would apply themselves to an attentive consideration, do set their thoughts more on words than things. Nay, because words are many of them learned before the ideas are known for which they stand: therefore some, not only children but men, speak several words no otherwise than parrots do, only because they have learned them, and have been accustomed to those sounds. But so far as words are of use and signification, so far is there a constant connexion between the sound and the idea, and a designation that the one stands for the other; without which application of them, they are nothing but so much insignificant noise.

8. Their Signification perfectly arbitrary, not the consequence of a natural connexion.

Words, by long and familiar use, as has been said, come to excite in men certain ideas so constantly and readily, that they are apt to suppose a natural connexion between them. But that they signify only men's peculiar ideas, and that BY A PERFECT ARBITRARY IMPOSITION, is evident, in that they often fail to excite in others (even that use the same language) the same ideas we take them to be signs of: and every man has so inviolable a liberty to make words stand for what ideas he pleases, that no one hath the power to make others have the same ideas in their minds that he has, when they use the same words that he does. And therefore the great Augustus himself, in the possession of that power which ruled the world, acknowledged he could not make a new Latin word: which was as much as to say, that he could not arbitrarily appoint what idea any sound should be a sign of, in the mouths and common language of his subjects. It is true, common use, by a tacit consent, appropriates certain sounds to certain ideas in all languages, which so far limits the signification of that sound, that unless a man applies it to the same idea, he does not speak properly: and let me add, that unless a man's words excite the same ideas in the hearer which he makes them stand for in speaking, he does not speak intelligibly. But whatever be the consequence of any man's using of words differently, either from their general meaning, or the particular sense of the person to whom he addresses them; this is certain, their signification, in his use of them, is limited to his ideas, and they can be signs of nothing else.

CHAPTER III.

OF GENERAL TERMS.

1. The greatest Part of Words are general terms.
All things that exist being particulars, it may perhaps be thought reasonable that words, which ought to be conformed to things, should be so too,—I mean in their signification: but yet we find quite the contrary. The far greatest part of words that make all languages are general terms: which has not been the effect of neglect or chance, but of reason and necessity.

2. That every particular Thing should have a Name for itself is impossible. First, It is impossible that every particular thing should have a distinct peculiar name. For, the signification and use of words depending on that connexion which the mind makes between its ideas and the sounds it uses as signs of them, it is necessary, in the application of names to things, that the mind should have distinct ideas of the things, and retain also the particular name that belongs to every one, with its peculiar appropriation to that idea. But it is beyond the power of human capacity to frame and retain distinct ideas of all the particular things we meet with: every bird and beast men saw; every tree and plant that affected the senses, could not find a place in the most capacious understanding. If it be looked on as an instance of a prodigious memory, that some generals have been able to call every soldier in their army by his proper name, we may easily find a reason why men have never attempted to give names to each sheep in their flock, or crow that flies over their heads; much less to call every leaf of plants, or grain of sand that came in their way, by a peculiar name.

3. And would be useless, if it were possible.
Secondly, If it were possible, it would yet be useless; because it would not serve to the chief end of language. Men would in vain heap up names of particular things, that would not serve them to communicate their thoughts. Men learn names, and use them in talk with others, only that they may be understood: which is then only done when, by use or consent, the sound I make by the organs of speech, excites in another man's mind who hears it, the idea I apply it to in mine, when I speak it. This cannot be done by names applied to particular things; whereof I alone having the ideas in my mind, the names of them could not be significant or intelligible to another, who was not acquainted with all those very particular things which had fallen under my notice.

4. A distinct name for every particular thing not fitted for enlargement of knowledge.

Thirdly, But yet, granting this also feasible, (which I think is not,) yet a distinct name for every particular thing would not be of any great use for the improvement of knowledge: which, though founded in particular things, enlarges itself by general views; to which things reduced into sorts, under general names, are properly subservient. These, with the names belonging to them, come within some compass, and do not multiply every moment, beyond what either the mind can contain, or use requires. And therefore, in these, men have for the most part stopped: but yet not so as to hinder themselves from distinguishing particular things by appropriated names, where convenience demands it. And therefore in their own species, which they have most to do with, and wherein they have often occasion to mention particular persons, they make use of proper names; and there distinct individuals have distinct denominations.

5. What things have proper Names, and why.

Besides persons, countries also, cities, rivers, mountains, and other the like distinctions of place have usually found peculiar names, and that for the same reason; they being such as men have often as occasion to mark particularly, and, as it were, set before others in their discourses with them. And I doubt not but, if we had reason to mention particular horses as often as as have reason to mention particular men, we should have proper names for the one, as familiar as for the other, and Bucephalus would be a word as much in use as Alexander. And therefore we see that, amongst jockeys, horses have their proper names to be known and distinguished by, as commonly as their servants: because, amongst them, there is often occasion to mention this or that particular horse when he is out of sight.

6. How general Words are made.

The next thing to be considered is,—How general words come to be made. For, since all things that exist are only particulars, how come we by general terms; or where find we those general natures they are supposed to stand for? Words become general by being made the signs of general ideas: and ideas become general, by separating from them the circumstances of time and place, and any other ideas that may determine them to this or that particular existence. By this way of abstraction they are made capable of representing more individuals than one; each of which having in it a conformity to that abstract idea, is (as we call it) of that sort.

7. Shown by the way we enlarge our complex ideas from infancy.

But, to deduce this a little more distinctly, it will not perhaps be amiss to trace our notions and names from their beginning, and observe by what degrees we proceed, and by what steps we enlarge our ideas from our first infancy. There is nothing more evident, than that the ideas of the persons children converse with (to instance in them alone) are, like the persons themselves, only particular. The ideas of the nurse and the mother are well framed in their minds; and, like pictures of them there, represent only those individuals. The names they first gave to them are confined to these individuals; and the names of NURSE and MAMMA, the child uses, determine themselves to those persons. Afterwards, when time and a larger acquaintance have made them observe that there are a great many other things in the world, that in some common agreements of shape, and several other qualities, resemble their father and mother, and those persons they have been used to, they frame an idea, which they find those many particulars do partake in; and to that they give, with others, the name MAN, for example. And thus they come to have a general name, and a general idea. Wherein they make nothing new; but only leave out of the complex idea they had of Peter and James, Mary and Jane, that which is peculiar to each, and retain only what is common to them all.

8. And further enlarge our complex ideas, by still leaving out properties contained in them.

By the same way that they come by the general name and idea of MAN, they easily advance to more general names and notions. For, observing that several things that differ from their idea of man, and cannot therefore be comprehended out under that name, have yet certain qualities wherein they agree with man, by retaining only those qualities, and uniting them into one idea, they have again another and more general idea; to which having given a name they make a term of a more comprehensive extension: which new idea is made, not by any new addition, but only as before, by leaving out the shape, and some other properties signified by the name man, and retaining only a body, with life, sense, and spontaneous motion, comprehended under the name animal.

9. General natures are nothing but abstract and partial ideas of more complex ones.

That this is the way whereby men first formed general ideas, and general names to them, I think is so evident, that there needs no other proof of it but the considering of a man's self, or others, and the ordinary proceedings of their minds in knowledge. And he that thinks GENERAL NATURES or NOTIONS are anything else but such abstract and partial ideas of more complex ones, taken at first from particular existences, will, I fear, be at a loss where to find them. For let any one effect, and then tell me, wherein does his idea of MAN differ from that of PETER and PAUL, or his idea of HORSE from that of BUCEPHALUS, but in the leaving out something that is peculiar to each individual, and retaining so much of those particular complex ideas of several particular existences as they are found to agree in? Of the complex ideas signified by the names MAN and HORSE, leaving out but those particulars wherein they differ, and retaining only those wherein they agree, and of those making a new distinct complex idea, and giving the name ANIMAL to it, one has a more general term, that comprehends with man several other creatures. Leave out of the idea of ANIMAL, sense and spontaneous motion, and the remaining complex idea, made up of the remaining simple ones of body, life, and nourishment, becomes a more general one, under the more comprehensive term, VIVENS. And, not to dwell longer upon this particular, so evident in itself; by the same way the mind proceeds to BODY, SUBSTANCE, and at last to BEING, THING, and such universal terms, which stand for any of our ideas whatsoever. To conclude: this whole mystery of genera and species, which make such a noise in the schools, and are with justice so little regarded out of them, is nothing else but ABSTRACT IDEAS, more or less comprehensive, with names annexed to them. In all which this is constant and unvariable, That every more general term stands for such an idea, and is but a part of any of those contained under it.

10. Why the Genus is ordinarily made Use of in Definitions.

This may show us the reason why, in the defining of words, which is nothing but declaring their signification, we make use of the GENUS, or next general word that comprehends it. Which is not out of necessity, but only to save the labour of enumerating the several simple ideas which the next general word or GENUS stands for; or, perhaps, sometimes the shame of not being able to do it. But though defining by GENUS and DIFFERENTIA (I crave leave to use these terms of art, though originally Latin, since they most properly suit those notions they are applied to), I say, though defining by the GENUS be the shortest way, yet I think it may be doubted whether it be the best. This I am sure, it is not the only, and so not absolutely necessary. For, definition being nothing but making another understand by words what idea the term defined stands for, a definition is best made by enumerating those simple ideas that are combined in the signification of the term defined: and if, instead of such an enumeration, men have accustomed themselves to use the next general term, it has not been out of necessity, or for greater clearness, but for quickness and dispatch sake. For I think that, to one who desired to know what idea the word MAN stood for; if it should be said, that man was a solid extended substance, having life, sense, spontaneous motion, and the faculty of reasoning, I doubt not but the meaning of the term man would be as well understood, and the idea it stands for be at least as clearly made known, as when it is defined to be a rational animal: which, by the several definitions of ANIMAL, VIVENS, and CORPUS, resolves itself into those enumerated ideas. I have, in explaining the term MAN, followed here the ordinary definition of the schools; which, though perhaps not the most, exact, yet serves well enough to my present purpose. And one may, in this instance, see what gave occasion to the rule, that a definition must consist of GENUS and DIFFERENTIA; and it suffices to show us the little necessity there is of such a rule, or advantage in the strict observing of it. For, definitions, as has been said, being only the explaining of one word by several others, so that the meaning or idea it stands for may be certainly known; languages are not always so made according to the rules of logic, that every term can have its signification exactly and clearly expressed by two others. Experience sufficiently satisfies us to the contrary; or else those who have made this rule have done ill, that they have given us so few definitions conformable to it. But of definitions more in the next chapter.

11. General and Universal are Creatures of the Understanding, and belong not to the Real Existence of things.

To return to general words: it is plain, by what has been said, that GENERAL and UNIVERSAL belong not to the real existence of things; but are the inventions and creatures of the understanding, made by it for its own use, and concern only signs, whether words or ideas. Words are general, as has been said, when used for signs of general ideas, and so are applicable indifferently to many particular things; and ideas are general when they are set up as the representatives of many particular things: but universality belongs not to things themselves, which are all of them particular in their existence, even those words and ideas which in their signification are general. When therefore we quit particulars, the generals that rest are only creatures of our own making; their general nature being nothing but the capacity they are put into, by the understanding, of signifying or representing many particulars. For the signification they have is nothing but a relation that, by the mind of man, is added to them.

12. Abstract Ideas are the Essences of Genera and Species.

The next thing therefore to be considered is, What kind of signification it is that general words have. For, as it is evident that they do not signify barely one particular thing; for then they would not be general terms, but proper names, so, on the other side, it is as evident they do not signify a plurality; for MAN and MEN would then signify the same; and the distinction of numbers (as the grammarians call them) would be superfluous and useless. That then which general words signify is a SORT of things; and each of them does that, by being a sign of an abstract idea in the mind; to which idea, as things existing are found to agree, so they come to be ranked under that name, or, which is all one, be of that sort. Whereby it is evident that the ESSENCES of the sorts, or, if the Latin word pleases better, SPECIES of things, are nothing else but these abstract ideas. For the having the essence of any species, being that which makes anything to be of that species; and the conformity to the idea to which the name is annexed being that which gives a right to that name; the having the essence, and the having that conformity, must needs be the same thing: since to be of any species, and to have a right to the name of that species, is all one. As, for example, to be a MAN, or of the SPECIES man, and to have right to the NAME man, is the same thing. Again, to be a man, or of the species man, and have the ESSENCE of a man, is the same thing. Now, since nothing can be a man, or have a right to the name man, but what has a conformity to the abstract idea the name man stands for, nor anything be a man, or have a right to the species man, but what has the essence of that species; it follows, that the abstract idea for which the name stands, and the essence of the species, is one and the same. From whence it is easy to observe, that the essences of the sorts of things, and, consequently, the sorting of things, is the workmanship of the understanding that abstracts and makes those general ideas.

13. They are the Workmanship of the Understanding, but have their Foundation in the Similitude of Things.

I would not here be thought to forget, much less to deny, that Nature, in the production of things, makes several of them alike: there is nothing more obvious, especially in the races of animals, and all things propagated by seed. But yet I think we may say, THE SORTING OF THEM UNDER NAMES IS THE WORKMANSHIP OF THE UNDERSTANDING, TAKING OCCASION, FROM THE SIMILITUDE IT OBSERVES AMONGST THEM, TO MAKE ABSTRACT GENERAL IDEAS, and set them up in the mind, with names annexed to them, as patterns or forms, (for, in that sense, the word FORM has a very proper signification,) to which as particular things existing are found to agree, so they come to be of that species, have that denomination, or are put into that CLASSIS. For when we say this is a man, that a horse; this justice, that cruelty; this a watch, that a jack; what do we else but rank things under different specific names, as agreeing to those abstract ideas, of which we have made those names the signs? And what are the essences of those species set out and marked by names, but those abstract ideas in the mind; which are, as it were, the bonds between particular things that exist, and the names they are to be ranked under? And when general names have any connexion with particular beings, these abstract ideas are the medium that unites them: so that the essences of species, as distinguished and denominated by us, neither are nor can be anything but those precise abstract ideas we have in our minds. And therefore the supposed real essences of substances, if different from our abstract ideas, cannot be the essences of the species WE rank things into. For two species may be one, as rationally as two different essences be the essence of one species: and I demand what are the alterations [which] may, or may not be made in a HORSE or LEAD, without making either of them to be of another species? In determining the species of things by OUR abstract ideas, this is easy to resolve: but if any one will regulate himself herein by supposed REAL essences, he will I suppose, be at a loss: and he will never be able to know when anything precisely ceases to be of the species of a HORSE or LEAD.

14. Each distinct abstract Idea is a distinct Essence.

Nor will any one wonder that I say these essences, or abstract ideas (which are the measures of name, and the boundaries of species) are the workmanship of the understanding, who considers that at least the complex ones are often, in several men, different collections of simple ideas; and therefore that is COVETOUSNESS to one man, which is not so to another. Nay, even in substances, where their abstract ideas seem to be taken from the things themselves, they are not constantly the same; no, not in that species which is most familiar to us, and with which we have the most intimate acquaintance: it having been more than once doubted, whether the FOETUS born of a woman were a MAN, even so far as that it hath been debated, whether it were or were not to be nourished and baptized: which could not be, if the abstract idea or essence to which the name man belonged were of nature's making; and were not the uncertain and various collection of simple ideas, which the understanding put together, and then, abstracting it, affixed a name to it. So that, in truth, every distinct abstract idea is a distinct essence; and the names that stand for such distinct ideas are the names of things essentially different. Thus a circle is as essentially different from an oval as a sheep from a goat; and rain is as essentially different from snow as water from earth: that abstract idea which is the essence of one being impossible to be communicated to the other. And thus any two abstract ideas, that in any part vary one from another, with two distinct names annexed to them, constitute two distinct sorts, or, if you please, SPECIES, as essentially different as any two of the most remote or opposite in the world.

15. Several significations of the word Essence.

But since the essences of things are thought by some (and not without reason) to be wholly unknown, it may not be amiss to consider the several significations of the word ESSENCE.

Real essences.

First, Essence may be taken for the very being of anything, whereby it is what it is. And thus the real internal, but generally (in substances) unknown constitution of things, whereon their discoverable qualities depend, may be called their essence. This is the proper original signification of the word, as is evident from the formation of it; essential in its primary notation, signifying properly, being. And in this sense it is still used, when we speak of the essence of PARTICULAR things, without giving them any name.

Nominal Essences.

Secondly, The learning and disputes of the schools having been much busied about genus and species, the word essence has almost lost its primary signification: and, instead of the real constitution of things, has been almost wholly applied to the artificial constitution of genus and species. It is true, there is ordinarily supposed a real constitution of the sorts of things; and it is past doubt there must be some real constitution, on which any collection of simple ideas co-existing must depend. But, it being evident that things are ranked under names into sorts or species, only as they agree to certain abstract ideas, to which we have annexed those names, the essence of each GENUS, or sort, comes to be nothing but that abstract idea which the general, or sortal (if I may have leave so to call it from sort, as I do general from genus,) name stands for. And this we shall find to be that which the word essence imports in its most familiar use.

These two sorts of essences, I suppose, may not unfitly be termed, the one the REAL, the other NOMINAL ESSENCE.

16. Constant Connexion between the Name and nominal Essence.

Between the NOMINAL ESSENCE and the NAME there is so near a connexion, that the name of any sort of things cannot be attributed to any particular being but what has this essence, whereby it answers that abstract idea whereof that name is the sign.

17. Supposition, that Species are distinguished by their real Essences useless.

Concerning the REAL ESSENCES of corporeal substances (to mention these only) there are, if I mistake not, two opinions. The one is of those who, using the word essence for they know not what, suppose a certain number of those essences, according to which all natural things are made, and wherein they do exactly every one of them partake, and so become of this or that species. The other and more rational opinion is of those who look on all natural things to have a real, but unknown, constitution of their insensible parts; from which flow those sensible qualities which serve us to distinguish them one from another, according as we have occasion to rank them into sorts, under common denominations. The former of these opinions, which supposes these essences as a certain number of forms or moulds, wherein all natural things that exist are cast, and do equally partake, has, I imagine, very much perplexed the knowledge of natural things. The frequent productions of monsters, in all the species of animals, and of changelings, and other strange issues of human birth, carry with them difficulties, not possible to consist with this hypothesis; since it is as impossible that two things partaking exactly of the same real essence should have different properties, as that two figures partaking of the same real essence of a circle should have different properties. But were there no other reason against it, yet the supposition of essences that cannot be known; and the making of them, nevertheless, to be that which distinguishes the species of things, is so wholly useless and unserviceable to any part of our knowledge, that that alone were sufficient to make us lay it by, and content ourselves with such essences of the sorts or species of things as come within the reach of our knowledge: which, when seriously considered, will be found, as I have said, to be nothing else but, those ABSTRACT complex ideas to which we have annexed distinct general names.

18. Real and nominal Essence

Essences being thus distinguished into nominal and real, we may further observe, that, in the species of simple ideas and modes, they are always the same; but in substances always quite different. Thus, a figure including a space between three lines, is the real as well as nominal essence of a triangle; it being not only the abstract idea to which the general name is annexed, but the very ESSENTIA or being of the thing itself; that foundation from which all its properties flow, and to which they are all inseparably annexed. But it is far otherwise concerning that parcel of matter which makes the ring on my finger; wherein these two essences are apparently different. For, it is the real constitution of its insensible parts, on which depend all those properties of colour, weight, fusibility, fixedness, &c., which are to be found in it; which constitution we know not, and so, having no particular idea of, having no name that is the sign of it. But yet it is its colour, weight, fusibility, fixedness, &c., which makes it to be gold, or gives it a right to that name, which is therefore its nominal essence. Since nothing can be called gold but what has a conformity of qualities to that abstract complex idea to which that name is annexed. But this distinction of essences, belonging particularly to substances, we shall, when we come to consider their names, have an occasion to treat of more fully.

19. Essences ingenerable and incorruptible.

That such abstract ideas, with names to them, as we have been speaking of are essences, may further appear by what we are told concerning essences, viz. that they are all ingenerable and incorruptible. Which cannot be true of the real constitutions of things, which begin and perish with them. All things that exist, besides their Author, are all liable to change; especially those things we are acquainted with, and have ranked into bands under distinct names or ensigns. Thus, that which was grass to-day is to-morrow the flesh of a sheep; and, within a few days after, becomes part of a man: in all which and the like changes, it is evident their real essence—i. e. that constitution whereon the properties of these several things depended—is destroyed, and perishes with them. But essences being taken for ideas established in the mind, with names annexed to them, they are supposed to remain steadily the same, whatever mutations the particular substances are liable to. For, whatever becomes of ALEXANDER and BUCEPHALUS, the ideas to which MAN and HORSE are annexed, are supposed nevertheless to remain the same; and so the essences of those species are preserved whole and undestroyed, whatever changes happen to any or all of the individuals of those species. By this means the essence of a species rests safe and entire, without the existence of so much as one individual of that kind. For, were there now no circle existing anywhere in the world, (as perhaps that figure exists not anywhere exactly marked out,) yet the idea annexed to that name would not cease to be what it is; nor cease to be as a pattern to determine which of the particular figures we meet with have or have not a right to the NAME circle, and so to show which of them, by having that essence, was of that species. And though there neither were nor had been in nature such a beast as an UNICORN, or such a fish as a MERMAID; yet, supposing those names to stand for complex abstract ideas that contained no inconsistency in them, the essence of a mermaid is as intelligible as that of a man; and the idea of an unicorn as certain, steady, and permanent as that of a horse. From what has been said, it is evident, that the doctrine of the immutability of essences proves them to be only abstract ideas; and is founded on the relation established between them and certain sounds as signs of them; and will always be true, as long as the same name can have the same signification.

20. Recapitulation.

To conclude. This is that which in short I would say, viz. that all the great business of GENERA and SPECIES, and their ESSENCES, amounts to no more but this:—That men making abstract ideas, and settling them in their minds with names annexed to them, do thereby enable themselves to consider things, and discourse of them, as it were in bundles, for the easier and readier improvement and communication of their knowledge, which would advance but slowly were their words and thoughts confined only to particulars.

An Essay Concerning Humane Understanding

CHAPTER IV.

OF THE NAMES OF SIMPLE IDEAS.

1. Names of simple Ideas, Modes, and Substances, have each something peculiar.

Though all words, as I have shown, signify nothing immediately but the ideas in the mind of the speaker; yet, upon a nearer survey, we shall find the names of SIMPLE IDEAS, MIXED MODES (under which I comprise RELATIONS too), and NATURAL SUBSTANCES, have each of them something peculiar and different from the other. For example:—

2. First, Names of simple Ideas, and of Substances intimate real Existence.

First, the names of SIMPLE IDEAS and SUBSTANCES, with the abstract ideas in the mind which they immediately signify, intimate also some real existence, from which was derived their original pattern. But the names of MIXED MODES terminate in the idea that is in the mind, and lead not the thoughts any further; as we shall see more at large in the following chapter.

3. Secondly, Names of simple Ideas and Modes signify always both real and nominal Essences.

Secondly, The names of simple ideas and modes signify always the real as well as nominal essence of their species. But the names of natural substances signify rarely, if ever, anything but barely the nominal essences of those species; as we shall show in the chapter that treats of the names of substances in particular.

4. Thirdly, Names of simple Ideas are undefinable.

Thirdly, The names of simple ideas are not capable of any definition; the names of all complex ideas are. It has not, that I know, been yet observed by anybody what words are, and what are not, capable of being defined; the want whereof is (as I am apt to think) not seldom the occasion of great wrangling and obscurity in men's discourses, whilst some demand definitions of terms that cannot be defined; and others think they ought not to rest satisfied in an explication made by a more general word, and its restriction, (or to speak in terms of art, by a genus and difference,) when, even after such definition, made according to rule, those who hear it have often no more a clear conception of the meaning of the word than they had before. This at least I think, that the showing what words are, and what are not, capable of definitions, and wherein consists a good definition, is not wholly besides our present purpose; and perhaps will afford so much light to the nature of these signs and our ideas, as to deserve a more particular consideration.

5. If all names were definable, it would be a Process IN INFINITUM.

I will not here trouble myself to prove that all terms are not definable, from that progress IN INFINITUM, which it will visibly lead us into, if we should allow that all names could be defined. For, if the terms of one definition were still to be defined by another, where at last should we stop? But I shall, from the nature of our ideas, and the signification of our words, show WHY SOME NAMES CAN, AND OTHERS CANNOT BE DEFINED; and WHICH THEY ARE.

6. What a Definition is.

I think it is agreed, that a DEFINITION is nothing else but THE SHOWING THE MEANING OF ONE WORD BY SEVERAL OTHER NOT SYNONYMOUS TERMS. The meaning of words being only the ideas they are made to stand for by him that uses them, the meaning of any term is then showed, or the word is defined, when, by other words, the idea it is made the sign of, and annexed to, in the mind of the speaker, is as it were represented, or set before the view of another; and thus its signification ascertained. This is the only use and end of definitions; and therefore the only measure of what is, or is not a good definition.

7. Simple Ideas, why undefinable.

This being premised, I say that the NAMES OF SIMPLE IDEAS, AND THOSE ONLY, ARE INCAPABLE OF BEING DEFINED. The reason whereof is this, That the several terms of a definition, signifying several ideas, they can all together by no means represent an idea which has no composition at all: and therefore a definition, which is properly nothing but the showing the meaning of one word by several others not signifying each the same thing, can in the names of simple ideas have no place.

8. Instances: Scholastic definitions of Motion.

The not observing this difference in our ideas, and their names, has produced that eminent trifling in the schools, which is so easy to be observed in the definitions they give us of some few of these simple ideas. For, as to the greatest part of them, even those masters of definitions were fain to leave them untouched, merely by the impossibility they found in it. What more exquisite jargon could the wit of man invent, than this definition:—'The act of a being in power, as far forth as in power;' which would puzzle any rational man, to whom it was not already known by its famous absurdity, to guess what word it could ever be supposed to be the explication of. If Tully, asking a Dutchman what BEWEEGINGE was, should have received this explication in his own language, that it was 'actus entis in potentia quatenus in potentia;' I ask whether any one can imagine he could thereby have understood what the word BEWEEGINGE signified, or have guessed what idea a Dutchman ordinarily had in his mind, and would signify to another, when he used that sound?

9. Modern definition of Motion.

Nor have the modern philosophers, who have endeavoured to throw off the jargon of the schools, and speak intelligibly, much better succeeded in defining simple ideas, whether by explaining their causes, or any otherwise. The atomists, who define motion to be 'a passage from one place to another,' what do they more than put one synonymous word for another? For what is PASSAGE other than MOTION? And if they were asked what passage was, how would they better define it than by motion? For is it not at least as proper and significant to say, Passage is a motion from one place to another, as to say, Motion is a passage, &c.? This is to translate, and not to define, when we change two words of the same signification one for another; which, when one is better understood than the other, may serve to discover what idea the unknown stands for; but is very far from a definition, unless we will say every English word in the dictionary is the definition of the Latin word it answers, and that motion is a definition of MOTUS. Nor will 'the successive application of the parts of the superficies of one body to those of another,' which the Cartesians give us, prove a much better definition of motion, when well examined.

10. Definitions of Light.

'The act of perspicuous, as far forth as perspicuous,' is another Peripatetic definition of a simple idea; which, though not more absurd than the former of motion, yet betrays its uselessness and insignificancy more plainly; because experience will easily convince any one that it cannot make the meaning of the word LIGHT (which it pretends to define) at all understood by a blind man, but the definition of motion appears not at first sight so useless, because it escapes this way of trial. For this simple idea, entering by the touch as well as sight, it is impossible to show an example of any one who has no other way to get the idea of motion, but barely by the definition of that name. Those who tell us that light is a great number of little globules, striking briskly on the bottom of the eye, speak more intelligibly than the Schools: but yet these words never so well understood would make the idea the word light stands for no more known to a man that understands it not before, than if one should tell him that light was nothing but a company of little tennis-balls, which fairies all day long struck with rackets against some men's foreheads, whilst they passed by others. For granting this explication of the thing to be true, yet the idea of the cause of light, if we had it never so exact, would no more give us the idea of light itself, as it is such a particular perception in us, than the idea of the figure and motion of a sharp piece of steel would give us the idea of that pain which it is able to cause in us. For the cause of any sensation, and the sensation itself, in all the simple ideas of one sense, are two ideas; and two ideas so different and distant one from another, that no two can be more so. And therefore, should Des Cartes's globules strike never so long on the retina of a man who was blind by a gutta serena, he would thereby never have any idea of light, or anything approaching it, though he understood never so well what little globules were, and what striking on another body was. And therefore the Cartesians very well distinguish between that light which is the cause of that sensation in us, and the idea which is produced in us by it, and is that which is properly light.

11. Simple Ideas, why undefinable, further explained.

Simple ideas, as has been shown, are only to be got by those impressions objects themselves make on our minds, by the proper inlets appointed to each sort. If they are not received this way, all the words in the world, made use of to explain or define any of their names, will never be able to produce in us the idea it stands for. For, words being sounds, can produce in us no other simple ideas than of those very sounds; nor excite any in us, but by that voluntary connexion which is known to be between them and those simple ideas which common use has made them the signs of. He that thinks otherwise, let him try if any words can give him the taste of a pine apple, and make him have the true idea of the relish of that celebrated delicious fruit. So far as he is told it has a resemblance with any tastes whereof he has the ideas already in his memory, imprinted there by sensible objects, not strangers to his palate, so far may he approach that resemblance in his mind. But this is not giving us that idea by a definition, but exciting in us other simple ideas by their known names; which will be still very different from the true taste of that fruit itself. In light and colours, and all other simple ideas, it is the same thing: for the signification of sounds is not natural, but only imposed and arbitrary. And no DEFINITION of light or redness is more fitted or able to produce either of those ideas in us, than the SOUND light or red, by itself. For, to hope to produce an idea of light or colour by a sound, however formed, is to expect that sounds should be visible, or colours audible; and to make the ears do the office of all the other senses. Which is all one as to say, that we might taste, smell, and see by the ears: a sort of philosophy worthy only of Sancho Panza, who had the faculty to see Dulcinea by hearsay. And therefore he that has not before received into his mind, by the proper inlet, the simple idea which any word stands for, can never come to know the signification of that word by any other words or sounds whatsoever, put together according to any rules of definition. The only way is, by applying to his senses the proper object; and so producing that idea in him, for which he has learned the name already. A studious blind man, who had mightily beat his head about visible objects, and made use of the explication of his books and friends, to understand those names of light and colours which often came in his way, bragged one day, That he now understood what SCARLET signified. Upon which, his friend demanding what scarlet was? The blind man answered, It was like the sound of a trumpet. Just such an understanding of the name of any other simple idea will he have, who hopes to get it only from a definition, or other words made use of to explain it.

12. The contrary shown in complex ideas, by instances of a Statue and Rainbow.

The case is quite otherwise in COMPLEX IDEAS; which, consisting of several simple ones, it is in the power of words, standing for the several ideas that make that composition, to imprint complex ideas in the mind which were never there before, and so make their names be understood. In such collections of ideas, passing under one name, definition, or the teaching the signification of one word by several others, has place, and may make us understand the names of things which never came within the reach of our senses; and frame ideas suitable to those in other men's minds, when they use those names: provided that none of the terms of the definition stand for any such simple ideas, which he to whom the explication is made has never yet had in his thought. Thus the word STATUE may be explained to a blind man by other words, when PICTURE cannot; his senses having given him the idea of figure, but not of colours, which therefore words cannot excite in him. This gained the prize to the painter against the statuary: each of which contending for the excellency of his art, and the statuary bragging that his was to be preferred, because it reached further, and even those who had lost their eyes could yet perceive the excellency of it. The painter agreed to refer himself to the judgment of a blind man; who being brought where there was a statue made by the one, and a picture drawn by the other; he was first led to the statue, in which he traced with his hands all the lineaments of the face and body, and with great admiration applauded the skill of the workman. But being led to the picture, and having his hands laid upon it, was told, that now he touched the head, and then the forehead, eyes, nose, &c., as his hand moved over the parts of the picture on the cloth, without finding any the least distinction: whereupon he cried out, that certainly that must needs be a very admirable and divine piece of workmanship, which could represent to them all those parts, where he could neither feel nor perceive anything.

13. Colours indefinable to the born-blind.

He that should use the word RAINBOW to one who knew all those colours, but yet had never seen that phenomenon, would, by enumerating the figure, largeness, position, and order of the colours, so well define that word that it might be perfectly understood. But yet that definition, how exact and perfect soever, would never make a blind man understand it; because several of the simple ideas that make that complex one, being such as he never received by sensation and experience, no words are able to excite them in his mind.

14. Complex Ideas definable only when the simple ideas of which they consist have been got from experience.

Simple ideas, as has been shown, can only be got by experience from those objects which are proper to produce in us those perceptions. When, by this means, we have our minds stored with them, and know the names for them, then we are in a condition to define, and by definition to understand, the names of complex ideas that are made up of them. But when any term stands for a simple idea that a man has never yet had in his mind, it is impossible by any words to make known its meaning to him. When any term stands for an idea a man is acquainted with, but is ignorant that that term is the sign of it, then another name of the same idea, which he has been accustomed to, may make him understand its meaning. But in no case whatsoever is any name of any simple idea capable of a definition.

15. Fourthly, Names of simple Ideas of less doubtful meaning than those of mixed modes and substances.

Fourthly, But though the names of simple ideas have not the help of definition to determine their signification, yet that hinders not but that they are generally less doubtful and uncertain than those of mixed modes and substances; because they, standing only for one simple perception, men for the most part easily and perfectly agree in their signification; and there is little room for mistake and wrangling about their meaning. He that knows once that whiteness is the name of that colour he has observed in snow or milk, will not be apt to misapply that word, as long as he retains that idea; which when he has quite lost, he is not apt to mistake the meaning of it, but perceives he understands it not. There is neither a multiplicity of simple ideas to be put together, which makes the doubtfulness in the names of mixed modes; nor a supposed, but an unknown, real essence, with properties depending thereon, the precise number whereof is also unknown, which makes the difficulty in the names of substances. But, on the contrary, in simple ideas the whole signification of the name is known at once, and consists not of parts, whereof more or less being put in, the idea may be varied, and so the signification of name be obscure, or uncertain.

16. Simple Ideas have few Ascents in linea praedicamentali.

Fifthly, This further may be observed concerning simple Simple ideas and their names, that they have but few ascents in linea praedicamentali, (as they call it,) from the lowest species to the summum genus. The reason whereof is, that the lowest species being but one simple idea, nothing can be left out of it, that so the difference being taken away, it may agree with some other thing in one idea common to them both; which, having one name, is the genus of the other two: v.g. there is nothing that can be left out of the idea of white and red to make them agree in one common appearance, and so have one general name; as RATIONALITY being left out of the complex idea of man, makes it agree with brute in the more general idea and name of animal. And therefore when, to avoid unpleasant enumerations, men would comprehend both white and red, and several other such simple ideas, under one general name, they have been fain to do it by a word which denotes only the way they get into the mind. For when white, red, and yellow are all comprehended under the genus or name colour, it signifies no more but such ideas as are produced in the mind only by the sight, and have entrance only through the eyes. And when they would frame yet a more general term to comprehend both colours and sounds, and the like simple ideas, they do it by a word that signifies all such as come into the mind only by one sense. And so the general term QUALITY, in its ordinary acceptation, comprehends colours, sounds, tastes, smells, and tangible qualities, with distinction from extension, number, motion, pleasure, and pain, which make impressions on the mind and introduce their ideas by more senses than one.

17. Sixthly, Names of simple Ideas not arbitrary, but perfectly taken from the existence of things.

Sixthly, The names of simple ideas, substances, and mixed modes have also this difference: that those of MIXED MODES stand for ideas perfectly arbitrary; those of SUBSTANCES are not perfectly so, but refer to a pattern, though with some latitude; and those of SIMPLE IDEAS are perfectly taken from the existence of things, and are not arbitrary at all. Which, what difference it makes in the significations of their names, we shall see in the following chapters.

Simple modes.

The names of SIMPLE MODES differ little from those of simple ideas.

CHAPTER V.

OF THE NAMES OF MIXED MODES AND RELATIONS.

1. Mixed modes stand for abstract Ideas, as other general Names.
The names of MIXED MODES, being general, they stand, as has been shewed, for sorts or species of things, each of which has its peculiar essence. The essences of these species also, as has been shewed, are nothing but the abstract ideas in the mind, to which the name is annexed. Thus far the names and essences of mixed modes have nothing but what is common to them with other ideas: but if we take a little nearer survey of them, we shall find that they have something peculiar, which perhaps may deserve our attention.

2. First, The abstract Ideas they stand for are made by the Understanding.
The first particularity I shall observe in them, is, that the abstract ideas, or, if you please, the essences, of the several species of mixed modes, are MADE BY THE UNDERSTANDING, wherein they differ from those of simple ideas: in which sort the mind has no power to make any one, but only receives such as are presented to it by the real existence of things operating upon it.

3. Secondly, Made arbitrarily, and without Patterns.
In the next place, these essences of the species of mixed modes are not only made by the mind, but MADE VERY ARBITRARILY, MADE WITHOUT PATTERNS, OR REFERENCE TO ANY REAL EXISTENCE. Wherein they differ from those of substances, which carry with them the supposition of some real being, from which they are taken, and to which they are conformable. But, in its complex ideas of mixed modes, the mind takes a liberty not to follow the existence of things exactly. It unites and retains certain collections, as so many distinct specific ideas; whilst others, that as often occur in nature, and are as plainly suggested by outward things, pass neglected, without particular names or specifications. Nor does the mind, in these of mixed modes, as in the complex idea of substances, examine them by the real existence of things; or verify them by patterns containing such peculiar compositions in nature. To know whether his idea of ADULTERY or INCEST be right, will a man seek it anywhere amongst things existing? Or is it true because any one has been witness to such an action? No: but it suffices here, that men have put

together such a collection into one complex idea, that makes the archetype and specific idea; whether ever any such action were committed in rerum natura or no.

4. How this is done.

To understand this right, we must consider wherein this making of these complex ideas consists; and that is not in the making any new idea, but putting together those which the mind had before. Wherein the mind does these three things: First, It chooses a certain number; Secondly, It gives them connexion, and makes them into one idea; Thirdly, It ties them together by a name. If we examine how the mind proceeds in these, and what liberty it takes in them, we shall easily observe how these essences of the species of mixed modes are the workmanship of the mind; and, consequently, that the species themselves are of men's making.

5. Evidently arbitrary, in that the Idea is often before the Existence.

Nobody can doubt but that these ideas of mixed modes are made by a voluntary collection of ideas, put together in the mind, independent from any original patterns in nature, who will but reflect that this sort of complex ideas may be made, abstracted, and have names given them, and so a species be constituted, before any one individual of that species ever existed. Who can doubt but the ideas of SACRILEGE or ADULTERY might be framed in the minds of men, and have names given them, and so these species of mixed modes be constituted, before either of them was ever committed; and might be as well discoursed of and reasoned about, and as certain truths discovered of them, whilst yet they had no being but in the understanding, as well as now, that they have but too frequently a real existence? Whereby it is plain how much the sorts of mixed modes are the creatures of the understanding, where they have a being as subservient to all the ends of real truth and knowledge, as when they really exist. And we cannot doubt but law-makers have often made laws about species of actions which were only the creatures of their own understandings; beings that had no other existence but in their own minds. And I think nobody can deny but that the RESURRECTION was a species of mixed modes in the mind, before it really existed.

6. Instances: Murder, Incest, Stabbing.

To see how arbitrarily these essences of mixed modes are made by the mind, we need but take a view of almost any of them. A little looking into them will satisfy us, that it is the mind that combines several scattered independent ideas into one complex one; and, by the common name it gives them, makes them the essence of a certain species, without regulating itself by any connexion they have in nature. For what greater connexion in nature has the idea of a man than the idea of a sheep with killing, that this is made a particular species of action, signified by the word MURDER, and the other not? Or what union is there in nature between the idea of the relation of a father with killing than that of a son or neighbour, that those are combined into one complex idea, and thereby made the essence of the distinct species PARRICIDE, whilst the other makes no distinct species at all? But, though they have made killing a man's father or mother a distinct species from killing his son or daughter, yet, in some other cases, son and daughter are taken in too, as well as father and mother: and they are all equally comprehended in the same species, as in that of INCEST. Thus the mind in mixed modes arbitrarily unites into complex ideas such as it finds convenient; whilst others that have altogether as much union in nature are left loose, and never combined into one idea, because they have no need of one name. It is evident then that the mind, by its free choice, gives a connexion to a certain number of ideas, which in nature have no more union with one another than others that it leaves out: why else is the part of the weapon the beginning of the wound is made with taken notice of, to make the distinct species called STABBING, and the figure and matter of the weapon left out? I do not say this is done without reason, as we shall see more by and by; but this I say, that it is done by the free choice of the mind, pursuing its own ends; and that, therefore, these species of mixed modes are the workmanship of the understanding. And there is nothing more evident than that, for the most part, in the framing these ideas, the mind searches not its patterns in nature, nor refers the ideas it makes to the real existence of things, but puts such together as may best serve its own purposes, without tying itself to a precise imitation of anything that really exists.

7. But still subservient to the End of Language, and not made at random.

But, though these complex ideas or essences of mixed modes depend on the mind, and are made by it with great liberty, yet they are not made at random, and jumbled together without any reason at all. Though these complex ideas be not always copied from nature, yet they are always suited to the end for which abstract ideas are made: and though they be combinations made of ideas that are loose enough, and have as little union in themselves as several other to which the mind never gives a connexion that combines them into one idea; yet they are always made for the convenience of communication, which is the chief end of language. The use of language is, by short sounds, to signify with ease and dispatch general conceptions; wherein not only abundance of particulars may be contained, but also a great variety of independent ideas collected into one complex one. In the making therefore of the species of mixed modes, men have had regard only to such combinations as they had occasion to mention one to another. Those they have combined into distinct complex ideas, and given names to; whilst others, that in nature have as near a union, are left loose and unregarded. For, to go no further than human actions themselves, if they would make distinct abstract ideas of all the varieties which might be observed in them, the number must be infinite, and the memory confounded with the plenty, as well as overcharged to little purpose. It suffices that men make and name so many complex ideas of these mixed modes as they find they have occasion to have names for, in the ordinary occurrence of their affairs. If they join to the idea of killing the idea of father or mother, and so make a distinct species from killing a man's son or neighbour, it is because of the different heinousness of the crime, and the distinct punishment is due to the murdering a man's father and mother, different to what ought to be inflicted on the murder of a son or neighbour; and therefore they find it necessary to mention it by a distinct name, which is the end of making that distinct combination. But though the ideas of mother and daughter are so differently treated, in reference to the idea of killing, that the one is joined with it to make a distinct abstract idea with a name, and so a distinct species, and the other not; yet, in respect of carnal knowledge, they are both taken in under INCEST: and that still for the same convenience of expressing under one name, and reckoning of one species, such unclean mixtures as have a peculiar turpitude beyond others; and this to avoid circumlocutions and tedious descriptions.

8. Whereof the intranslatable Words of divers Languages are a Proof. A moderate skill in different languages will easily satisfy one of the truth of this, it being so obvious to observe great store of words in one language which have not any that answer them in another. Which plainly shows that those of one country, by their customs and manner of life, have found occasion to make several complex ideas, and given names to them, which others never collected into specific ideas. This could not have happened if these species were the steady workmanship of nature, and not collections made and abstracted by the mind, in order to naming, and for the convenience of communication. The terms of our law, which are not empty sounds, will hardly find words that answer them in the Spanish or Italian, no scanty languages; much less, I think, could any one translate them into the Caribbee or Westoe tongues: and the VERSURA of the Romans, or

CORBAN of the Jews, have no words in other languages to answer them; the reason whereof is plain, from what has been said. Nay, if we look a little more nearly into this matter, and exactly compare different languages, we shall find that, though they have words which in translations and dictionaries are supposed to answer one another, yet there is scarce one often amongst the names of complex ideas, especially of mixed modes, that stands for the same precise idea which the word does that in dictionaries it is rendered by. There are no ideas more common and less compounded than the measures of time, extension, and weight; and the Latin names, HORA, PES, LIBRA, are without difficulty rendered by the English names, HOUR, FOOT, and POUND: but yet there is nothing more evident than that the ideas a Roman annexed to these Latin names, were very far different from those which an Englishman expresses by those English ones. And if either of these should make use of the measures that those of the other language designed by their names, he would be quite out in his account. These are too sensible proofs to be doubted; and we shall find this much more so in the names of more abstract and compounded ideas, such as are the greatest part of those which make up moral discourses: whose names, when men come curiously to compare with those they are translated into, in other languages, they will find very few of them exactly to correspond in the whole extent of their significations.

9. This shows Species to be made for Communication.

The reason why I take so particular notice of this is, that we may not be mistaken about GENERA and SPECIES, and their ESSENCES, as if they were things regularly and constantly made by nature, and had a real existence in things; when they appear, upon a more wary survey, to be nothing else but an artifice of the understanding, for the easier signifying such collections of ideas as it should often have occasion to communicate by one general term; under which divers particulars, as far forth as they agreed to that abstract idea, might be comprehended. And if the doubtful signification of the word SPECIES may make it sound harsh to some, that I say the species of mixed modes are 'made by the understanding'; yet, I think, it can by nobody be denied that it is the mind makes those abstract complex ideas to which specific names are given. And if it be true, as it is, that the mind makes the patterns for sorting and naming of things, I leave it to be considered who makes the boundaries of the sort or species; since with me SPECIES and SORT have no other difference than that of a Latin and English idiom.

10. In mixed Modes it is the Name that ties the Combination of simple ideas together, and makes it a Species.

The near relation that there is between SPECIES, ESSENCES, and their GENERAL NAME, at least in mixed modes, will further appear when we consider, that it is the name that seems to preserve those essences, and give them their lasting duration. For, the connexion between the loose parts of those complex ideas being made by the mind, this union, which has no particular foundation in nature, would cease again, were there not something that did, as it were, hold it together, and keep the parts from scattering. Though therefore it be the mind that makes the collection, it is the name which is as it were the knot that ties them fast together. What a vast variety of different ideas does the word TRIUMPHUS hold together, and deliver to us as one species! Had this name been never made, or quite lost, we might, no doubt, have had descriptions of what passed in that solemnity: but yet, I think, that which holds those different parts together, in the unity of one complex idea, is that very word annexed to it; without which the several parts of that would no more be thought to make one thing, than any other show, which having never been made but once, had never been united into one complex idea, under one denomination. How much, therefore, in mixed modes, the unity necessary to any essence depends on the mind; and how much the continuation and fixing of that unity depends on the name in common use annexed to it, I leave to be considered by those who look upon essences and species as real established things in nature.

11.

Suitable to this, we find that men speaking of mixed modes, seldom imagine or take any other for species of them, but such as are set out by name: because they, being of man's making only, in order to naming, no such species are taken notice of, or supposed to be, unless a name be joined to it, as the sign of man's having combined into one idea several loose ones; and by that name giving a lasting union to the parts which would otherwise cease to have any, as soon as the mind laid by that abstract idea, and ceased actually to think on it. But when a name is once annexed to it, wherein the parts of that complex idea have a settled and permanent union, then is the essence, as it were, established, and the species looked on as complete. For to what purpose should the memory charge itself with such compositions, unless it were by abstraction to make them general? And to what purpose make them general, unless it were that they might have general names for the convenience of discourse and communication? Thus we see, that killing a man with a sword or a hatchet are looked on as no distinct species of action; but if the point of the sword first enter the body, it passes for a distinct species, where it has a distinct name, as in England, in whose language it is called STABBING: but in another country, where it has not happened to be specified under a peculiar name, it passes not for a distinct species. But in the species of corporeal substances, though it be the mind that makes the nominal essence, yet, since those ideas which are combined in it are supposed to have an union in nature whether the mind joins them or not, therefore those are looked on as distinct species, without any operation of the mind, either abstracting, or giving a name to that complex idea.

12. For the Originals of our mixed Modes, we look no further than the Mind; which also shows them to be the Workmanship of the Understanding.

Conformable also to what has been said concerning the essences of the species of mixed modes, that they are the creatures of the understanding rather than the works of nature; conformable, I say, to this, we find that their names lead our thoughts to the mind, and no further. When we speak of JUSTICE, or GRATITUDE, we frame to ourselves no imagination of anything existing, which we would conceive; but our thoughts terminate in the abstract ideas of those virtues, and look not further; as they do when we speak of a HORSE, or IRON, whose specific ideas we consider not as barely in the mind, but as in things themselves, which afford the original patterns of those ideas. But in mixed modes, at least the most considerable parts of them, which are moral beings, we consider the original patterns as being in the mind, and to those we refer for the distinguishing of particular beings under names. And hence I think it is that these essences of the species of mixed modes are by a more particular name called NOTIONS; as, by a peculiar right, appertaining to the understanding.

13. Their being made by the Understanding without Patterns, shows the Reason why they are so compounded.

Hence, likewise, we may learn why the complex ideas of mixed modes are commonly more compounded and decompounded than those of natural substances. Because they being the workmanship of the understanding, pursuing only its own ends, and the conveniency of expressing in short those ideas it would make known to another, it does with great liberty unite often into one abstract idea things that, in their nature, have no coherence; and so under one term bundle together a great variety of compounded and decompounded ideas. Thus the name of PROCESSION: what a great mixture of independent ideas of persons, habits, tapers, orders, motions, sounds, does it contain in that complex one, which the mind of man has arbitrarily put together, to express by that one name? Whereas the complex ideas of the sorts of substances are usually made up of only a small number of simple ones; and in the species of animals, these two, viz. shape and voice, commonly make the whole nominal essence.

14. Names of mixed Modes stand alway for their real Essences, which are the workmanship of our minds.

Another thing we may observe from what has been said is, That the names of mixed modes always signify (when they have any determined signification) the REAL essences of their species. For, these abstract ideas being the workmanship of the mind, and not referred to the real existence of things, there is no supposition of anything more signified by that name, but barely that complex idea the mind itself has formed; which is all it would have expressed by it; and is that on which all the properties of the species depend, and from which alone they all flow: and so in these the real and nominal essence is the same; which, of what concernment it is to the certain knowledge of general truth, we shall see hereafter.

15. Why their Names are usually got before their Ideas.

This also may show us the reason why for the most part the names of mixed modes are got before the ideas they stand for are perfectly known. Because there being no species of these ordinarily taken notice of but what have names, and those species, or rather their essences, being abstract complex ideas, made arbitrarily by the mind, it is convenient, if not necessary, to know the names, before one endeavour to frame these complex ideas: unless a man will fill his head with a company of abstract complex ideas, which, others having no names for, he has nothing to do with, but to lay by and forget again. I confess that, in the beginning of languages, it was necessary to have the idea before one gave it the name: and so it is still, where, making a new complex idea, one also, by giving it a new name, makes a new word. But this concerns not languages made, which have generally pretty well provided for ideas which men have frequent occasion to have and communicate; and in such, I ask whether it be not the ordinary method, that children learn the names of mixed modes before they have their ideas? What one of a thousand ever frames the abstract ideas of GLORY and AMBITION, before he has heard the names of them? In simple ideas and substances I grant it is otherwise; which, being such ideas as have a real existence and union in nature, the ideas and names are got one before the other, as it happens.

16. Reason of my being so large on this Subject.
What has been said here of MIXED MODES is, with very little difference, applicable also to RELATIONS; which, since every man himself may observe, I may spare myself the pains to enlarge on: especially, since what I have here said concerning Words in this third Book, will possibly be thought by some to this be much more than what so slight a subject required. I allow it might be brought into a narrower compass; but I was willing to stay my reader on an argument that appears to me new and a little out of the way, (I am sure it is one I thought not of when I began to write,) that, by searching it to the bottom, and turning it on every side, some part or other might meet with every one's thoughts, and give occasion to the most averse or negligent to reflect on a general miscarriage, which, though of great consequence, is little taken notice of. When it is considered what a pudder is made about ESSENCES, and how much all sorts of knowledge, discourse, and conversation are pestered and disordered by the careless and confused use and application of words, it will perhaps be thought worth while thoroughly to lay it open. And I shall be pardoned if I have dwelt long on an argument which I think, therefore, needs to be inculcated, because the faults men are usually guilty of in this kind, are not only the greatest hindrances of true knowledge, but are so well thought of as to pass for it. Men would often see what a small pittance of reason and truth, or possibly none at all, is mixed with those huffing opinions they are swelled with; if they would but look beyond fashionable sounds, and observe what IDEAS are or are not comprehended under those words with which they are so armed at all points, and with which they so confidently lay about them. I shall imagine I have done some service to truth, peace, and learning, if, by any enlargement on this subject, I can make men reflect on their own use of language; and give them reason to suspect, that, since it is frequent for others, it may also be possible for them, to have sometimes very good and approved words in their mouths and writings, with very uncertain, little, or no signification. And therefore it is not unreasonable for them to be wary herein themselves, and not to be unwilling to have them examined by others. With this design, therefore, I shall go on with what I have further to say concerning this matter.

CHAPTER VI.

OF THE NAMES OF SUBSTANCES.

1. The common Names of Substances stand for Sorts.
The common names of substances, as well as other general terms, stand for SORTS: which is nothing else but the being made signs of such complex ideas wherein several particular substances do or might agree, by virtue of which they are capable of being comprehended in one common conception, and signified by one name. I say do or might agree: for though there be but one sun existing in the world, yet the idea of it being abstracted, so that more substances (if there were several) might each agree in it, it is as much a sort as if there were as many suns as there are stars. They want not their reasons who think there are, and that each fixed star would answer the idea the name sun stands for, to one who was placed in a due distance: which, by the way, may show us how much the sorts, or, if you please, GENERA and SPECIES of things (for those Latin terms signify to me no more than the English word sort) depend on such collections of ideas as men have made, and not on the real nature of things; since it is not impossible but that, in propriety of speech, that might be a sun to one which is a star to another.
2. The Essence of each Sort of substance is our abstract Idea to which the name is annexed.
The measure and boundary of each sort or species, whereby it is constituted that particular sort, and distinguished from others, is that we call its ESSENCE, which is nothing but that abstract idea to which the name is annexed; so that everything contained in that idea is essential to that sort. This, though it be all the essence of natural substances that WE know, or by which we distinguish them into sorts, yet I call it by a peculiar name, the NOMINAL ESSENCE, to distinguish it from the real constitution of substances, upon which depends this nominal essence, and all the properties of that sort; which, therefore, as has been said, may be called the REAL ESSENCE: v.g. the nominal essence of gold is that complex idea the word gold stands for, let it be, for instance, a body yellow, of a certain weight, malleable, fusible, and fixed. But the real essence is the constitution of the insensible parts of that body, on which those qualities and all the other properties of gold depend. How far these two are different, though they are both called essence, is obvious at first sight to discover.
3. The nominal and real Essence different.

For, though perhaps voluntary motion, with sense and reason, joined to a body of a certain shape, be the complex idea to which I and others annex the name MAN, and so be the nominal essence of the species so called: yet nobody will say that complex idea is the real essence and source of all those operations which are to be found in any individual of that sort. The foundation of all those qualities which are the ingredients of our complex idea, is something quite different: and had we such a knowledge of that constitution of man; from which his faculties of moving, sensation, and reasoning, and other powers flow, and on which his so regular shape depends, as it is possible angels have, and it is certain his Maker has, we should have a quite other idea of his essence than what now is contained in our definition of that species, be it what it will: and our idea of any individual man would be as far different from what it is now, as is his who knows all the springs and wheels and other contrivances within of the famous clock at Strasburg, from that which a gazing countryman has of it, who barely sees the motion of the hand, and hears the clock strike, and observes only some of the outward appearances.

4. Nothing essential to Individuals.

That ESSENCE, in the ordinary use of the word, relates to sorts, and that it is considered in particular beings no further than as they are ranked into sorts, appears from hence: that, take but away the abstract ideas by which we sort individuals, and rank them under common names, and then the thought of anything essential to any of them instantly vanishes: we have no notion of the one without the other, which plainly shows their relation. It is necessary for me to be as I am; God and nature has made me so: but there is nothing I have is essential to me. An accident or disease may very much alter my colour or shape; a fever or fall may take away my reason or memory, or both; and an apoplexy leave neither sense, nor understanding, no, nor life. Other creatures of my shape may be made with more and better, or fewer and worse faculties than I have; and others may have reason and sense in a shape and body very different from mine. None of these are essential to the one or the other, or to any individual whatever, till the mind refers it to some sort or species of things; and then presently, according to the abstract idea of that sort, something is found essential. Let any one examine his own thoughts, and he will find that as soon as he supposes or speaks of essential, the consideration of some species, or the complex idea signified by some general name, comes into his mind; and it is in reference to that that this or that quality is said to be essential. So that if it be asked, whether it be essential to me or any other particular corporeal being, to have reason? I say, no; no more than it is essential to this white thing I write on to have words in it. But if that particular being be to be counted of the sort MAN, and to have the name MAN given it, then reason is essential to it; supposing reason to be a part of the complex idea the name man stands for: as it is essential to this thing I write on to contain words, if I will give it the name TREATISE, and rank it under that species. So that essential and not essential relate only to our abstract ideas, and the names annexed to them; which amounts to no more than this, That whatever particular thing has not in it those qualities which are contained in the abstract idea which any general term stands for, cannot be ranked under that species, nor be called by that name; since that abstract idea is the very essence of that species.

5. The only essences perceived by us in individual substances are those qualities which entitle them to receive their names.

Thus, if the idea of BODY with some people be bare extension or space, then solidity is not essential to body: if others make the idea to which they give the name BODY to be solidity and extension, then solidity is essential to body. That therefore, and that alone, is considered as essential, which makes a part of the complex idea the name of a sort stands for; without which no particular thing can be reckoned of that sort, nor be entitled to that name. Should there be found a parcel of matter that had all the other qualities that are in iron, but wanted obedience to the loadstone, and would neither be drawn by it nor receive direction from it, would any one question whether it wanted anything essential? It would be absurd to ask, Whether a thing really existing wanted anything essential to it. Or could it be demanded, Whether this made an essential or specific difference or no, since WE have no other measure of essential or specific but our abstract ideas? And to talk of specific differences in NATURE, without reference to general ideas in names, is to talk unintelligibly. For I would ask any one, What is sufficient to make an essential difference in nature between any two particular beings, without any regard had to some abstract idea, which is looked upon as the essence and standard of a species? All such patterns and standards being quite laid aside, particular beings, considered barely in themselves, will be found to have all their qualities equally essential; and everything in each individual will be essential to it; or, which is more, nothing at all. For, though it may be reasonable to ask, Whether obeying the magnet be essential to iron? yet I think it is very improper and insignificant to ask, whether it be essential to the particular parcel of matter I cut my pen with; without considering it under the name IRON, or as being of a certain species. And if, as has been said, our abstract ideas, which have names annexed to them, are the boundaries of species, nothing can be essential but what is contained in those ideas.

6. Even the real essences of individual substances imply potential sorts.

It is true, I have often mentioned a REAL ESSENCE, distinct in substances from those abstract ideas of them, which I call their nominal essence. By this real essence I mean, that real constitution of anything, which is the foundation of all those properties that are combined in, and are constantly found to co-exist with the nominal essence; that particular constitution which everything has within itself, without any relation to anything without it. But essence, even in this sense, RELATES TO A SORT, AND SUPPOSES A SPECIES. For, being that real constitution on which the properties depend, it necessarily supposes a sort of things, properties belonging only to species, and not to individuals: v. g. supposing the nominal essence of gold to be a body of such a peculiar colour and weight, with malleability and fusibility, the real essence is that constitution of the parts of matter on which these qualities and their union depend; and is also the foundation of its solubility in aqua regia and other properties, accompanying that complex idea. Here are essences and properties, but all upon supposition of a sort or general abstract idea, which is considered as immutable; but there is no individual parcel of matter to which any of these qualities are so annexed as to be essential to it or inseparable from it. That which is essential belongs to it as a condition whereby it is of this or that sort: but take away the consideration of its being ranked under the name of some abstract idea, and then there is nothing necessary to it, nothing inseparable from it. Indeed, as to the real essences of substances, we only suppose their being, without precisely knowing what they are; but that which annexes them still to the species is the nominal essence, of which they are the supposed foundation and cause.

7. The nominal Essence bounds the Species to us.

The next thing to be considered is, by which of those essences it is that substances are determined into sorts or species; and that, it is evident, is by the nominal essence. For it is that alone that the name, which is the mark of the sort, signifies. It is impossible, therefore, that anything should determine the sorts of things, which WE rank under general names, but that idea which that name is designed as a mark for; which is that, as has been shown, which we call nominal essence. Why do we say this is a horse, and that a mule; this is an animal, that an herb? How comes any particular thing to be of this or that sort, but because it has that nominal essence; or, which is all one, agrees to that abstract idea, that name is annexed to? And I desire any one but to reflect on his own thoughts, when he hears or speaks any of those or other names of substances, to know what sort of essences they stand for.

8. The nature of Species as formed by us.

And that the species of things to us are nothing but the ranking them under distinct names, according to the complex ideas in US, and not according to precise, distinct, real essences in THEM, is plain from hence:—That we find many of the individuals that are ranked into one sort, called by one common name, and so received as being of one species, have yet qualities, depending on their real constitutions, as far different one from another as from others from which they are accounted to differ specifically. This, as it is easy to be observed by all who have to do with natural bodies, so chemists especially are often, by sad experience, convinced of it, when they, sometimes in vain, seek for the same qualities in one parcel of sulphur, antimony, or vitriol, which they have found in others. For, though they are bodies of the same species, having the same nominal essence, under the same name, yet do they often, upon severe ways of examination, betray qualities so different one from another, as to frustrate the expectation and labour of very wary chemists. But if things were distinguished into species, according to their real essences, it would be as impossible to find different properties in any two individual substances of the same species, as it is to find different properties in two circles, or two equilateral triangles. That is properly the essence to US, which determines every particular to this or that CLASSIS; or, which is the same thing, to this or that general name: and what can that be else, but that abstract idea to which that name is annexed; and so has, in truth, a reference, not so much to the being of particular things, as to their general denominations?

9. Not the real Essence, or texture of parts, which we know not.

Nor indeed can we rank and sort things, and consequently (which is the end of sorting) denominate them, by their real essences; because we know them not. Our faculties carry us no further towards the knowledge and distinction of substances, than a collection of THOSE SENSIBLE IDEAS WHICH WE OBSERVE IN THEM; which, however made with the greatest diligence and exactness we are capable of, yet is more remote from the true internal constitution from which those qualities flow, than, as I said, a countryman's idea is from the inward contrivance of that famous clock at Strasburg, whereof he only sees the outward figure and motions. There is not so contemptible a plant or animal, that does not confound the most enlarged understanding. Though the familiar use of things about us take off our wonder, yet it cures not our ignorance. When we come to examine the stones we tread on, or the iron we daily handle, we presently find we know not their make; and can give no reason of the different qualities we find in them. It is evident the internal constitution, whereon their properties depend, is unknown to us: for to go no further than the grossest and most obvious we can imagine amongst them, What is that texture of parts, that real essence, that makes lead and antimony fusible, wood and stones not? What makes lead and iron malleable, antimony and stones not? And yet how infinitely these come short of the fine contrivances and inconceivable real essences of plants or animals, every one knows. The workmanship of the all-wise and powerful God in the great fabric of the universe, and every part thereof, further exceeds the capacity and comprehension of the most inquisitive and intelligent man, than the best contrivance of the most ingenious man doth the conceptions of the most ignorant of rational creatures. Therefore we in vain pretend to range things into sorts, and dispose them into certain classes under names, by their real essences, that are so far from our discovery or comprehension. A blind man may as soon sort things by their colours, and he that has lost his smell as well distinguish a lily and a rose by their odours, as by those internal constitutions which he knows not. He that thinks he can distinguish sheep and goats by their real essences, that are unknown to him, may be pleased to try his skill in those species called CASSIOWARY and QUERECHINCHIO; and by their internal real essences determine the boundaries of those species, without knowing the complex idea of sensible qualities that each of those names stand for, in the countries where those animals are to be found.

10. Not the substantial Form, which know Not.

Those, therefore, who have been taught that the several species of substances had their distinct internal SUBSTANTIAL FORMS, and that it was those FORMS which made the distinction of substances into their true species and genera, were led yet further out of the way by having their minds set upon fruitless inquiries after 'substantial forms'; wholly unintelligible, and whereof we have scarce so much as any obscure or confused conception in general.

11. That the Nominal Essence is that only whereby we distinguish Species of Substances, further evident, from our ideas of finite Spirits and of God. That our ranking and distinguishing natural substances into species consists in the nominal essences the mind makes, and not in the real

essences to be found in the things themselves, is further evident from our ideas of spirits. For the mind getting, only by reflecting on its own operations, those simple ideas which it attributes to spirits, it hath or can have no other notion of spirit but by attributing all those operations it finds in itself to a sort of beings; without consideration of matter. And even the most advanced notion we have of GOD is but attributing the same simple ideas which we have got from reflection on what we find in ourselves, and which we conceive to have more perfection in them than would be in their absence; attributing, I say, those simple ideas to Him in an unlimited degree. Thus, having got from reflecting on ourselves the idea of existence, knowledge, power and pleasure—each of which we find it better to have than to want; and the more we have of each the better—joining all these together, with infinity to each of them, we have the complex idea of an eternal, omniscient, omnipotent, infinitely wise and happy being. And though we are told that there are different species of angels; yet we know not how to frame distinct specific ideas of them: not out of any conceit that the existence of more species than one of spirits is impossible; but because having no more simple ideas (nor being able to frame more) applicable to such beings, but only those few taken from ourselves, and from the actions of our own minds in thinking, and being delighted, and moving several parts of our bodies; we can no otherwise distinguish in our conceptions the several species of spirits, one from another, but by attributing those operations and powers we find in ourselves to them in a higher or lower degree; and so have no very distinct specific ideas of spirits, except only of GOD, to whom we attribute both duration and all those other ideas with infinity; to the other spirits, with limitation: nor, as I humbly conceive, do we, between GOD and them in our ideas, put any difference, by any number of simple ideas which we have of one and not of the other, but only that of infinity. All the particular ideas of existence, knowledge, will, power, and motion, &c., being ideas derived from the operations of our minds, we attribute all of them to all sorts of spirits, with the difference only of degrees; to the utmost we can imagine, even infinity, when we would frame as well as we can an idea of the First Being; who yet, it is certain, is infinitely more remote, in the real excellency of his nature, from the highest and perfectest of all created beings, than the greatest man, nay, purest seraph, is from the most contemptible part of matter; and consequently must infinitely exceed what our narrow understandings can conceive of Him.

12. Of finite Spirits there are probably numberless Species in a continuous series of gradations.

It is not impossible to conceive, nor repugnant to reason, that there may be many species of spirits, as much separated and diversified one from another by distinct properties whereof we have no ideas, as the species of sensible things are distinguished one from another by qualities which we know and observe in them. That there should be more species of intelligent creatures above us, than there are of sensible and material below us, is probable to me from hence: that in all the visible corporeal world, we see no chasms or gaps. All quite down from us the descent is by easy steps, and a continued series of things, that in each remove differ very little one from the other. There are fishes that have wings, and are not strangers to the airy region: and there are some birds that are inhabitants of the water, whose blood is cold as fishes, and their flesh so like in taste that the scrupulous are allowed them on fish-days. There are animals so near of kin both to birds and beasts that they are in the middle between both: amphibious animals link the terrestrial and aquatic together; seals live at land and sea, and porpoises have the warm blood and entrails of a hog; not to mention what is confidently reported of mermaids, or sea-men. There are some brutes that seem to have as much knowledge and reason as some that are called men: and the animal and vegetable kingdoms are so nearly joined, that, if you will take the lowest of one and the highest of the other, there will scarce be perceived any great difference between them: and so on, till we come to the lowest and the most inorganical parts of matter, we shall find everywhere that the several species are linked together, and differ but in almost insensible degrees. And when we consider the infinite power and wisdom of the Maker, we have reason to think that it is suitable to the magnificent harmony of the universe, and the great design and infinite goodness of the Architect, that the species of creatures should also, by gentle degrees, ascend upward from us toward his infinite perfection, as we see they gradually descend from us downwards: which if it be probable, we have reason then to be persuaded that there are far more species of creatures above us than there are beneath; we being, in degrees of perfection, much more remote from the infinite being of God than we are from the lowest state of being, and that which approaches nearest to nothing. And yet of all those distinct species, for the reasons abovesaid, we have no clear distinct ideas.

13. The Nominal Essence that of the Species, as conceived by us, proved from Water and Ice.

But to return to the species of corporeal substances. If I should ask any one whether ice and water were two distinct species of things, I doubt not but I should be answered in the affirmative: and it cannot be denied but he that says they are two distinct species is in the right. But if an Englishman bred in Jamaica, who perhaps had never seen nor heard of ice, coming into England in the winter, find the water he put in his basin at night in a great part frozen in the morning, and, not knowing any peculiar name it had, should call it hardened water; I ask whether this would be a new species to him, different from water? And I think it would be answered here, It would not be to him a new species, no more than congealed jelly, when it is cold, is a distinct species from the same jelly fluid and warm; or than liquid gold in the furnace is a distinct species from hard gold in the hands of a workman. And if this be so, it is plain that OUR DISTINCT SPECIES are NOTHING BUT DISTINCT COMPLEX IDEAS, WITH DISTINCT NAMES ANNEXED TO THEM. It is true every substance that exists has its peculiar constitution, whereon depend those sensible qualities and powers we observe in it; but the ranking of things into species (which is nothing but sorting them under several titles) is done by us according to the ideas that WE have of them: which, though sufficient to distinguish them by names, so that we may be able to discourse of them when we have them not present before us; yet if we suppose it to be done by their real internal constitutions, and that things existing are distinguished by nature into species, by real essences, according as we distinguish them into species by names, we shall be liable to great mistakes.

14. Difficulties in the supposition of a certain number of real Essences

To distinguish substantial beings into species, according to the usual supposition, that there are certain precise essences or forms of things, whereby all the individuals existing are, by nature distinguished into species, these things are necessary:—

15. A crude supposition.

First, To be assured that nature, in the production of things, always designs them to partake of certain regulated established essences, which are to be the models of all things to be produced. This, in that crude sense it is usually proposed, would need some better explication, before it can fully be assented to.

16. Monstrous births.

Secondly, It would be necessary to know whether nature always attains that essence it designs in the production of things. The irregular and monstrous births, that in divers sorts of animals have been observed, will always give us reason to doubt of one or both of these.

17. Are monsters really a distinct species?

Thirdly, It ought to be determined whether those we call monsters be really a distinct species, according to the scholastic notion of the word species; since it is certain that everything that exists has its particular constitution. And yet we find that some of these monstrous productions have few or none of those qualities which are supposed to result from, and accompany, the essence of that species from whence they derive their originals, and to which, by their descent, they seem to belong.

18. Men can have no ideas of Real Essences.

Fourthly, The real essences of those things which we distinguish into species, and as so distinguished we name, ought to be known; i.e. we ought to have ideas of them. But since we are ignorant in these four points, the supposed real essences of things stand US not in stead for the distinguishing substances into species.

19. Our Nominal Essences of Substances not perfect collections of the properties that flow from the Real Essence.

Fifthly, The only imaginable help in this case would be, that, having framed perfect complex ideas of the properties of things flowing from their different real essences, we should thereby distinguish them into species. But neither can this be done. For, being ignorant of the real essence itself, it is impossible to know all those properties that flow from it, and are so annexed to it, that any one of them being away, we may certainly conclude that that essence is not there, and so the thing is not of that species. We can never know what is the precise number of properties depending on the real essence of gold, any one of which failing, the real essence of gold, and consequently gold, would not be there, unless we knew the real essence of gold itself, and by that determined that species. By the word GOLD here, I must be understood to design a particular piece of matter; v. g. the last guinea that was coined. For, if it should stand here, in its ordinary signification, for that complex idea which I or any one else calls gold, i. e. for the nominal essence of gold, it would be jargon. So hard is it to show the various meaning and imperfection of words, when we have nothing else but words to do it by.

20. Hence names independent of Real Essence.

By all which it is clear, that our distinguishing substances into species by names, is not at all founded on their real essences; nor can we pretend to range and determine them exactly into species, according to internal essential differences.

21. But stand for such collections of simple ideas as we have made the Name stand for.

But since, as has been remarked, we have need of GENERAL words, though we know not the real essences of things; all we can do is, to collect such a number of simple ideas as, by examination, we find to be united together in things existing, and thereof to make one complex idea. Which, though it be not the real essence of any substance that exists, is yet the specific essence to which our name belongs, and is convertible with it; by which we may at least try the truth of these nominal essences. For example: there be that say that the essence of body is EXTENSION; if it be so, we can never mistake in putting the essence of anything for the thing itself. Let us then in discourse put extension for body, and when we would say that body moves, let us say that extension moves, and see how ill it will look. He that should say that one extension by impulse moves another extension, would, by the bare expression, sufficiently show the absurdity of such a notion. The essence of anything in respect of us, is the whole complex idea comprehended and marked by that name; and in substances, besides the several distinct simple ideas that make them up, the confused one of substance, or of an unknown support and cause of their union, is always a part: and therefore the essence of body is not bare extension, but an extended solid thing; and so to say, an extended solid thing moves, or impels another, is all one, and as intelligible, as to say, BODY moves or impels. Likewise, to say that a rational animal is capable of conversation, is all one as to say a man; but no one will say that rationality is capable of conversation, because it makes not the whole essence to which we give the name man.

22. Our Abstract Ideas are to us the Measures of the Species we make in instance in that of Man.

There are creatures in the world that have shapes like ours, but are hairy, and want language and reason. There are naturals amongst us that have perfectly our shape, but want reason, and some of them language too. There are creatures, as it is said, (sit fides penes authorem, but there appears no contradiction that there should be such,) that, with language and reason and a shape in other things agreeing with ours, have hairy tails; others where the males have no beards, and others where the females have. If it be asked whether these be all men or no, all of human species? it is plain, the question refers only to the nominal essence: for those of them to whom the definition of the word man, or the complex idea signified by that name, agrees, are men, and the other not. But if the inquiry be made concerning the supposed real essence; and whether the internal constitution and frame of these several creatures be specifically different, it is wholly impossible for us to answer, no part of that going into our specific idea: only we have reason to think, that where the faculties or outward frame so much differs, the internal constitution is not exactly the same. But what difference in the real internal constitution makes a specific difference it is in vain to inquire; whilst our measures of species be, as they are, only our abstract ideas, which we know; and not that internal constitution, which makes no part of them. Shall the difference of hair only on the skin be a mark of a different internal specific constitution between a changeling and a drill, when they agree in shape, and want of reason and speech? And shall not the want of reason and speech be a sign to us of different real constitutions and species between a changeling and a reasonable man? And so of the rest, if we pretend that distinction of species or sorts is fixedly established by the real frame and secret constitutions of things.

23. Species in Animals not distinguished by Generation.

Nor let any one say, that the power of propagation in animals by the mixture of male and female, and in plants by seeds, keeps the supposed real species distinct and entire, For, granting this to be true, it would help us in the distinction of the species of things no further than the tribes of animals and vegetables. What must we do for the rest? But in those too it is not sufficient: for if history lie not, women have conceived by drills; and what real species, by that measure, such a production will be in nature will be a new question: and we have reason to think this is not impossible, since mules and jumarts, the one from the mixture of an ass and a mare, the other from the mixture of a bull and a mare, are so frequent in the world. I once saw a creature that was the issue of a cat and a rat, and had the plain marks of both about it; wherein nature appeared to have followed the pattern of neither sort alone, but to have jumbled them both together. To which he that shall add the monstrous productions that are so frequently to be met with in nature, will find it hard, even in the race of animals, to determine by the pedigree of what species every animal's issue is; and be at a loss about the real essence, which he thinks certainly conveyed by generation, and has alone a right to the specific name. But further, if the species of animals and plants are to be distinguished only by propagation, must I go to the Indies to see the sire and dam of the one, and the plant from which the seed was gathered that produced the other, to know whether this be a tiger or that tea?

24. Not by substantial Forms.

Upon the whole matter, it is evident that it is their own collections of sensible qualities that men make the essences of THEIR several sorts of substances; and that their real internal structures are not considered by the greatest part of men in the sorting them. Much less were any SUBSTANTIAL FORMS ever thought on by any but those who have in this one part of the world learned the language of the schools: and yet those ignorant men, who pretend not any insight into the real essences, nor trouble themselves about substantial forms, but are content with knowing things one from another by their sensible qualities, are often better acquainted with their differences; can more nicely distinguish them from their uses; and better know what they expect from each, than those learned quick-sighted men, who look so deep into them, and talk so confidently of something more hidden and essential.

25. The specific Essences that are common made by Men.

But supposing that the REAL essences of substances were discoverable by those that would severely apply themselves to that inquiry, yet we could not reasonably think that the ranking of things under general names was regulated by those internal real constitutions, or anything else but their OBVIOUS appearances; since languages, in all countries, have been established long before sciences. So that they have not been philosophers or logicians, or such who have troubled themselves about forms and essences, that have made the general names that are in use amongst the several nations of men: but those more or less comprehensive terms have, for the most part, in all languages, received their birth and signification from ignorant and illiterate people, who sorted and denominated things by those sensible qualities they found in them; thereby to signify them, when absent, to others, whether they had an occasion to mention a sort or a particular thing.

26. Therefore very various and uncertain in the ideas of different men.

Since then it is evident that we sort and name substances by their nominal and not by their real essences, the next thing to be considered is how, and by whom these essences come to be made. As to the latter, it is evident they are made by the mind, and not by nature: for were they Nature's workmanship, they could not be so various and different in several men as experience tells us they are. For if we will examine it, we shall not find the nominal essence of any one species of substances in all men the same: no, not of that which of all others we are the most intimately acquainted with. It could not possibly be that the abstract idea to which the name MAN is given should be different in several men, if it were of Nature's making; and that to one it should be animal rationale, and to another, animal implume bipes latis unguibus. He that annexes the name man to a complex idea, made up of sense and spontaneous motion, joined to a body of such a shape, has thereby one essence of the species man; and he that, upon further examination, adds rationality, has another essence of the species he calls man: by which means the same individual will be a true man to the one which is not so to the other. I think there is scarce any one will allow this upright figure, so well known, to be the essential difference of the species man; and yet how far men determine of the sorts of animals rather by their shape than descent, is very visible; since it has been more than once debated, whether several human foetuses should be preserved or received to baptism or no, only because of the difference of their outward configuration from the ordinary make of children, without knowing whether they were not as capable of reason as infants cast in another mould: some whereof, though of an approved shape, are never capable of as much appearance of reason all their lives as is to be found in an ape, or an elephant, and never give any signs of being acted by a rational soul. Whereby it is evident, that the outward figure, which only was found wanting, and not the faculty of reason, which nobody could know would be wanting in its due season, was made essential to the human species. The learned divine and lawyer must, on such occasions, renounce his sacred definition of animal rationale, and substitute some other essence of the human species. [Monsieur Menage furnishes us with an example worth the taking notice of on this occasion: 'When the abbot of Saint Martin,' says he, 'was born, he had so little of the figure of a man, that it bespake him rather a monster. It was for some time under deliberation, whether he should be baptized or no. However, he was baptized, and declared a man provisionally [till time should show what he would prove]. Nature had moulded him so untowardly, that he was called all his life the Abbot Malotru; i.e. ill-shaped. He was of Caen. (Menagiana, 278, 430.) This child, we see, was very near being excluded out of the species of man, barely by his shape. He escaped very narrowly as he was; and it is certain, a figure a little more oddly turned had cast him, and he had been executed, as a thing not to be allowed to pass for a man. And yet there can be no reason given why, if the lineaments of his face had been a little altered, a rational soul could not have been lodged in him; why a visage somewhat longer, or a nose flatter, or a wider mouth, could not have consisted, as well as the rest of his ill figure, with such a soul, such parts, as made him, disfigured as he was, capable to be a dignitary in the church.]

27. Nominal Essences of particular substances are undetermined by nature, and therefore various as men vary.

Wherein, then, would I gladly know, consist the precise and unmovable boundaries of that species? It is plain, if we examine, there is no such thing made by Nature, and established by her amongst men. The real essence of that or any other sort of substances, it is evident, we know not; and therefore are so undetermined in our nominal essences, which we make ourselves, that, if several men were to be asked concerning some oddly-shaped foetus, as soon as born, whether it were a man or no, it is past doubt one should meet with different answers. Which could not happen, if the nominal essences, whereby we limit and distinguish the species of substances, were not made by man with some liberty; but were exactly copied from precise boundaries set by nature, whereby it distinguished all substances into certain species. Who would undertake to resolve what species that monster was of which is mentioned by Licetus (lib. i. c. 3), with a man's head and hog's body? Or those other which to the bodies of men had the heads of beasts, as dogs, horses, &c. If any of these creatures had lived, and could have spoke, it would have increased the difficulty. Had the upper part to the middle been of human shape, and all below swine, had it been murder to destroy it? Or must the bishop have been consulted, whether it were man enough to be admitted to the font or no? As I have been told it happened in France some years since, in somewhat a like case. So uncertain are the boundaries of species of animals to us, who have no other measures than the complex ideas of our own collecting: and so far are we from certainly knowing what a MAN is; though perhaps it will be judged great ignorance to make any doubt about it. And yet I think I may say, that the certain boundaries of that species are so far from being determined, and the precise number of simple ideas which make the nominal essence so far from being settles and perfectly known, that very material doubts may still arise about it. And I imagine none of the definitions of the word MAN which we yet have, nor descriptios of that sort of animal, are so perfect and exact as to satisfy a considerate inquisitive person; much less to obtain a general consent, and to be that which men would everywhere stick by, in the decision of cases, and determining of life and death, baptism or no baptism, in productions that mights happen.

28. But not so arbitrary as Mixed Modes.

But though these nominal essences of substances are made by the mind, they are not yet made so arbitrarily as those of mixed modes. To the making of any nominal essence, it is necessary, First, that the ideas whereof it consists have such a union as to make but one idea, how compounded soever. Secondly, that the particular ideas so united be exactly the same, neither more nor less. For if two abstract complex ideas differ either in number or sorts of their component parts, they make two different, and not one and the same essence. In the first of these, the mind, in making its complex ideas of substances, only follows nature; and puts none together which are not supposed to have a union in nature. Nobody joins the voice of a sheep with the shape of a horse; nor the colour of lead with the weight and fixedness of gold, to be the complex ideas of any real substances; unless he has a mind to fill his head with chimeras, and his discourse with unintelligible words. Men observing certain qualities always joined and existing together, therein copied nature; and of ideas so united made their complex ones of substances. For, though men may make what complex ideas they please, and give what names to them they will; yet, if they will be understood WHEN THEY SPEAK OF THINGS REALLY EXISTING, they must in some degree conform their ideas to the things they would speak of; or else men's language will be like that of Babel; and every man's words, being intelligible only to himself, would no longer serve to conversation and the ordinary affairs of life, if the ideas they stand for be not some way answering the common appearances and agreement of substances as they really exist.

29. Our Nominal Essences of substances usually consist of a few obvious qualities observed in things.

Secondly, Though the mind of man, in making its complex ideas of substances, never puts any together that do not really, or are not supposed to, co-exist; and so it truly borrows that union from nature: yet the number it combines depends upon the various care, industry, or fancy of him that makes it. Men generally content themselves with some few sensible obvious qualities; and often, if not always, leave out others as material and as firmly united as those that they take. Of sensible substances there are two sorts: one of organized bodies, which are propagated by seed; and in these the SHAPE is that which to us is the leading quality, and most characteristical part, that determines the species. And therefore in vegetables and animals, an extended solid substance of such a certain figure usually serves the turn. For however some men seem to prize their definition of animal rationale, yet should there a creature be found that had language and reason, but partaked not of the usual shape of a man, I believe it would hardly pass for a man, how much soever it were animal rationale. And if Balaam's ass had all his life discoursed as rationally as he did once with his master, I doubt yet whether any one would have thought him worthy the name man, or allowed him to be of the same species with himself. As in vegetables and animals it is the shape, so in most other bodies, not propagated by seed, it is the COLOUR we most fix on, and are most led by. Thus where we find the colour of gold, we are apt to imagine all the other qualities comprehended in our complex idea to be there also: and we commonly take these two obvious qualities, viz. shape and colour, for so presumptive ideas of several species, that in a good picture, we readily say, this is a lion, and that a rose; this is a gold, and that a silver goblet, only by the different figures and colours represented to the eye by the pencil.

30. Yet, imperfect as they thus are, they serve for common converse. But though this serves well enough for gross and confused conceptions, and inaccurate ways of talking and thinking; yet MEN ARE FAR ENOUGH FROM HAVING AGREED ON THE PRECISE NUMBER OF SIMPLE IDEAS OR QUALITIES BELONGING TO ANY SORT OF THINGS, SIGNIFIED BY ITS NAME. Nor is it a wonder; since it requires much time, pains, and skill, strict inquiry, and long examination to find out what, and how many, those simple ideas are, which are constantly and inseparably united in nature, and are always to be found together in the same subject. Most men, wanting either time, inclination, or industry enough for this, even to some tolerable degree, content themselves with some few obvious and outward appearances of things, thereby readily to distinguish and sort them for the common affairs of life: and so, without further examination, give them names, or take up the names already in use. Which, though in common conversation they pass well enough for the signs of some few obvious qualities co-existing, are yet far enough from comprehending, in a settled signification, a precise number of simple ideas, much less all those which are united in nature. He that shall consider, after so much stir about genus and species, and such a deal of talk of specific differences, how few words we have yet settled definitions of, may with reason imagine, that those FORMS which there hath been so much noise made about are only chimeras, which give us no light into the specific natures of things. And he that shall consider how far the names of substances are from having significations wherein all who use them do

agree, will have reason to conclude that, though the nominal essences of substances are all supposed to be copied from nature, yet they are all, or most of them, very imperfect. Since the composition of those complex ideas are, in several men, very different: and therefore that these boundaries of species are as men, and not as Nature, makes them, if at least there are in nature any such prefixed bounds. It is true that many particular substances are so made by Nature, that they have agreement and likeness one with another, and so afford a foundation of being ranked into sorts. But the sorting of things by us, or the making of determinate species, being in order to naming and comprehending them under general terms, I cannot see how it can be properly said, that Nature sets the boundaries of the species of things: or, if it be so, our boundaries of species are not exactly conformable to those in nature. For we, having need of general names for present use, stay not for a perfect discovery of all those qualities which would BEST show us their most material differences and agreements; but we ourselves divide them, by certain obvious appearances, into species, that we may the easier under general names communicate our thoughts about them. For, having no other knowledge of any substance but of the simple ideas that are united in it; and observing several particular things to agree with others in several of those simple ideas; we make that collection our specific idea, and give it a general name; that in recording our thoughts, and in our discourse with others, we may in one short word designate all the individuals that agree in that complex idea, without enumerating the simple ideas that make it up; and so not waste our time and breath in tedious descriptions: which we see they are fain to do who would discourse of any new sort of things they have not yet a name for.

31. Essences of Species under the same Name very different in different minds.

But however these species of substances pass well enough in ordinary conversation, it is plain that this complex idea wherein they observe several individuals to agree, is by different men made very differently; by some more, and others less accurately. In some, this complex idea contains a greater, and in others a smaller number of qualities; and so is apparently such as the mind makes it. The yellow shining colour makes gold to children; others add weight, malleableness, and fusibility; and others yet other qualities, which they find joined with that yellow colour, as constantly as its weight and fusibility. For in all these and the like qualities, one has as good a right to be put into the complex idea of that substance wherein they are all joined as another. And therefore different men, leaving out or putting in several simple ideas which others do not, according to their various examination, skill, or observation of that subject, have different essences of gold, which must therefore be of their own and not of nature's making.

32. The more general our Ideas of Substances are, the more incomplete and partial they are.

If the number of simple ideas that make the nominal essence of the lowest species, or first sorting, of individuals, depends on the mind of man, variously collecting them, it is much more evident that they do so in the more comprehensive classes, which, by the masters of logic, are called genera. These are complex ideas designedly imperfect: and it is visible at first sight, that several of those qualities that are to be found in the things themselves are purposely left out of generical ideas. For, as the mind, to make general ideas comprehending several particulars, leaves out those of time and place, and such other, that make them incommunicable to more than one individual; so to make other yet more general ideas, that may comprehend different sorts, it leaves out those qualities that distinguish them, and puts into its new collection only such ideas as are common to several sorts. The same convenience that made men express several parcels of yellow matter coming from Guinea and Peru under one name, sets them also upon making of one name that may comprehend both gold and silver, and some other bodies of different sorts. This is done by leaving out those qualities, which are peculiar to each sort, and retaining a complex idea made up of those that are common to them all. To which the name METAL being annexed, there is a genus constituted; the essence whereof being that abstract idea, containing only malleableness and fusibility, with certain degrees of weight and fixedness, wherein some bodies of several kinds agree, leaves out the colour and other qualities peculiar to gold and silver, and the other sorts comprehended under the name metal. Whereby it is plain that men follow not exactly the patterns set them by nature, when they make their general ideas of substances; since there is no body to be found which has barely malleableness and fusibility in it, without other qualities as inseparable as those. But men, in making their general ideas, seeking more the convenience of language, and quick dispatch by short and comprehensive signs, than the true and precise nature of things as they exist, have, in the framing their abstract ideas, chiefly pursued that end; which was to be furnished with store of general and variously comprehensive names. So that in this whole business of genera and species, the genus, or more comprehensive, is but a partial conception of what is in the species; and the species but a partial idea of what is to be found in each individual. If therefore any one will think that a man, and a horse, and an animal, and a plant, &c., are distinguished by real essences made by nature, he must think nature to be very liberal of these real essences, making one for body, another for an animal, and another for a horse; and all these essences liberally bestowed upon Bucephalus. But if we would rightly consider what is done in all these genera and species, or sorts, we should find that there is no new thing made; but only more or less comprehensive signs, whereby we may be enabled to express in a few syllables great numbers of particular things, as they agree in more or less general conceptions, which we have framed to that purpose. In all which we may observe, that the more general term is always the name of a less complex idea; and that each genus is but a partial conception of; the species comprehended under it. So that if these abstract general ideas be thought to be complete, it can only be in respect of a certain established relation between them and certain names which are made use of to signify them; and not in respect of anything existing, as made by nature.

33. This all accommodated to the end of the Speech.

This is adjusted to the true end of speech, which is to be the easiest and shortest way of communicating our notions. For thus he that would discourse of things, as they agreed in the complex idea of extension and solidity, needed but use the word BODY to denote all such. He that to these would join others, signified by the words life, sense, and spontaneous motion, needed but use the word ANIMAL to signify all which partaked of those ideas, and he that had made a complex idea of a body, with life, sense, and motion, with the faculty of reasoning, and a certain shape joined to it, needed but use the short monosyllable MAN, to express all particulars that correspond to that complex idea. This is the proper business of genus and species: and this men do without any consideration of real essences, or substantial forms; which come not within the reach of our knowledge when we think of those things, nor within the signification of our words when we discourse with others.

34. Instance in Cassowaries.

Were I to talk with any one of a sort of birds I lately saw in St. James's Park, about three or four feet high, with a covering of something between feathers and hair, of a dark brown colour, without wings, but in the place thereof two or three little branches coming down like sprigs of Spanish broom, long great legs, with feet only of three claws, and without a tail; I must make this description of it, and so may make others understand me.

But when I am told that the name of it is CASSUARIS, I may then use that word to stand in discourse for all my complex idea mentioned in that description; though by that word, which is now become a specific name, I know no more of the real essence or constitution of that sort of animals than I did before; and knew probably as much of the nature of that species of birds before I learned the name, as many Englishmen do of swans or herons, which are specific names, very well known, of sorts of birds common in England.

35. Men determine the Sorts of Substances, which may be sorted variously. From what has been said, it is evident that MEN make sorts of things. For, it being different essences alone that make different species, it is plain that they who make those abstract ideas which are the nominal essences do thereby make the species, or sort. Should there be a body found, having all the other qualities of gold except malleableness, it would no doubt be made a question whether it were gold or not, i.e. whether it were of that species. This could be determined only by that abstract idea to which every one annexed the name gold: so that it would be true gold to him, and belong to that species, who included not malleableness in his nominal essence, signified by the sound gold; and on the other side it would not be true gold, or of that species, to him who included malleableness in his specific idea. And who, I pray, is it that makes these diverse species, even under one and the same name, but men that make two different abstract ideas, consisting not exactly of the same collection of qualities? Nor is it a mere supposition to imagine that a body may exist wherein the other obvious qualities of gold may be without malleableness; since it is certain that gold itself will be sometimes so eager, (as artists call it,) that it will as little endure the hammer as glass itself. What we have said of the putting in, or leaving out of malleableness, in the complex idea the name gold is by any one annexed to, may be said of its peculiar weight, fixedness, and several other the like qualities: for whatever is left out, or put in, it is still the complex idea to which that name is annexed that makes the species: and as any particular parcel of matter answers that idea, so the name of the sort belongs truly to it; and it is of that species. And thus anything is true gold, perfect metal. All which determination of the species, it is plain, depends on the understanding of man, making this or that complex idea.

36. Nature makes the Similitudes of Substances.

This, then, in short, is the case: Nature makes many PARTICULAR THINGS, which do agree one with another in many sensible qualities, and probably too in their internal frame and constitution: but it is not this real essence that distinguishes them into species; it is men who, taking occasion from the qualities they find united in them, and wherein they observe often several individuals to agree, range them into sorts, in order to their naming, for the convenience of comprehensive signs; under which individuals, according to their conformity to this or that abstract idea, come to be ranked as under ensigns: so that this is of the blue, that the red regiment; this is a man, that a drill: and in this, I think, consists the whole business of genus and species.

37. The manner of sorting particular beings the work of fallible men, though nature makes things alike.

I do not deny but nature, in the constant production of particular beings, makes them not always new and various, but very much alike and of kin one to another: but I think it nevertheless true, that the boundaries of the species, whereby men sort them, are made by men; since the essences of the species, distinguished by different names, are, as has been proved, of man's making, and seldom adequate to the internal nature of the things they are taken from. So that we may truly say, such a manner of sorting of things is the workmanship of men.

38. Each abstract Idea, with a name to it, makes a nominal Essence.

One thing I doubt not but will seem very strange in this doctrine, which is, that from what has been said it will follow, that each abstract idea, with a name to it, makes a distinct species. But who can help it, if truth will have it so? For so it must remain till somebody can show us the species of things limited and distinguished by something else; and let us see that general terms signify not our abstract ideas, but something different from them. I would fain know why a shock and a hound are not as distinct species as a spaniel and an elephant. We have no other idea of the different essence of an elephant and a spaniel, than we have of the different essence of a shock and a hound; all the essential difference, whereby we know and distinguish them one from another, consisting only in the different collection of simple ideas, to which we have given those different names.

39. How Genera and Species are related to naming.

How much the making of species and genera is in order to general names; and how much general names are necessary, if not to the being, yet at least to the completing of a species, and making it pass for such, will appear, besides what has been said above concerning ice and water, in a very familiar example. A silent and a striking watch are but one species, to those who have but one name for them: but he that has the name WATCH for one, and CLOCK for the other, and distinct complex ideas to which those names belong, to HIM they are different species. It will be said perhaps, that the inward contrivance and constitution is different between these two, which the watchmaker has a clear idea of. And yet it is plain they are but one species to him, when he has but one name for them. For what is sufficient in the inward contrivance to make a new species? There are some watches that are made with four wheels, others with five; is this a specific difference to the workman? Some have strings and physics, and others none; some have the balance loose, and others regulated by a spiral spring, and others by hogs' bristles. Are any or all of these enough to make a specific difference to the workman, that knows each of these and several other different contrivances in the internal constitutions of watches? It is certain each of these hath a real difference from the rest; but whether it be an essential, a specific difference or no, relates only to the complex idea to which the name watch is given: as long as they all agree in the idea which that name stands for, and that name does not as a generical name comprehend different species under it, they are not essentially nor specifically different. But if any one will make minuter divisions, from differences that he knows in the internal frame of watches, and to such precise complex ideas give names that shall prevail; they will then be new species, to them who have those ideas with names to them, and can by those differences distinguish watches into these several sorts; and then WATCH will be a generical name. But yet they would be no distinct species to men ignorant of clock-work, and the inward contrivances of watches, who had no other idea but the outward shape and bulk, with the marking of the hours by the hand. For to them all those other names would be but synonymous terms for the same idea, and signify no more, nor no other thing but a watch. Just thus I think it is in natural things. Nobody will doubt that the wheels or springs (if I may so say) within, are different in a RATIONAL MAN and a CHANGELING; no more than that there is a difference in the frame between a DRILL and a CHANGELING. But whether one or both these differences be essential or specifical, is only to be known to us by their agreement or disagreement with the complex idea that the name man stands for: for by that alone can it be determined whether one, or both, or neither of those be a man.

40. Species of Artificial Things less confused than Natural.

From what has been before said, we may see the reason why, in the species of artificial things, there is generally less confusion and uncertainty than in natural. Because an artificial thing being a production of man, which the artificer designed, and therefore well knows the idea of, the name of it is supposed to stand for no other idea, nor to import any other essence, than what is certainly to be known, and easy enough to be apprehended. For the idea or essence of the several sorts of artificial things, consisting for the most part in nothing but the determinate figure of sensible parts, and sometimes motion depending thereon, which the artificer fashions in matter, such as he finds for his turn; it is not beyond the reach of our faculties to attain a certain idea thereof; and so settle the signification of the names whereby the species of artificial things are distinguished, with less doubt, obscurity, and equivocation than we can in things natural, whose differences and operations depend upon contrivances beyond the reach of our discoveries.

41. Artificial Things of distinct Species.

I must be excused here if I think artificial things are of distinct species as well as natural: since I find they are as plainly and orderly ranked into sorts, by different abstract ideas, with general names annexed to them, as distinct one from another as those of natural substances. For why should we not think a watch and pistol as distinct species one from another, as a horse and a dog; they being expressed in our minds by distinct ideas, and to others by distinct appellations?

42. Substances alone, of all our several sorts of ideas, have proper Names.

This is further to be observed concerning substances, that they alone of all our several sorts of ideas have particular or proper names, whereby one only particular thing is signified. Because in simple ideas, modes, and relations, it seldom happens that men have occasion to mention often this or that particular when it is absent. Besides, the greatest part of mixed modes, being actions which perish in their birth, are not capable of a lasting duration, as substances which are the actors; and wherein the simple ideas that make up the complex ideas designed by the name have a lasting union.

43. Difficult to lead another by words into the thoughts of things stripped of those abstract ideas we give them.

I must beg pardon of my reader for having dwelt so long upon this subject, and perhaps with some obscurity. But I desire it may be considered, how difficult it is to lead another by words into the thoughts of things, stripped of those specific differences we give them: which things, if I name not, I say nothing; and if I do name them, I thereby rank them into some sort or other, and suggest to the mind the usual abstract idea of that species; and so cross my purpose. For, to talk of a man, and to lay by, at the same time, the ordinary signification of the name man, which is our complex idea usually annexed to it; and bid the reader consider man, as he is in himself, and as he is really distinguished from others in his internal constitution, or real essence, that is, by something he knows not what, looks like trifling: and yet thus one must do who would speak of the supposed real essences and species of things, as thought to be made by nature, if it be but only to make it understood, that there is no such thing signified by the general names which substances are called by. But because it is difficult by known familiar names to do this, give me leave to endeavour by an example to make the different consideration the mind has of specific names and ideas a little more clear; and to show how the complex ideas of modes are referred sometimes to archetypes in the minds of other intelligent beings, or, which is the same, to the signification annexed by others to their received names; and sometimes to no archetypes at all. Give me leave also to show how the mind always refers its ideas of substances, either to the substances themselves, or to the signification of their names, as to the archetypes; and also to make plain the nature of species or sorting of things, as apprehended and made use of by us; and of the essences belonging to those species: which is perhaps of more moment to discover the extent and certainty of our knowledge than we at first imagine.

44. Instances of mixed Modes names KINNEAH and NIOUPH.

Let us suppose Adam, in the state of a grown man, with a good understanding, but in a strange country, with all things new and unknown about him; and no other faculties to attain the knowledge of them but what one of this age has now. He observes Lamech more melancholy than usual, and imagines it to be from a suspicion he has of his wife Adah, (whom he most ardently loved) that she had too much kindness for another man. Adam discourses these his thoughts to Eve, and desires her to take care that Adah commit not folly: and in these discourses with Eve he makes use of these two new words KINNEAH and NIOUPH. In time, Adam's mistake appears, for he finds Lamech's trouble proceeded from having killed a man: but yet the two names KINNEAH and NIOUPH, (the one standing for suspicion in a husband of his wife's disloyalty to him; and the other for the act of committing disloyalty,) lost not their distinct significations. It is plain then, that here were two distinct complex ideas of mixed modes, with names to them, two distinct species of actions essentially different; I ask wherein consisted the essences of these two distinct species of actions? And it is plain it consisted in a precise combination of simple ideas, different in one from the other. I ask, whether the complex idea in Adam's mind, which he called KINNEAH, were adequate or not? And it is plain it was; for it being a combination of simple ideas, which he, without any regard to any archetype, without respect to anything as a pattern, voluntarily put together, abstracted, and gave the name KINNEAH to, to express in short to others, by that one sound, all the simple ideas contained and united in that complex one; it must necessarily follow that it was an adequate idea. His own choice having made that combination, it had all in it he intended it should, and so could not but be perfect, could not but be adequate; it being referred to no other archetype which it was supposed to represent.

45. These words, KINNEAH and NIOUPH, by degrees grew into common use, and then the case was somewhat altered. Adam's children had the same faculties, and thereby the same power that he had, to make what complex ideas of mixed modes they pleased in their own minds; to abstract them, and make what sounds they pleased the signs of them: but the use of names being to make our ideas within us known to others, that cannot be done, but when the same sign stands for the same idea in two who would communicate their thoughts and discourse together. Those, therefore, of Adam's children, that found these two words, KINNEAH and NIOUPH, in familiar use, could not take them for insignificant sounds, but must needs conclude they stood for something; for certain ideas, abstract ideas, they being general names; which abstract ideas were the essences of the species distinguished by those names. If therefore, they would use these words as names of species already established and agreed on, they were obliged to conform the ideas in their minds, signified by these names, to the ideas that they stood for in other men's minds, as to their patterns and archetypes; and then indeed their ideas of these complex modes were liable to be inadequate, as being very apt (especially those that consisted of combinations of many simple ideas) not to be exactly conformable to the ideas in other men's minds, using the same names; though for this there be usually a remedy at hand, which is to ask the meaning of any word we understand not of him that uses it: it being as impossible to know certainly what the words jealousy and adultery (which I think answer [Hebrew] and [Hebrew]) stand for in another man's mind, with whom I would discourse about them; as it was impossible, in the beginning of language, to know what KINNEAH and NIOUPH stood for in another man's mind, without explication; they being voluntary signs in every one.

46. Instances of a species of Substance named ZAHAB.

Let us now also consider, after the same manner, the names of substances in their first application. One of Adam's children, roving in the mountains, lights on a glittering substance which pleases his eye. Home he carries it to Adam, who, upon consideration of it, finds it to be hard, to have a bright yellow colour, and an exceeding great weight. These perhaps, at first, are all the qualities he takes notice of in it; and abstracting this complex idea, consisting of a substance having that peculiar bright yellowness, and a weight very great in proportion to its bulk, he gives the name ZAHAB, to denominate and mark all substances that have these sensible qualities in them. It is evident now, that, in this case, Adam acts quite differently from what he did before, in forming those ideas of mixed modes to which he gave the names KINNEAH and NIOUPH. For there he put ideas together only by his own imagination, not taken from the existence of anything; and to them he gave names to denominate all things that should happen to agree to those his abstract ideas, without considering whether any such thing did exist or not: the standard there was of his own making. But in the forming his idea of this new substance, he takes the quite contrary course; here he has a standard made by nature; and therefore, being to represent that to himself, by the idea he has of it, even when it is absent, he puts in no simple idea into his complex one, but what he has the perception of from the thing itself. He takes care that his idea be conformable to this archetype, and intends the name should stand for an idea so conformable.

47.

This piece of matter, thus denominated ZAHAB by Adam, being quite different from any he had seen before, nobody, I think, will deny to be a distinct species, and to have its peculiar essence; and that the name ZAHAB is the mark of the species, and a name belonging to all things partaking in that essence. But here it is plain the essence Adam made the name ZAHAB stand for was nothing but a body hard, shining, yellow, and very heavy. But the inquisitive mind of man, not content with the knowledge of these, as I may say, superficial qualities, puts Adam upon further examination of this matter. He therefore knocks, and beats it with flints, to see what was discoverable in the inside: he finds it yield to blows, but not easily separate into pieces: he finds it will bend without breaking. Is not now ductility to be added to his former idea, and made part of the essence of the species that name ZAHAB stands for? Further trials discover fusibility and fixedness. Are not they also, by the same reason that any of the others were, to be put into the complex idea signified by the name ZAHAB? If not, what reason will there be shown more for the one than the other? If these must, then all the other properties, which any further trials shall discover in this matter, ought by the same reason to make a part of the ingredients of the complex idea which the name ZAHAB stands for, and so be the essence of the species marked by that name. Which properties, because they are endless, it is plain that the idea made after this fashion, by this archetype, will be always inadequate.

48. The Abstract Ideas of Substances always imperfect and therefore various.

But this is not all. It would also follow that the names of substances would not only have, as in truth they have, but would also be supposed to have different significations, as used by different men, which would very much cumber the use of language. For if every distinct quality that were discovered in any matter by any one were supposed to make a necessary part of the complex idea signified by the common name given to it, it must follow, that men must suppose the same word to signify different things in different men: since they cannot doubt but different men may have discovered several qualities, in substances of the same denomination, which others know nothing of.

49. Therefore to fix the Nominal Species Real Essence supposed.

To avoid this therefore, they have supposed a real essence belonging to every species, from which these properties all flow, and would have their name of the species stand for that. But they, not having any idea of that real essence in substances, and their words signifying nothing but the ideas they have, that which is done by this attempt is only to put the name or sound in the place and stead of the thing having that real essence, without knowing what the real essence is, and this is that which men do when they speak of species of things, as supposing them made by nature, and distinguished by real essences.

50. Which Supposition is of no Use.

For, let us consider, when we affirm that 'all gold is fixed,' either it means that fixedness is a part of the definition, i. e., part of the nominal essence the word gold stands for; and so this affirmation, 'all gold is fixed,' contains nothing but the signification of the term gold. Or else it means, that fixedness, not being a part of the definition of the gold, is a property of that substance itself: in which case it is plain that the word gold stands in the place of a substance, having the real essence of a species of things made by nature. In which way of substitution it has so confused and uncertain a signification, that, though this proposition—'gold is fixed'—be in that sense an affirmation of something real; yet it is a truth will always fail us in its particular application, and so is of no real use or certainty. For let it be ever so true, that all gold, i. e. all that has the real essence of gold, is fixed, what serves this for, whilst we know not, in this sense, WHAT IS

OR IS NOT GOLD? For if we know not the real essence of gold, it is impossible we should know what parcel of matter has that essence, and so whether IT be true gold or no.

51. Conclusion.

To conclude: what liberty Adam had at first to make any complex ideas of MIXED MODES by no other pattern but by his own thoughts, the same have all men ever since had. And the same necessity of conforming his ideas of SUBSTANCES to things without him, as to archetypes made by nature, that Adam was under, if he would not wilfully impose upon himself, the same are all men ever since under too. The same liberty also that Adam had of affixing any new name to any idea, the same has any one still, (especially the beginners of languages, if we can imagine any such;) but only with this difference, that, in places where men in society have already established a language amongst them, the significations of words are very warily and sparingly to be altered. Because men being furnished already with names for their ideas, and common use having appropriated known names to certain ideas, an affected misapplication of them cannot but be very ridiculous. He that hath new notions will perhaps venture sometimes on the coining of new terms to express them: but men think it a boldness, and it is uncertain whether common use will ever make them pass for current. But in communication with others, it is necessary that we conform the ideas we make the vulgar words of any language stand for to their known proper significations, (which I have explained at large already,) or else to make known that new signification we apply them to.

CHAPTER VII.

OF PARTICLES.

1. Particles connect Parts, or whole Sentences together.
Besides words which are names of ideas in the mind, there are a great many others that are made use of to signify the CONNEXION that the mind gives to ideas, or to propositions, one with another. The mind, in communicating its thoughts to others, does not only need signs of the ideas it has then before it, but others also, to show or intimate some particular action of its own, at that time, relating to those ideas. This it does several ways; as _I_S and _I_S NOT, are the general marks, of the mind, affirming or denying. But besides affirmation or negation, without which there is in words no truth or falsehood, the mind does, in declaring its sentiments to others, connect not only the parts of propositions, but whole sentences one to another, with their several relations and dependencies, to make a coherent discourse.

2. In right use of Particles consists the Art of Well-speaking
The words whereby it signifies what connexion it gives to the several affirmations and negations, that it unites in one continued reasoning or narration, are generally called PARTICLES: and it is in the right use of these that more particularly consists the clearness and beauty of a good style. To think well, it is not enough that a man has ideas clear and distinct in his thoughts, nor that he observes the agreement or disagreement of some of them; but he must think in train, and observe the dependence of his thoughts and reasonings upon one another. And to express well such methodical and rational thoughts, he must have words to show what connexion, restriction, distinction, opposition, emphasis, &c., he gives to each respective part of his discourse. To mistake in any of these, is to puzzle instead of informing his hearer: and therefore it is, that those words which are not truly by themselves the names of any ideas are of such constant and indispensable use in language, and do much contribute to men's well expressing themselves.

3. They say what Relation the Mind gives to its own Thoughts.
This part of grammar has been perhaps as much neglected as some others over-diligently cultivated. It is easy for men to write, one after another, of cases and genders, moods and tenses, gerunds and supines: in these and the like there has been great diligence used; and particles themselves, in some languages, have been, with great show of exactness, ranked into their

several orders. But though PREPOSITIONS and CONJUNCTIONS, &c., are names well known in grammar, and the particles contained under them carefully ranked into their distinct subdivisions; yet he who would show the right use of particles, and what significancy and force they have, must take a little more pains, enter into his own thoughts, and observe nicely the several postures of his mind in discoursing.

4. They are all marks of some action or intimation of the mind.

Neither is it enough, for the explaining of these words, to render them, as is usual in dictionaries, by words of another tongue which come nearest to their signification: for what is meant by them is commonly as hard to be understood in one as another language. They are all marks of some action or intimation of the mind; and therefore to understand them rightly, the several views, postures, stands, turns, limitations, and exceptions, and several other thoughts of the mind, for which we have either none or very deficient names, are diligently to be studied. Of these there is a great variety, much exceeding the number of particles that most languages have to express them by: and therefore it is not to be wondered that most of these particles have divers and sometimes almost opposite significations. In the Hebrew tongue there is a particle consisting of but one single letter, of which there are reckoned up, as I remember, seventy, I am sure above fifty, several significations.

5. Instance in But.

'But' is a particle, none more familiar in our language: and he that says it is a discretive conjunction, and that it answers to sed Latin, or mais in French, thinks he has sufficiently explained it. But yet it seems to me to intimate several relations the mind gives to the several propositions or parts of them which it joins by this monosyllable.

First, 'But to say no more:' here it intimates a stop of the mind in the course it was going, before it came quite to the end of it.

Secondly, 'I saw but two plants;' here it shows that the mind limits the sense to what is expressed, with a negation of all other.

Thirdly,'You pray; but it is not that God would bring you to the true religion.'

Fourthly, 'But that he would confirm you in your own.' The first of these BUTS intimates a supposition in the mind of something otherwise than it should be; the latter shows that the mind makes a direct opposition between that and what goes before it.

Fifthly, 'All animals have sense, but a dog is an animal:' here it signifies little more but that the latter proposition is joined to the former, as the minor of a syllogism.

6. This Matter of the use of Particles but lightly touched here.

To these, I doubt not, might be added a great many other significations of this particle, if it were my business to examine it in its full latitude, and consider it in all the places it is to be found: which if one should do, I doubt whether in all those manners it is made use of, it would deserve the title of DISCRETIVE, which grammarians give to it. But I intend not here a full explication of this sort of signs. The instances I have given in this one may give occasion to reflect on their use and force in language, and lead us into the contemplation of several actions of our minds in discoursing, which it has found a way to intimate to others by these particles, some whereof constantly, and others in certain constructions, have the sense of a whole sentence contained in them.

CHAPTER VIII.

OF ABSTRACT AND CONCRETE TERMS.

1. Abstract Terms predicated one on another and why.
The ordinary words of language, and our common use of them, would have given us light into the nature of our ideas, if they had been but considered with attention. The mind, as has been shown, has a power to abstract its ideas, and so they become essences, general essences, whereby the sorts of things are distinguished. Now each abstract idea being distinct, so that of any two the one can never be the other, the mind will, by its intuitive knowledge, perceive their difference, and therefore in propositions no two whole ideas can ever be affirmed one of another. This we see in the common use of language, which permits not any two abstract words, or names of abstract ideas, to be affirmed one of another. For how near of kin soever they may seem to be, and how certain soever it is that man is an animal, or rational, or white, yet every one at first hearing perceives the falsehood of these propositions: HUMANITY IS ANIMALITY, or RATIONALITY, or WHITENESS: and this is as evident as any of the most allowed maxims. All our affirmations then are only in concrete, which is the affirming, not one abstract idea to be another, but one abstract idea to be joined to another; which abstract ideas, in substances, may be of any sort; in all the rest are little else but of relations; and in substances the most frequent are of powers: v.g. 'a man is white,' signifies that the thing that has the essence of a man has also in it the essence of whiteness, which is nothing but a power to produce the idea of whiteness in one whose eyes can discover ordinary objects: or, 'a man is rational,' signifies that the same thing that hath the essence of a man hath also in it the essence of rationality, i.e. a power of reasoning.

2. They show the Difference of our Ideas.
This distinction of names shows us also the difference of our ideas: for if we observe them, we shall find that OUR SIMPLE IDEAS HAVE ALL ABSTRACT AS WELL AS CONCRETE NAMES: the one whereof is (to speak the language of grammarians) a substantive, the other an adjective; as whiteness, white; sweetness, sweet. The like also holds in our ideas of modes and relations; as justice, just; equality, equal: only with this difference, that some of the concrete names of relations amongst men chiefly are substantives; as, paternitas, pater; whereof it were easy to render a reason. But as to our ideas of substances, we have very few or no

abstract names at all. For though the Schools have introduced animalitas, humanitas, corporietas, and some others; yet they hold no proportion with that infinite number of names of substances, to which they never were ridiculous enough to attempt the coining of abstract ones: and those few that the Schools forged, and put into the mouths of their scholars, could never yet get admittance into common use, or obtain the license of public approbation. Which seems to me at least to intimate the confession of all mankind, that they have no ideas of the real essences of substances, since they have not names for such ideas: which no doubt they would have had, had not their consciousness to themselves of their ignorance of them kept them from so idle an attempt. And therefore, though they had ideas enough to distinguish gold from a stone, and metal from wood; yet they but timorously ventured on such terms, as aurietas and saxietas, metallietas and lignietas, or the like names, which should pretend to signify the real essences of those substances whereof they knew they had no ideas. And indeed it was only the doctrine of SUBSTANTIAL FORMS, and the confidence of mistaken pretenders to a knowledge that they had not, which first coined and then introduced animalitas and humanitas, and the like; which yet went very little further than their own Schools, and could never get to be current amongst understanding men. Indeed, humanitas was a word in familiar use amongst the Romans; but in a far different sense, and stood not for the abstract essence of any substance; but was the abstracted name of a mode, and its concrete humanus, not homo.

CHAPTER IX.

OF THE IMPERFECTION OF WORDS.

1. Words are used for recording and communicating our Thoughts.
From what has been said in the foregoing chapters, it is easy to perceive what imperfection there is in language, and how the very nature of words makes it almost unavoidable for many of them to be doubtful and uncertain in their significations. To examine the perfection or imperfection of words, it is necessary first to consider their use and end: for as they are more or less fitted to attain that, so they are more or less perfect. We have, in the former part of this discourse often, upon occasion, mentioned a double use of words.

First, One for the recording of our own thoughts.

Secondly, The other for the communicating of our thoughts to others.

2. Any Words will serve for recording.

As to the first of these, FOR THE RECORDING OUR OWN THOUGHTS FOR THE HELP OF OUR OWN MEMORIES, whereby, as it were, we talk to ourselves, any words will serve the turn. For since sounds are voluntary and indifferent signs of any ideas, a man may use what words he pleases to signify his own ideas to himself: and there will be no imperfection in them, if he constantly use the same sign for the same idea: for then he cannot fail of having his meaning understood, wherein consists the right use and perfection of language.

3. Communication by Words either for civil or philosophical purposes.

Secondly, As to COMMUNICATION BY WORDS, that too has a double use.

I. Civil.

II. Philosophical. First, By, their CIVIL use, I mean such a communication of thoughts and ideas by words, as may serve for the upholding common conversation and commerce, about the ordinary affairs and conveniences of civil life, in the societies of men, one amongst another.

Secondly, By the PHILOSOPHICAL use of words, I mean such a use of them as may serve to convey the precise notions of things, and to express in general propositions certain and undoubted truths, which the mind may rest upon and be satisfied with in its search after true knowledge. These two uses are very distinct; and a great deal less exactness will serve in the one than in the other, as we shall see in what follows.

4. The imperfection of Words is the Doubtfulness or ambiguity of their Signification, which is caused by the sort of ideas they stand for.

The chief end of language in communication being to be understood, words serve not well for that end, neither in civil nor philosophical discourse, when any word does not excite in the hearer the same idea which it stands for in the mind of the speaker. Now, since sounds have no natural connexion with our ideas, but have all their signification from the arbitrary imposition of men, the doubtfulness and uncertainty of their signification, which is the imperfection we here are speaking of, has its cause more in the ideas they stand for than in any incapacity there is in one sound more than in another to signify any idea: for in that regard they are all equally perfect.

That then which makes doubtfulness and uncertainty in the signification of some more than other words, is the difference of ideas they stand for.

5. Natural Causes of their Imperfection, especially in those that stand for Mixed Modes, and for our ideas of Substances.

Words having naturally no signification, the idea which each stands for must be learned and retained, by those who would exchange thoughts, and hold intelligible discourse with others, in any language. But this is the hardest to be done where,

First, The ideas they stand for are very complex, and made up of a great number of ideas put together.

Secondly, Where the ideas they stand for have no certain connexion in nature; and so no settled standard anywhere in nature existing, to rectify and adjust them by.

Thirdly, When the signification of the word is referred to a standard, which standard is not easy to be known.

Fourthly, Where the signification of the word and the real essence of the thing are not exactly the same.

These are difficulties that attend the signification of several words that are intelligible. Those which are not intelligible at all, such as names standing for any simple ideas which another has not organs or faculties to attain; as the names of colours to a blind man, or sounds to a deaf man, need not here be mentioned.

In all these cases we shall find an imperfection in words; which I shall more at large explain, in their particular application to our several sorts of ideas: for if we examine them, we shall find that the NAMES OF _M_IXED _M_ODES ARE MOST LIABLE TO DOUBTFULNESS AND IMPERFECTION, FOR THE TWO FIRST OF THESE REASONS;

and the NAMES OF _S_UBSTANCES CHIEFLY FOR THE TWO LATTER.

6. The Names of mixed Modes doubtful.

First, The names of MIXED MODES are, many of them, liable to great uncertainty and obscurity in their signification.

I. Because the Ideas they stand for are so complex.

Because of that GREAT COMPOSITION these complex ideas are often made up of. To make words serviceable to the end of communication, it is necessary, as has been said, that they excite in the hearer exactly the same idea they stand for in the mind of the speaker. Without this, men fill one another's heads with noise and sounds; but convey not thereby their thoughts, and lay not before one another their ideas, which is the end of discourse and language. But when a word stands for a very complex idea that is compounded and decompounded, it is not easy for men to form and retain that idea so exactly, as to make the name in common use stand for the same precise idea, without any the least variation. Hence it comes to pass that men's names of very compound ideas, such as for the most part are moral words, have seldom in two different men the same precise signification; since one man's complex idea seldom agrees with another's, and often differs from his own—from that which he had yesterday, or will have tomorrow.

7. Secondly because they have no Standards in Nature.

Because the names of mixed modes for the most part WANT STANDARDS IN NATURE, whereby men may rectify and adjust their significations; therefore they are very various and doubtful. They are assemblages of ideas put together at the pleasure of the mind, pursuing its own ends of discourse, and suited to its own notions; whereby it designs not to copy anything really existing, but to denominate and rank things as they come to agree with those archetypes or forms it has made. He that first brought the word SHAM, or WHEEDLE, or BANTER, in use, put together as he thought fit those ideas he made it stand for; and as it is with any new names of modes that are now brought into any language, so it was with the old ones when they were first made use of. Names, therefore, that stand for collections of ideas which the mind makes at pleasure must needs be of doubtful signification, when such collections are nowhere to be found constantly united in nature, nor any patterns to be shown whereby men may adjust them. What the word MURDER, or SACRILEGE, &c., signifies can never be known from things themselves: there be many of the parts of those complex ideas which are not visible in the action itself; the intention of the mind, or the relation of holy things, which make a part of murder or sacrilege, have no necessary connexion with the outward and visible action of him that commits either: and the pulling the trigger of the gun with which the murder is committed, and is all the action that perhaps is visible, has no natural connexion with those other ideas that make up the complex one named murder. They have their union and combination only from the understanding which unites them under one name: but, uniting them without any rule or pattern, it cannot be but that the signification of the name that stands for such voluntary collections should be often various in the minds of different men, who have scarce any standing rule to regulate themselves and their notions by, in such arbitrary ideas.

8. Common use, or propriety not a sufficient Remedy.

It is true, common use, that is, the rule of propriety may be supposed here to afford some aid, to settle the signification of language; and it cannot be denied but that in some measure it does. Common use regulates the meaning of words pretty well for common conversation; but nobody having an authority to establish the precise signification of words, nor determine to what ideas any one shall annex them, common use is not sufficient to adjust them to Philosophical Discourses; there being scarce any name of any very complex idea (to say nothing of others) which, in common use, has not a great latitude, and which, keeping within the bounds of propriety, may not be made the sign of far different ideas. Besides, the rule and measure of propriety itself being nowhere established, it is often matter of dispute, whether this or that way of using a word be propriety of speech or no. From all which it is evident, that the names of such kind of very complex ideas are naturally liable to this imperfection, to be of doubtful and uncertain signification; and even in men that have a mind to understand one another, do not always stand for the same idea in speaker and hearer. Though the names GLORY and GRATITUDE be the same in every man's mouth through a whole country, yet the complex collective idea which every one thinks on or intends by that name, is apparently very different in men using the same language.

9. The way of learning these Names contributes also to their Doubtfulness.

The way also wherein the names of mixed modes are ordinarily learned, does not a little contribute to the doubtfulness of their signification. For if we will observe how children learn languages, we shall find that, to make them understand what the names of simple ideas or substances stand for, people ordinarily show them the thing whereof they would have them have the idea; and then repeat to them the name that stands for it; as WHITE,

SWEET, MILK, SUGAR, CAT, DOG. But as for mixed modes, especially the most material of them, MORAL WORDS, the sounds are usually learned first; and then, to know what complex ideas they stand for, they are either beholden to the explication of others, or (which happens for the most part) are left to their own observation and industry; which being little laid out in the search of the true and precise meaning of names, these moral words are in most men's mouths little more than bare sounds; or when they have any, it is for the most part but a very loose and undetermined, and, consequently, obscure and confused signification. And even those themselves who have with more attention settled their notions, do yet hardly avoid the inconvenience to have them stand for complex ideas different from those which other, even intelligent and studious men, make them the signs of. Where shall one find any, either controversial debate, or familiar discourse, concerning honour, faith, grace, religion, church, &c., wherein it is not easy to observe the different notions men have of them? Which is nothing but this, that they are not agreed in the signification of those words, nor have in their minds the same complex ideas which they make them stand for, and so all the contests that follow thereupon are only about the meaning of a sound. And hence we see that, in the interpretation of laws, whether divine or human, there is no end; comments beget comments, and explications make new matter for explications; and of limiting, distinguishing, varying the signification of these moral words there is no end. These ideas of men's making are, by men still having the same power, multiplied in infinitum. Many a man who was pretty well satisfied of the meaning of a text of Scripture, or clause in the code, at first reading, has, by consulting commentators, quite lost the sense of it, and by these elucidations given rise or increase to his doubts, and drawn obscurity upon the place. I say not this that I think commentaries needless; but to show how uncertain the names of mixed modes naturally are, even in the mouths of those who had both the intention and the faculty of speaking as clearly as language was capable to express their thoughts.

10. Hence unavoidable Obscurity in ancient Authors.

What obscurity this has unavoidably brought upon the writings of men who have lived in remote ages, and different countries, it will be needless to take notice. Since the numerous volumes of learned men, employing their thoughts that way, are proofs more than enough, to show what attention, study, sagacity, and reasoning are required to find out the true meaning of ancient authors. But, there being no writings we have any great concernment to be very solicitous about the meaning of, but those that contain either truths we are required to believe, or laws we are to obey, and draw inconveniences on us when we mistake or transgress, we may be less anxious about the sense of other authors; who, writing but their own opinions, we are under no greater necessity to know them, than they to know ours. Our good or evil depending not on their decrees, we may safely be ignorant of their notions: and therefore in the reading of them, if they do not use their words with a due clearness and perspicuity, we may lay them aside, and without any injury done them, resolve thus with ourselves, Si non vis intelligi, debes negligi.

11. Names of Substances of doubtful Signification, because the ideas they stand for relate to the reality of things.

If the signification of the names of mixed modes be uncertain, because there be no real standards existing in nature to which those ideas are referred, and by which they may be adjusted, the names of SUBSTANCES are of a doubtful signification, for a contrary reason, viz. because the ideas they stand for are supposed conformable to the reality of things, and are referred to as standards made by Nature. In our ideas of substances we have not the liberty, as in mixed modes, to frame what combinations we think fit, to be the characteristical notes to rank and denominate things by. In these we must follow Nature, suit our complex ideas to real existences, and regulate the signification of their names by the things themselves, if we will have our names to be signs of them, and stand for them. Here, it is true, we have patterns to follow; but patterns that will make the signification of their names very uncertain: for names must be of a very unsteady and various meaning, if the ideas they stand for be referred to standards without us, that either cannot be known at all, or can be known but imperfectly and uncertainly.

12. Names of Substances referred, I. To real Essences that cannot be known.

The names of substances have, as has been shown, a double reference in their ordinary use.

First, Sometimes they are made to stand for, and so their signification is supposed to agree to, THE REAL CONSTITUTION OF THINGS, from which all their properties flow, and in which they all centre. But this real constitution, or (as it is apt to be called) essence, being utterly unknown to us, any sound that is put to stand for it must be very uncertain in its application; and it will be impossible to know what things are or ought to be called a HORSE, or ANTIMONY, when those words are put for real essences that we have no ideas of at all. And therefore in this supposition, the names of substances being referred to standards that cannot be known, their significations can never be adjusted and established by those standards.

13. Secondly, To co-existing Qualities, which are known but imperfectly. Secondly, The simple ideas that are FOUND TO CO-EXIST IN SUBSTANCES being that which their names immediately signify, these, as united in the several sorts of things, are the proper standards to which their names are referred, and by which their significations may be best rectified. But neither will these archetypes so well serve to this purpose as to leave these names without very various and uncertain significations. Because these simple ideas that co-exist, and are united in the same subject, being very numerous, and having all an equal right to go into the complex specific idea which the specific name is to stand for, men, though they propose to themselves the very same subject to consider, yet frame very different ideas about it; and so the name they use for it unavoidably comes to have, in several men, very different significations. The simple qualities which make up the complex ideas, being most of them powers, in relation to changes which they are apt to make in, or receive from other bodies, are almost infinite. He that shall but observe what a great variety of alterations any one of the baser metals is apt to receive, from the different application only of fire; and how much a greater number of changes any of them will receive in the hands of a chymist, by the application of other bodies, will not think it strange that I count the properties of any sort of bodies not easy to be collected, and completely known, by the ways of inquiry which our faculties are capable of. They being therefore at least so many, that no man can know the precise and definite number, they are differently discovered by different men, according to their various skill, attention, and ways of handling; who therefore cannot choose but have different ideas of the same substance, and therefore make the signification of its common name very various and uncertain. For the complex ideas of substances, being made up of such simple ones as are supposed to co-exist in nature, every one has a right to put into his complex idea those qualities he has found to be united together. For, though in the substance of gold one satisfies himself with colour and weight, yet another thinks solubility in aqua regia as necessary to be joined with that colour in his idea of gold, as any one does its fusibility; solubility in aqua regia being a quality as constantly joined with its colour and weight as fusibility or any other; others put into it ductility or fixedness, &c., as they have been taught by tradition or experience. Who of all these has established the right signification of the word, gold? Or

who shall be the judge to determine? Each has his standard in nature, which he appeals to, and with reason thinks he has the same right to put into his complex idea signified by the word gold, those qualities, which, upon trial, he has found united; as another who has not so well examined has to leave them out; or a third, who has made other trials, has to put in others. For the union in nature of these qualities being the true ground of their union in one complex idea, who can say one of them has more reason to be put in or left out than another? From hence it will unavoidably follow, that the complex ideas of substances in men using the same names for them, will be very various, and so the significations of those names very uncertain.

14. Thirdly, To co-existing Qualities which are known but imperfectly.

Besides, there is scarce any particular thing existing, which, in some of its simple ideas, does not communicate with a greater, and in others a less number of particular beings: who shall determine in this case which are those that are to make up the precise collection that is to be signified by the specific name? or can with any just authority prescribe, which obvious or common qualities are to be left out; or which more secret, or more particular, are to be put into the signification of the name of any substance? All which together, seldom or never fail to produce that various and doubtful signification in the names of substances, which causes such uncertainty, disputes, or mistakes, when we come to a philosophical use of them.

15. With this imperfection, they may serve for civil, but not well for philosophical Use.

It is true, as to civil and common conversation, the general names of substances, regulated in their ordinary signification by some obvious qualities, (as by the shape and figure in things of known seminal propagation, and in other substances, for the most part by colour, joined with some other sensible qualities,) do well enough to design the things men would be understood to speak of: and so they usually conceive well enough the substances meant by the word gold or apple, to distinguish the one from the other. But in PHILOSOPHICAL inquiries and debates, where general truths are to be established, and consequences drawn from positions laid down, there the precise signification of the names of substances will be found not only not to be well established but also very hard to be so. For example: he that shall make malleability, or a certain degree of fixedness, a part of his complex idea of gold, may make propositions concerning gold, and draw consequences from them, that will truly and clearly follow from gold, taken in such a signification: but yet

such as another man can never be forced to admit, nor be convinced of their truth, who makes not malleableness, or the same degree of fixedness, part of that complex idea that the name gold, in his use of it, stands for.
16. Instance, Liquor.
This is a natural and almost unavoidable imperfection in almost all the names of substances, in all languages whatsoever, which men will easily find when, once passing from confused or loose notions, they come to more strict and close inquiries. For then they will be convinced how doubtful and obscure those words are in their signification, which in ordinary use appeared very clear and determined. I was once in a meeting of very learned and ingenious physicians, where by chance there arose a question, whether any liquor passed through the filaments of the nerves. The debate having been managed a good while, by variety of arguments on both sides, I (who had been used to suspect, that the greatest part of disputes were more about the signification of words than a real difference in the conception of things) desired, that, before they went any further on in this dispute, they would first examine and establish amongst them, what the word LIQUOR signified. They at first were a little surprised at the proposal; and had they been persons less ingenious, they might perhaps have taken it for a very frivolous or extravagant one: since there was no one there that thought not himself to understand very perfectly what the word liquor stood for; which I think, too, none of the most perplexed names of substances. However, they were pleased to comply with my motion; and upon examination found that the signification of that word was not so settled or certain as they had all imagined; but that each of them made it a sign of a different complex idea. This made them perceive that the main of their dispute was about the signification of that term; and that they differed very little in their opinions concerning SOME fluid and subtle matter, passing through the conduits of the nerves; though it was not so easy to agree whether it was to be called LIQUOR or no, a thing, which, when considered, they thought it not worth the contending about.
17. Instance, Gold.
How much this is the case in the greatest part of disputes that men are engaged so hotly in, I shall perhaps have an occasion in another place to take notice. Let us only here consider a little more exactly the fore-mentioned instance of the word GOLD, and we shall see how hard it is precisely to determine its signification. I think all agree to make it stand for a body of a certain yellow shining colour; which being the idea to which children have annexed that name, the shining yellow part of a peacock's

tail is properly to them gold. Others finding fusibility joined with that yellow colour in certain parcels of matter, make of that combination a complex idea to which they give the name gold, to denote a sort of substances; and so exclude from being gold all such yellow shining bodies as by fire will be reduced to ashes; and admit to be of that species, or to be comprehended under that name gold, only such substances as having that shining yellow colour, will by fire be reduced to fusion, and not to ashes. Another, by the same reason, adds the weight, which, being a quality as straightly joined with that colour as its fusibility, he thinks has the same reason to be joined in its idea, and to be signified by its name: and therefore the other made up of body, of such a colour and fusibility, to be imperfect; and so on of all the rest: wherein no one can show a reason why some of the inseparable qualities, that are always united in nature, should be put into the nominal essence, and others left out, or why the word gold, signifying that sort of body the ring on his finger is made of, should determine that sort rather by its colour, weight, and fusibility, than by its colour, weight, and solubility in aqua regia: since the dissolving it by that liquor is as inseparable from it as the fusion by fire, and they are both of them nothing but the relation which that substance has to two other bodies, which have a power to operate differently upon it. For by what right is it that fusibility comes to be a part of the essence signified by the word gold, and solubility but a property of it? Or why is its colour part of the essence, and its malleableness but a property? That which I mean is this, That these being all but properties, depending on its real constitution, and nothing but powers, either active or passive, in reference to other bodies, no one has authority to determine the signification of the word gold (as referred to such a body existing in nature) more to one collection of ideas to be found in that body than to another: whereby the signification of that name must unavoidably be very uncertain. Since, as has been said, several people observe several properties in the same substance; and I think I may say nobody all. And therefore we have but very imperfect descriptions of things, and words have very uncertain significations.

18. The Names of simple Ideas the least doubtful.

From what has been said, it is easy to observe what has been before remarked, viz. that the NAMES OF SIMPLE IDEAS are, of all others, the least liable to mistakes, and that for these reasons. First, Because the ideas they stand for, being each but one single perception, are much easier got, and more clearly retained, than the more complex ones, and therefore are not liable to the uncertainty which usually attends those compounded ones of substances and mixed modes, in which the precise number of simple ideas that make them up are not easily agreed, so readily kept in mind. And, Secondly, Because they are never referred to any other essence, but barely that perception they immediately signify: which reference is that which renders the signification of the names of substances naturally so perplexed, and gives occasion to so many disputes. Men that do not perversely use their words, or on purpose set themselves to cavil, seldom mistake, in any language which they are acquainted with, the use and signification of the name of simple ideas. WHITE and SWEET, YELLOW and BITTER, carry a very obvious meaning with them, which every one precisely comprehends, or easily perceives he is ignorant of, and seeks to be informed. But what precise collection of simple ideas MODESTY or FRUGALITY stand for, in another's use, is not so certainly known. And however we are apt to think we well enough know what is meant by GOLD or IRON; yet the precise complex idea others make them the signs of is not so certain: and I believe it is very seldom that, in speaker and hearer, they stand for exactly the same collection. Which must needs produce mistakes and disputes, when they are made use of in discourses, wherein men have to do with universal propositions, and would settle in their minds universal truths, and consider the consequences that follow from them.

19. And next to them, simple Modes.

By the same rule, the names of SIMPLE MODES are, next to those of simple ideas, least liable to doubt and uncertainty; especially those of figure and number, of which men have so clear and distinct ideas. Who ever that had a mind to understand them mistook the ordinary meaning of SEVEN, or a TRIANGLE? And in general the least compounded ideas in every kind have the least dubious names.

20. The most doubtful are the Names of very compounded mixed Modes and Substances.

Mixed modes, therefore, that are made up but of a few and obvious simple ideas, have usually names of no very uncertain signification. But the names of mixed modes, which comprehend a great number of simple ideas, are commonly of a very doubtful and undetermined meaning, as has been shown. The names of substances, being annexed to ideas that are neither the real essences, nor exact representations of the patterns they are referred to, are liable to yet greater imperfection and uncertainty, especially when we come to a philosophical use of them.

21. Why this Imperfection charged upon Words.

The great disorder that happens in our names of substances, proceeding, for the most part, from our want of knowledge, and inability to penetrate into their real constitutions, it may probably be wondered why I charge this as an imperfection rather upon our words than understandings. This exception has so much appearance of justice, that I think myself obliged to give a reason why I have followed this method. I must confess, then, that, when I first began this Discourse of the Understanding, and a good while after, I had not the least thought that any consideration of words was at all necessary to it. But when, having passed over the original and composition of our ideas, I began to examine the extent and certainty of our knowledge, I found it had so near a connexion with words, that, unless their force and manner of signification were first well observed, there could be very little said clearly and pertinently concerning knowledge: which being conversant about truth, had constantly to do with propositions. And though it terminated in things, yet it was for the most part so much by the intervention of words, that they seemed scarce separable from our general knowledge. At least they interpose themselves so much between our understandings, and the truth which it would contemplate and apprehend, that, like the medium through which visible objects pass, the obscurity and disorder do not seldom cast a mist before our eyes, and impose upon our understandings. If we consider, in the fallacies men put upon themselves, as well as others, and the mistakes in men's disputes and notions, how great a part is owing to words, and their uncertain or mistaken significations, we shall have reason to think this no small obstacle in the way to knowledge; which I conclude we are the more carefully to be warned of, because it has been so far from being taken notice of as an inconvenience, that the arts of improving it have been made the business of men's study, and obtained the reputation of learning and subtilty, as we shall see in the following chapter. But I am apt to imagine, that, were the imperfections of language, as the instrument of knowledge, more thoroughly weighed, a great many of the controversies that make such a noise in the world, would of themselves cease; and the way to knowledge, and perhaps peace too, lie a great deal opener than it does.

22. This should teach us Moderation in imposing our own Sense of old Authors.

Sure I am that the signification of words in all languages, depending very much on the thoughts, notions, and ideas of him that uses them, must unavoidably be of great uncertainty to men of the same language and country. This is so evident in the Greek authors, that he that shall peruse their writings will find in almost every one of them, a distinct language, though the same words. But when to this natural difficulty in every country, there shall be added different countries and remote ages, wherein the speakers and writers had very different notions, tempers, customs, ornaments, and figures of speech, &c., every one of which influenced the signification of their words then, though to us now they are lost and unknown; it would become us to be charitable one to another in our interpretations or misunderstandings of those ancient writings; which, though of great concernment to be understood, are liable to the unavoidable difficulties of speech, which (if we except the names of simple ideas, and some very obvious things) is not capable, without a constant defining the terms, of conveying the sense and intention of the speaker, without any manner of doubt and uncertainty to the hearer. And in discourses of religion, law, and morality, as they are matters of the highest concernment, so there will be the greatest difficulty.

23. Especially of the Old and New Testament Scriptures.

The volumes of interpreters and commentators on the Old and New Testament are but too manifest proofs of this. Though everything said in the text be infallibly true, yet the reader may be, nay, cannot choose but be, very fallible in the understanding of it. Nor is it to be wondered, that the will of God, when clothed in words, should be liable to that doubt and uncertainty which unavoidably attends that sort of conveyance, when even his Son, whilst clothed in flesh, was subject to all the frailties and inconveniences of human nature, sin excepted. And we ought to magnify his goodness, that he hath spread before all the world such legible characters of his works and providence, and given all mankind so sufficient a light of reason, that they to whom this written word never came, could not (whenever they set themselves to search) either doubt of the being of a God, or of the obedience due to him. Since then the precepts of Natural Religion are plain, and very intelligible to all mankind, and seldom come to be controverted; and other revealed truths, which are conveyed to us by books and languages, are liable to the common and natural obscurities and difficulties incident to words; methinks it would become us to be more careful and diligent in observing the former, and less magisterial, positive, and imperious, in imposing our own sense and interpretations of the latter.

CHAPTER X.

OF THE ABUSE OF WORDS.

1. Woeful abuse of Words.

Besides the imperfection that is naturally in language, and the obscurity and confusion that is so hard to be avoided in the use of words, there are several WILFUL faults and neglects which men are guilty of in this way of communication, whereby they render these signs less clear and distinct in their signification than naturally they need to be.

2. First, Words are often employed without any, or without clear Ideas.

FIRST, In this kind the first and most palpable abuse is, the using of words without clear and distinct ideas; or, which is worse, signs without anything signified. Of these there are two sorts:—

I. Some words introduced without clear ideas annexed to them, even in their first original.

One may observe, in all languages, certain words that, if they be examined, will be found in their first original, and their appropriated use, not to stand for any clear and distinct ideas. These, for the most part, the several sects of philosophy and religion have introduced. For their authors or promoters, either affecting something singular, and out of the way of common apprehensions, or to support some strange opinions, or cover some weakness of their hypothesis, seldom fail to coin new words, and such as, when they come to be examined, may justly be called INSIGNIFICANT TERMS. For, having either had no determinate collection of ideas annexed to them when they were first invented; or at least such as, if well examined, will be found inconsistent, it is no wonder, if, afterwards, in the vulgar use of the same party, they remain empty sounds, with little or no signification, amongst those who think it enough to have them often in their mouths, as the distinguishing characters of their Church or School, without much troubling their heads to examine what are the precise ideas they stand for. I shall not need here to heap up instances; every man's reading and conversation will sufficiently furnish him. Or if he wants to be better stored, the great mint-masters of this kind of terms, I mean the Schoolmen and Metaphysicians (under which I think the disputing natural and moral philosophers of these latter ages may be comprehended) have wherewithal abundantly to content him.

3. II. Other Words, to which ideas were annexed at first, used afterwards without distinct meanings.

Others there be who extend this abuse yet further, who take so little care to lay by words, which, in their primary notation have scarce any clear and distinct ideas which they are annexed to, that, by an unpardonable negligence, they familiarly use words which the propriety of language HAS affixed to very important ideas, without any distinct meaning at all. WISDOM, GLORY, GRACE, &c., are words frequent enough in every man's mouth; but if a great many of those who use them should be asked what they mean by them, they would be at a stand, and not know what to answer: a plain proof, that, though they have learned those sounds, and have them ready at their tongues ends, yet there are no determined ideas laid up in their minds, which are to be expressed to others by them.

4. This occasioned by men learning Names before they have the Ideas the names belong to.

Men having been accustomed from their cradles to learn words which are easily got and retained, before they knew or had framed the complex ideas to which they were annexed, or which were to be found in the things they were thought to stand for, they usually continue to do so all their lives; and without taking the pains necessary to settle in their minds determined ideas, they use their words for such unsteady and confused notions as they have, contenting themselves with the same words other people use; as if their very sound necessarily carried with it constantly the same meaning. This, though men make a shift with in the ordinary occurrences of life, where they find it necessary to be understood, and therefore they make signs till they are so; yet this insignificancy in their words, when they come to reason concerning either their tenets or interest, manifestly fills their discourse with abundance of empty unintelligible noise and jargon, especially in moral matters, where the words for the most part standing for arbitrary and numerous collections of ideas, not regularly and permanently united in nature, their bare sounds are often only thought on, or at least very obscure and uncertain notions annexed to them. Men take the words they find in use amongst their neighbours; and that they may not seem ignorant what they stand for, use them confidently, without much troubling their heads about a certain fixed meaning; whereby, besides the ease of it, they obtain this advantage, That, as in such discourses they seldom are in the right, so they are as seldom to be convinced that they are in the wrong; it being all one to go about to draw those men out of their mistakes who have no settled notions, as to dispossess a vagrant of his habitation who has no settled abode. This I guess to be so; and every one may observe in himself and others whether it be so or not.

5. Secondly Unsteady Application of them.

SECONDLY, Another great abuse of words is INCONSTANCY in the use of them. It is hard to find a discourse written on any subject, especially of controversy, wherein one shall not observe, if he read with attention, the same words (and those commonly the most material in the discourse, and upon which the argument turns) used sometimes for one collection of simple ideas, and sometimes for another; which is a perfect abuse of language. Words being intended for signs of my ideas, to make them known to others, not by any natural signification, but by a voluntary imposition, it is plain cheat and abuse, when I make them stand sometimes for one thing and sometimes for another; the wilful doing whereof can be imputed to nothing but great folly, or greater dishonesty. And a man, in his accounts with another may, with as much fairness make the characters of numbers stand sometimes for one and sometimes for another collection of units: v.g. this character 3, stand sometimes for three, sometimes for four, and sometimes for eight, as in his discourse or reasoning make the same words stand for different collections of simple ideas. If men should do so in their reckonings, I wonder who would have to do with them? One who would speak thus in the affairs and business of the world, and call 8 sometimes seven, and sometimes nine, as best served his advantage, would presently have clapped upon him, one of the two names men are commonly disgusted with. And yet in arguings and learned contests, the same sort of proceedings passes commonly for wit and learning; but to me it appears a greater dishonesty than the misplacing of counters in the casting up a debt; and the cheat the greater, by how much truth is of greater concernment and value than money.

6. Thirdly, Affected Obscurity, as in the Peripatetic and other sects of Philosophy.

THIRDLY. Another abuse of language is an AFFECTED OBSCURITY; by either applying old words to new and unusual significations; or introducing new and ambiguous terms, without defining either; or else putting them so together, as may confound their ordinary meaning. Though the Peripatetick philosophy has been most eminent in this way, yet other sects have not been wholly clear of it. There are scarce any of them that are not cumbered with some difficulties (such is the imperfection of human knowledge,) which they have been fain to cover with obscurity of terms, and to confound the signification of words, which, like a mist before people's eyes, might hinder their weak parts from being discovered. That BODY and EXTENSION in common use, stand for two distinct ideas, is plain to any one that will but reflect a little. For were their signification precisely the same, it would be as proper, and as intelligible to say, 'the body of an extension,' as the 'extension of a body;' and yet there are those who find it necessary to confound their signification. To this abuse, and the mischiefs of confounding the signification of words, logic, and the liberal sciences as they have been handled in the schools, have given reputation; and the admired Art of Disputing hath added much to the natural imperfection of languages, whilst it has been made use of and fitted to perplex the signification of words, more than to discover the knowledge and truth of things: and he that will look into that sort of learned writings, will find the words there much more obscure, uncertain, and undetermined in their meaning, than they are in ordinary conversation.

7. Logic and Dispute have much contributed to this.

This is unavoidably to be so, where men's parts and learning are estimated by their skill in disputing. And if reputation and reward shall attend these conquests, which depend mostly on the fineness and niceties of words, it is no wonder if the wit of man so employed, should perplex, involve, and subtilize the signification of sounds, so as never to want something to say in opposing or defending any question; the victory being adjudged not to him who had truth on his side, but the last word in the dispute.

8. Calling it Subtlety.

This, though a very useless skill, and that which I think the direct opposite to the ways of knowledge, hath yet passed hitherto under the laudable and esteemed names of SUBTLETY and ACUTENESS, and has had the applause of the schools, and encouragement of one part of the learned men of the world. And no wonder, since the philosophers of old, (the disputing and wrangling philosophers I mean, such as Lucian wittily and with reason taxes,) and the Schoolmen since, aiming at glory and esteem, for their great and universal knowledge, easier a great deal to be pretended to than really acquired, found this a good expedient to cover their ignorance, with a curious and inexplicable web of perplexed words, and procure to themselves the admiration of others, by unintelligible terms, the apter to produce wonder because they could not be understood; whilst it appears in all history, that these profound doctors were no wiser nor more useful than their neighbours, and brought but small advantage to human life or the societies wherein they lived; unless the coining of new words, where they produced no new things to apply them to, or the perplexing or obscuring the signification of old ones, and so bringing all things into question and dispute, were a thing profitable to the life of man, or worthy commendation and reward.

9. This Learning very little benefits Society.

For, notwithstanding these learned disputants, these all-knowing doctors, it was to the unscholastic statesman that the governments of the world owed their peace, defence, and liberties; and from the illiterate and contemned mechanic (a name of disgrace) that they received the improvements of useful arts. Nevertheless, this artificial ignorance, and learned gibberish, prevailed mightily in these last ages, by the interest and artifice of those who found no easier way to that pitch of authority and dominion they have attained, than by amusing the men of business, and ignorant, with hard words, or employing the ingenious and idle in intricate disputes about unintelligible terms, and holding them perpetually entangled in that endless labyrinth. Besides, there is no such way to gain admittance, or give defence to strange and absurd doctrines, as to guard them round about with legions of obscure, doubtful, and undefined words. Which yet make these retreats more like the dens of robbers, or holes of foxes, than the fortresses of fair warriors; which, if it be hard to get them out of, it is not for the strength that is in them, but the briars and thorns, and the obscurity of the thickets they are beset with. For untruth being unacceptable to the mind of man, there is no other defence left for absurdity but obscurity.

10. But destroys the instruments of Knowledge and communication.

Thus learned ignorance, and this art of keeping even inquisitive men from true knowledge, hath been propagated in the world, and hath much perplexed, whilst it pretended to inform the understanding. For we see that other well-meaning and wise men, whose education and parts had not acquired that ACUTENESS, could intelligibly express themselves to one another; and in its plain use make a benefit of language. But though unlearned men well enough understood the words white and black; &c., and had constant notions of the ideas signified by those words; yet there were philosophers found who had learning and subtlety enough to prove that snow was black; i.e. to prove that white was black. Whereby they had the advantage to destroy the instruments and means of discourse, conversation, instruction, and society; whilst, with great art and subtlety, they did no more but perplex and confound the signification of words, and thereby render language less useful than the real defects of it had made it; a gift which the illiterate had not attained to.

11. As useful as to confound the sound that the Letters of the Alphabet stand for.

These learned men did equally instruct men's understandings, and profit their lives, as he who should alter the signification of known characters, and, by a subtle device of learning, far surpassing the capacity of the illiterate, dull, and vulgar, should in his writing show that he could put A for B, and D for E, &c., to the no small admiration and benefit of for his reader. It being as senseless to put BLACK, which is a word agreed on to stand for one sensible idea, to put it, I say, for another, or the contrary idea; i.e. to call SNOW BLACK, as to put this mark A, which is a character agreed on to stand for one modification of sound, made by a certain motion of the organs of speech, for B, which is agreed on to stand for another modification of sound, made by another certain mode of the organs of speech.

12. This Art has perplexed Religion and Justice.

Nor hath this mischief stopped in logical niceties, or curious empty speculations; it hath invaded the great concernments of human life and society; obscured and perplexed the material truths of law and divinity; brought confusion, disorder, and uncertainty into the affairs of mankind; and if not destroyed, yet in a great measure rendered useless, these two great rules, religion and justice. What have the greatest part of the comments and disputes upon the laws of God and man served for, but to make the meaning more doubtful, and perplex the sense? What have been the effect of those multiplied curious distinctions, and acute niceties, but obscurity and uncertainty, leaving the words more unintelligible, and the reader more at a loss? How else comes it to pass that princes, speaking or writing to their servants, in their ordinary commands are easily understood; speaking to their people, in their laws, are not so? And, as I remarked before, doth it not often happen that a man of an ordinary capacity very well understands a text, or a law, that he reads, till he consults an expositor, or goes to counsel; who, by that time he hath done explaining them, makes the words signify either nothing at all, or what he pleases.

13. and ought not to pass for Learning.

Whether any by-interests of these professions have occasioned this, I will not here examine; but I leave it to be considered, whether it would not be well for mankind, whose concernment it is to know things as they are, and to do what they ought, and not to spend their lives in talking about them, or tossing words to and fro;—whether it would not be well, I say, that the use of words were made plain and direct; and that language, which was given us for the improvement of knowledge and bond of society, should not be employed to darken truth and unsettle people's rights; to raise mists, and render unintelligible both morality and religion? Or that at least, if this will happen, it should not be thought learning or knowledge to do so?

14. IV. Fourthly, by taking Words for Things.

FOURTHLY, Another great abuse of words is, the TAKING THEM FOR THINGS. This, though it in some degree concerns all names in general, yet more particularly affects those of substances. To this abuse those men are most subject who most confine their thoughts to any one system, and give themselves up into a firm belief of the perfection of any received hypothesis: whereby they come to be persuaded that the terms of that sect are so suited to the nature of things, that they perfectly correspond with their real existence. Who is there that has been bred up in the Peripatetick philosophy, who does not think the Ten Names, under which are ranked the Ten Predicaments, to be exactly conformable to the nature of things? Who is there of that school that is not persuaded that SUBSTANTIAL FORMS, VEGETATIVE SOULS, ABHORRENCE OF A VACUUM, INTENTIONAL SPECIES, &c., are something real? These words men have learned from their very entrance upon knowledge, and have found their masters and systems lay great stress upon them: and therefore they cannot quit the opinion, that they are conformable to nature, and are the representations of something that really exists. The Platonists have their SOUL OF THE WORLD, and the Epicureans their ENDEAVOR TOWARDS MOTION in their atoms when at rest. There is scarce any sect in philosophy has not a distinct set of terms that others understand not. But yet this gibberish, which, in the weakness of human understanding, serves so well to palliate men's ignorance, and cover their errors, comes, by familiar use amongst those of the same tribe, to seem the most important part of language, and of all other the terms the most significant: and should AERIAL and OETHERIAL VEHICLES come once, by the prevalency of that doctrine, to be generally received anywhere, no doubt those terms would make impressions on men's minds, so as to establish them in the persuasion of the reality of such things, as much as Peripatetick FORMS and INTENTIONAL SPECIES have heretofore done. 15. Instance, in Matter.

How much names taken for things are apt to mislead the understanding, the attentive reading of philosophical writers would abundantly discover; and that perhaps in words little suspected of any such misuse. I shall instance in one only, and that a very familiar one. How many intricate disputes have there been about MATTER, as if there were some such thing really in nature, distinct from BODY; as it is evident the word matter stands for an idea distinct from the idea of body? For if the ideas these two terms stood for were precisely the same, they might indifferently in all places be put for one another. But we see that though it be proper to say, There is one matter of all bodies, one cannot say, There is one body of all matters: we familiarly say one body is bigger than another; but it sounds harsh (and I think is never used) to say one matter is bigger than another. Whence comes this, then? Viz. from hence: that, though matter and body be not really distinct, but wherever there is the one there is the other; yet matter and body stand for two different conceptions, whereof the one is incomplete, and but a part of the other. For body stands for a solid extended figured substance, whereof matter is but a partial and more confused conception; it seeming to me to be used for the substance and solidity of body, without taking in its extension and figure: and therefore it is that, speaking of matter, we speak of it always as one, because in truth it expressly contains nothing but the idea of a solid substance, which is everywhere the same, everywhere uniform. This being our idea of matter, we no more conceive or speak of different MATTERS in the world than we do of different solidities; though we both conceive and speak of different bodies, because extension and figure are capable of variation. But, since solidity cannot exist without extension and figure, the taking matter to be the name of something really existing under that precision, has no doubt produced those obscure and unintelligible discourses and disputes, which have filled the heads and books of philosophers concerning materia prima; which imperfection or abuse, how far it may concern a great many other general terms I leave to be considered. This, I think, I may at least say, that we should have a great many fewer disputes in the world, if words were taken for what they are, the signs of our ideas only; and not for things themselves. For, when we argue about MATTER, or any the like term, we truly argue only about the idea we express by that sound, whether that precise idea agree to anything really existing in nature or no. And if men would tell what ideas they make their words stand for, there could not be half that obscurity or wrangling in the search or support of truth that there is.

16. This makes Errors lasting.

But whatever inconvenience follows from this mistake of words, this I am sure, that, by constant and familiar use, they charm men into notions far remote from the truth of things. It would be a hard matter to persuade any one that the words which his father, or schoolmaster, the parson of the parish, or such a reverend doctor used, signified nothing that really existed in nature: which perhaps is none of the least causes that men are so hardly drawn to quit their mistakes, even in opinions purely philosophical, and where they have no other interest but truth. For the words they have a long time been used to, remaining firm in their minds, it is no wonder that the wrong notions annexed to them should not be removed.

17. Fifthly, by setting them in the place of what they cannot signify.

V. FIFTHLY, Another abuse of words is, THE SETTING THEM IN THE PLACE OF THINGS WHICH THEY DO OR CAN BY NO MEANS SIGNIFY. We may observe that, in the general names of substances, whereof the NOMINAL essences are only known to us, when we put them into propositions, and affirm or deny anything about them, we do most commonly tacitly suppose or intend, they should stand for the REAL essence of a certain sort of substances. For, when a man says gold is malleable, he means and would insinuate something more than this, That what I call gold is malleable, (though truly it amounts to no more,) but would have this understood, viz. That gold, i.e. what has the real essence of gold, is malleable; which amounts to thus much, that malleableness depends on, and is inseparable from the real essence of gold. But a man, not knowing wherein that real essence consists, the connexion in his mind of malleableness is not truly with an essence he knows not, but only with the sound gold he puts for it. Thus, when we say that ANIMAL RATIONALE is, and animal imflume bipes latis unguibus is not a good definition of a man; it is plain we suppose the name man in this case to stand for the real essence of a species, and would signify that 'a rational animal' better described that real essence than 'a two-legged animal with broad nails, and without feathers.' For else, why might not Plato as properly make the word [word in Greek], or MAN, stand for his complex idea, made up of the idea of a body, distinguished from others by a certain shape and other outward appearances, as Aristotle make the complex idea to which he gave the name [word in Greek], or MAN, of body and the faculty of reasoning joined together; unless the name [word in Greek], or MAN, were supposed to stand for something else than what it signifies; and to be put in the place of some other thing than the idea a man professes he would express by it?

18. VI. Putting them for the real Essences of Substances.

It is true the names of substances would be much more useful, and propositions made in them much more certain, were the real essences of substances the ideas in our minds which those words signified. And it is for want of those real essences that our words convey so little knowledge or certainty in our discourses about them; and therefore the mind, to remove that imperfection as much as it can, makes them, by a secret supposition, to stand for a thing having that real essence, as if thereby it made some nearer approaches to it. For, though the word MAN or GOLD signify nothing truly but a complex idea of properties united together in one sort of substances; yet there is scarce anybody, in the use of these words, but often supposes each of those names to stand for a thing having the real essence on which these properties depend. Which is so far from diminishing the imperfection of our words, that by a plain abuse it adds to it, when we would make them stand for something, which, not being in our complex idea, the name we use can no ways be the sign of.

19. Hence we think Change of our Complex Ideas of Substances not to change their Species.

This shows us the reason why in MIXED MODES any of the ideas that make the composition of the complex one being left out or changed, it is allowed to be another thing, i.e. to be of another species, as is plain in CHANCE-MEDLEY, MANSLAUGHTER, MURDER, PARRICIDE, &c. The reason whereof is, because the complex idea signified by that name is the real as well as nominal essence; and there is no secret reference of that name to any other essence but that. But in SUBSTANCES, it is not so. For though in that called GOLD, one puts into his complex idea what another leaves out, and vice versa: yet men do not usually think that therefore the species is changed: because they secretly in their minds refer that name, and suppose it annexed to a real immutable essence of a thing existing, on which those properties depend. He that adds to his complex idea of gold that of fixedness and solubility in AQUA REGIA, which he put not in it before, is not thought to have changed the species; but only to have a more perfect idea, by adding another simple idea, which is always in fact joined with those other, of which his former complex idea consisted. But this reference of the name to a thing, whereof we have not the idea, is so far from helping at all, that it only serves the more to involve us in difficulties. For by this tacit reference to the real essence of that species of bodies, the word GOLD (which, by standing for a more or less perfect collection of simple ideas, serves to design that sort of body well enough in civil discourse) comes to have no signification at all, being put for somewhat whereof we have no idea at all, and so can signify nothing at all, when the body itself is away. For however it may be thought all one, yet, if well considered, it will be found a quite different thing, to argue about gold in name, and about a parcel in the body itself, v.g. a piece of leaf-gold laid before us; though in discourse we are fain to substitute the name for the thing.

20. The Cause of this Abuse, a supposition of Nature's working always regularly, in setting boundaries to Species.

That which I think very much disposes men to substitute their names for the real essences of species, is the supposition before mentioned, that nature works regularly in the production of things, and sets the boundaries to each of those species, by giving exactly the same real internal constitution to each individual which we rank under one general name. Whereas any one who observes their different qualities can hardly doubt, that many of the individuals, called by the same name, are, in their internal constitution, as different one from another as several of those which are ranked under different specific names. This supposition, however, that the same precise and internal constitution goes always with the same specific name, makes men forward to take those names for the representatives of those real essences; though indeed they signify nothing but the complex ideas they have in their minds when they use them. So that, if I may so say, signifying one thing, and being supposed for, or put in the place of another, they cannot but, in such a kind of use, cause a great deal of uncertainty in men's discourses; especially in those who have thoroughly imbibed the doctrine of SUBSTANTIAL FORMS, whereby they firmly imagine the several species of things to be determined and distinguished.

21. This Abuse contains two false Suppositions.

But however preposterous and absurd it be to make our names stand for ideas we have not, or (which is all one) essences that we know not, it being in effect to make our words the signs of nothing; yet it is evident to any one who ever so little reflects on the use men make of their words, that there is nothing more familiar. When a man asks whether this or that thing he sees, let it be a drill, or a monstrous foetus, be a MAN or no; it is evident the question is not, Whether that particular thing agree to his complex idea expressed by the name man: but whether it has in it the real essence of a species of things which he supposes his name man to stand for. In which way of using the names of substances, there are these false suppositions contained:—

First, that there are certain precise essences according to which nature makes all particular things, and by which they are distinguished into species. That everything has a real constitution, whereby it is what it is, and on which its sensible qualities depend, is past doubt: but I think it has been proved that this makes not the distinction of species as WE rank them, nor the boundaries of their names.

Secondly, this tacitly also insinuates, as if we had IDEAS of these proposed essences. For to what purpose else is it, to inquire whether this or that thing have the real essence of the species man, if we did not suppose that there were such a specifick essence known? Which yet is utterly false. And therefore such application of names as would make them stand for ideas which we have not, must needs cause great disorder in discourses and reasonings about them, and be a great inconvenience in our communication by words.

22. VI. Sixthly, by proceeding upon the supposition that the words we use have a certain and evident Signification which other men cannot but understand.

SIXTHLY, there remains yet another more general, though perhaps less observed, abuse of words; and that is, that men having by a long and familiar use annexed to them certain ideas, they are apt to imagine SO NEAR AND NECESSARY A CONNEXION BETWEEN THE NAMES AND SIGNIFICATION THEY USE THEM IN, that they forwardly suppose one cannot but understand what their meaning is; and therefore one ought to acquiesce in the words delivered, as if it were past doubt that, in the use of those common received sounds, the speaker and hearer had necessarily the same precise ideas. Whence presuming, that when they have in discourse used any term, they have thereby, as it were, set before others the very thing they talked of. And so likewise taking the words of others, as naturally standing for just what they themselves have been accustomed to apply them to, they never trouble themselves to explain their own, or understand clearly others' meaning. From whence commonly proceeds noise, and wrangling, without improvement or information; whilst men take words to be the constant regular marks of agreed notions, which in truth are no more but the voluntary and unsteady signs of their own ideas. And yet men think it strange, if in discourse, or (where it is often absolutely necessary) in dispute, one sometimes asks the meaning of their terms: though the arguings one may every day observe in conversation make it evident, that there are few names of complex ideas which any two men use for the same just precise collection. It is hard to name a word which will not be a clear instance of this. LIFE is a term, none more familiar. Any one almost would take it for an affront to be asked what he meant by it. And yet if it comes in question, whether a plant that lies ready formed in the seed have life; whether the embryo in an egg before incubation, or a man in a swoon without sense or motion, be alive or no; it is easy to perceive that a clear, distinct, settled idea does not always accompany the use of so known a word as that of life is. Some gross and confused conceptions men indeed ordinarily have, to which they apply the common words of their language; and such a loose use of their words serves them well enough in their ordinary discourses or affairs. But this is not sufficient for philosophical inquiries. Knowledge and reasoning require precise determinate ideas. And though men will not be so importunately dull as not to understand what others say, without demanding an explication of their terms; nor so troublesomely critical as to correct others in the use of the words they receive from them: yet, where truth and knowledge are concerned in the case, I know not what fault it can be, to desire the explication of words whose sense seems dubious; or why a man should be ashamed to own his ignorance in what sense another man uses his words; since he has no other way of certainly knowing it but by being informed. This abuse of taking words upon trust has nowhere spread so far, nor with so ill effects, as amongst men of letters. The multiplication and obstinacy of disputes, which have so laid waste the intellectual world, is owing to nothing more than to this ill use of words. For though it be generally believed that there is great diversity of opinions in the volumes and variety of controversies the world is distracted with; yet the most I can find that the contending learned men of different parties do, in their arguings one with another, is, that they speak different languages. For I am apt to imagine, that when any of them, quitting terms, think upon things, and know what they think, they think all the same: though perhaps what they would have be different.

23. The Ends of Language: First, To convey our Ideas.

To conclude this consideration of the imperfection and abuse of language. The ends of language in our discourse with others being chiefly these three: First, to make known one man's thoughts or ideas to another; Secondly, to do so with as much ease and quickness as possible; and, Thirdly, thereby to convey the knowledge of things: language is either abused or deficient, when it fails of any of these three.

First, Words fail in the first of these ends, and lay not open one man's ideas to another's view: 1. When men have names in their mouths without any determinate ideas in their minds whereof they are the signs: or, 2. When they apply the common received names of any language to ideas, to which the common use of that language does not apply them: or 3. When they apply them very unsteadily, making them stand now for one, and by and by for another idea.

24. Secondly, To do it with Quickness.

Secondly, Men fail of conveying their thoughts with the quickness and ease that may be, when they have complex ideas without having any distinct names for them. This is sometimes the fault of the language itself, which has not in it a sound yet applied to such a signification; and sometimes the fault of the man, who has not yet learned the name for that idea he would show another.

25. Thirdly, Therewith to convey the Knowledge of Things.

Thirdly, there is no knowledge of things conveyed by men's words, when their ideas agree not to the reality of things. Though it be a defect that has its original in our ideas, which are not so conformable to the nature of things as attention, study and application might make them, yet it fails not to extend itself to our words too, when we use them as signs of real beings, which yet never had any reality or existence.

26. How Men's Words fail in all these: First, when used without any ideas.

First, He that hath words of any language, without distinct ideas in his mind to which he applies them, does, so far as he uses them in discourse, only make a noise without any sense or signification; and how learned soever he may seem, by the use of hard words or learned terms, is not much more advanced thereby in knowledge, than he would be in learning, who had nothing in his study but the bare titles of books, without possessing the contents of them. For all such words, however put into discourse, according to the right construction of grammatical rules, or the harmony of well-turned periods, do yet amount to nothing but bare sounds, and nothing else.

27. Secondly, when complex ideas are without names annexed to them.

Secondly, He that has complex ideas, without particular names for them, would be in no better case than a bookseller, who had in his warehouse volumes that lay there unbound, and without titles, which he could therefore make known to others only by showing the loose sheets, and communicate them only by tale. This man is hindered in his discourse, for want of words to communicate his complex ideas, which he is therefore forced to make known by an enumeration of the simple ones that compose them; and so is fain often to use twenty words, to express what another man signifies in one.

28. Thirdly, when the same sign is not put for the same idea.

Thirdly, He that puts not constantly the same sign for the same idea, but uses the same word sometimes in one and sometimes in another signification, ought to pass in the schools and conversation for as fair a man, as he does in the market and exchange, who sells several things under the same name.

29. Fourthly, when words are diverted from their common use.

Fourthly, He that applies the words of any language to ideas different from those to which the common use of that country applies them, however his own understanding may be filled with truth and light, will not by such words be able to convey much of it to others, without defining his terms. For however the sounds are such as are familiarly known, and easily enter the ears of those who are accustomed to them; yet standing for other ideas than those they usually are annexed to, and are wont to excite in the mind of the hearers, they cannot make known the thoughts of him who thus uses them.

30. Fifthly, when they are names of fantastical imaginations.

Fifthly, He that imagined to himself substances such as never have been, and filled his head with ideas which have not any correspondence with the real nature of things, to which yet he gives settled and defined names, may fill his discourse, and perhaps another man's head, with the fantastical imaginations of his own brain, but will be very far from advancing thereby one jot in real and true knowledge.

31. Summary.

He that hath names without ideas, wants meaning in his words, and speaks only empty sounds. He that hath complex ideas without names for them, wants liberty and dispatch in his expressions, and is necessitated to use periphrases. He that uses his words loosely and unsteadily will either be not minded or not understood. He that applies his names to ideas different from their common use, wants propriety in his language, and speaks gibberish. And he that hath the ideas of substances disagreeing with the real existence of things, so far wants the materials of true knowledge in his understanding, and hath instead thereof chimeras.

32. How men's words fail when they stand for Substances.

In our notions concerning Substances, we are liable to all the former inconveniences: v. g. he that uses the word TARANTULA, without having any imagination or idea of what it stands for, pronounces a good word; but so long means nothing at all by it. 2. He that, in a newly-discovered country, shall see several sorts of animals and vegetables, unknown to him before, may have as true ideas of them, as of a horse or a stag; but can speak of them only by a description, till he shall either take the names the natives call them by, or give them names himself. 3. He that uses the word BODY sometimes for pure extension, and sometimes for extension and solidity together, will talk very fallaciously. 4. He that gives the name HORSE to that idea which common usage calls MULE, talks improperly, and will not be understood. 5. He that thinks the name CENTAUR stands for some real being, imposes on himself, and mistakes words for things.

33. How when they stand for Modes and Relations.

In Modes and Relations generally, we are liable only to the four first of these inconveniences; viz. 1. I may have in my memory the names of modes, as GRATITUDE or CHARITY, and yet not have any precise ideas annexed in my thoughts to those names, 2. I may have ideas, and not know the names that belong to them: v. g. I may have the idea of a man's drinking till his colour and humour be altered, till his tongue trips, and his eyes look red, and his feet fail him; and yet not know that it is to be called DRUNKENNESS. 3. I may have the ideas of virtues or vices, and names also, but apply them amiss: v. g. when I apply the name FRUGALITY to that idea which others call and signify by this sound, COVETOUSNESS. 4. I may use any of those names with inconstancy. 5. But, in modes and relations, I cannot have ideas disagreeing to the existence of things: for modes being complex ideas, made by the mind at pleasure, and relation being but by way of considering or comparing two things together, and so also an idea of my own making, these ideas can scarce be found to disagree with anything existing; since they are not in the mind as the copies of things regularly made by nature, nor as properties inseparably flowing from the internal constitution or essence of any substance; but, as it were, patterns lodged in my memory, with names annexed to them, to denominate actions and relations by, as they come to exist. But the mistake is commonly in my giving a wrong name to my conceptions; and so using words in a different sense from other people: I am not understood, but am thought to have wrong ideas of them, when I give wrong names to them. Only if I put in my ideas of mixed modes or relations any inconsistent ideas together, I fill my head also with chimeras; since such ideas, if well examined, cannot so much as exist in the mind, much less any real being ever be denominated from them.

34. Seventhly, Language is often abused by Figurative Speech.

Since wit and fancy find easier entertainment in the world than dry truth and real knowledge, figurative speeches and allusion in language will hardly be admitted as an imperfection or abuse of it. I confess, in discourses where we seek rather pleasure and delight than information and improvement, such ornaments as are borrowed from them can scarce pass for faults. But yet if we would speak of things as they are, we must allow that all the art of rhetoric, besides order and clearness; all the artificial and figurative application of words eloquence hath invented, are for nothing else but to insinuate wrong ideas, move the passions, and thereby mislead the judgment; and so indeed are perfect cheats: and therefore, however laudable or allowable oratory may render them in harangues and popular addresses, they are certainly, in all discourses that pretend to inform or instruct, wholly to be avoided; and where truth and knowledge are concerned, cannot but be thought a great fault, either of the language or person that makes use of them. What and how various they are, will be superfluous here to take notice; the books of rhetoric which abound in the world, will instruct those who want to be informed: only I cannot but observe how little the preservation and improvement of truth and knowledge is the care and concern of mankind; since the arts of fallacy are endowed and preferred. It is evident how much men love to deceive and be deceived, since rhetoric, that powerful instrument of error and deceit, has its established professors, is publicly taught, and has always been had in great reputation: and I doubt not but it will be thought great boldness, if not brutality, in me to have said thus much against it. Eloquence, like the fair sex, has too prevailing beauties in it to suffer itself ever to be spoken against. And it is in vain to find fault with those arts of deceiving, wherein men find pleasure to be deceived.

CHAPTER XI.

OF THE REMEDIES OF THE FOREGOING IMPERFECTIONS AND ABUSES OF WORDS.

1. Remedies are worth seeking.
The natural and improved imperfections of languages we have seen above at large: and speech being the great bond that holds society together, and the common conduit, whereby the improvements of knowledge are conveyed from one man and one generation to another, it would well deserve our most serious thoughts to consider, what remedies are to be found for the inconveniences above mentioned.
2. Are not easy to find.
I am not so vain as to think that any one can pretend to attempt the perfect reforming the languages of the world, no not so much as of his own country, without rendering himself ridiculous. To require that men should use their words constantly in the same sense, and for none but determined and uniform ideas, would be to think that all men should have the same notions, and should talk of nothing but what they have clear and distinct ideas of: which is not to be expected by any one who hath not vanity enough to imagine he can prevail with men to be very knowing or very silent. And he must be very little skilled in the world, who thinks that a voluble tongue shall accompany only a good understanding; or that men's talking much or little should hold proportion only to their knowledge.
3. But yet necessary to those who search after Truth.
But though the market and exchange must be left to their own ways of talking, and gossipings not be robbed of their ancient privilege: though the schools, and men of argument would perhaps take it amiss to have anything offered, to abate the length or lessen the number of their disputes; yet methinks those who pretend seriously to search after or maintain truth, should think themselves obliged to study how they might deliver themselves without obscurity, doubtfulness, or equivocation, to which men's words are naturally liable, if care be not taken.
4. Misuse of Words the great Cause of Errors.
For he that shall well consider the errors and obscurity, the mistakes and confusion, that are spread in the world by an ill use of words, will find some reason to doubt whether language, as it has been employed, has contributed more to the improvement or hindrance of knowledge amongst

mankind. How many are there, that, when they would think on things, fix their thoughts only on words, especially when they would apply their minds to moral matters? And who then can wonder if the result of such contemplations and reasonings, about little more than sounds, whilst the ideas they annex to them are very confused and very unsteady, or perhaps none at all; who can wonder, I say, that such thoughts and reasonings end in nothing but obscurity and mistake, without any clear judgment or knowledge?

5. Has made men more conceited and obstinate.

This inconvenience, in an ill use of words, men suffer in their own private meditations: but much more manifest are the disorders which follow from it, in conversation, discourse, and arguings with others. For language being the great conduit, whereby men convey their discoveries, reasonings, and knowledge, from one to another, he that makes an ill use of it, though he does not corrupt the fountains of knowledge, which are in things themselves, yet he does, as much as in him lies, break or stop the pipes whereby it is distributed to the public use and advantage of mankind. He that uses words without any clear and steady meaning, what does he but lead himself and others into errors? And he that designedly does it, ought to be looked on as an enemy to truth and knowledge. And yet who can wonder that all the sciences and parts of knowledge have been so overcharged with obscure and equivocal terms, and insignificant and doubtful expressions, capable to make the most attentive or quick-sighted very little, or not at all, the more knowing or orthodox: since subtlety, in those who make profession to teach or defend truth, hath passed so much for a virtue: a virtue, indeed, which, consisting for the most part in nothing but the fallacious and illusory use of obscure or deceitful terms, is only fit to make men more conceited in their ignorance, and more obstinate in their errors.

6. Addicted to Wrangling about sounds.

Let us look into the books of controversy of any kind, there we shall see that the effect of obscure, unsteady, or equivocal terms is nothing but noise and wrangling about sounds, without convincing or bettering a man's understanding. For if the idea be not agreed on, betwixt the speaker and hearer, for which the words stand, the argument is not about things, but names. As often as such a word whose signification is not ascertained betwixt them, comes in use, their understandings have no other object wherein they agree, but barely the sound; the things that they think on at that time, as expressed by that word, being quite different.

7. Instance, Bat and Bird.

Whether a BAT be a BIRD or no, is not a question, Whether a bat be another thing than indeed it is, or have other qualities than indeed it has; for that would be extremely absurd to doubt of. But the question is, (i) Either between those that acknowledged themselves to have but imperfect ideas of one or both of this sort of things, for which these names are supposed to stand. And then it is a real inquiry concerning the NATURE of a bird or a bat, to make their yet imperfect ideas of it more complete; by examining whether all the simple ideas to which, combined together, they both give name bird, be all to be found in a bat: but this is a question only of inquirers (not disputers) who neither affirm nor deny, but examine: Or, (2) It is a question between disputants; whereof the one affirms, and the other denies that a bat is a bird. And then the question is barely about the signification of one or both these WORDS; in that they not having both the same complex ideas to which they give these two names, one holds and the other denies, that these two names may be affirmed one of another. Were they agreed in the signification of these two names, it were impossible they should dispute about them. For they would presently and clearly see (were that adjusted between them,) whether all the simple ideas of the more general name bird were found in the complex idea of a bat or no; and so there could be no doubt whether a bat were a bird or no. And here I desire it may be considered, and carefully examined, whether the greatest part of the disputes in the world are not merely verbal, and about the signification of words; and whether, if the terms they are made in were defined, and reduced in their signification (as they must be where they signify anything) to determined collections of the simple ideas they do or should stand for, those disputes would not end of themselves, and immediately vanish. I leave it then to be considered, what the learning of disputation is, and how well they are employed for the advantage of themselves or others, whose business is only the vain ostentation of sounds; i. e. those who spend their lives in disputes and controversies. When I shall see any of those combatants strip all his terms of ambiguity and obscurity, (which every one may do in the words he uses himself,) I shall think him a champion for knowledge, truth, and peace, and not the slave of vain-glory, ambition, or a party.

8. Remedies.

To remedy the defects of speech before mentioned to some degree, and to prevent the inconveniences that follow from them, I imagine the observation of these following rules may be of use, till somebody better able shall judge it worth his while to think more maturely on this matter, and oblige the world with his thoughts on it.

First Remedy: To use no Word without an Idea annexed to it.

First, A man shall take care to use no word without a signification, no name without an idea for which he makes it stand. This rule will not seem altogether needless to any one who shall take the pains to recollect how often he has met with such words as INSTINCT, SYMPATHY, and ANTIPATHY, &c., in the discourse of others, so made use of as he might easily conclude that those that used them had no ideas in their minds to which they applied them, but spoke them only as sounds, which usually served instead of reasons on the like occasions. Not but that these words, and the like, have very proper significations in which they may be used; but there being no natural connexion between any words and any ideas, these, and any other, may be learned by rote, and pronounced or writ by men who have no ideas in their minds to which they have annexed them, and for which they make them stand; which is necessary they should, if men would speak intelligibly even to themselves alone.

9. Second Remedy: To have distinct, determinate Ideas annexed to Words, especially in mixed Modes.

Secondly, It is not enough a man uses his words as signs of some ideas: those he annexes them to, if they be simple, must be clear and distinct; if complex, must be determinate, i.e. the precise collection of simple ideas settled in the mind, with that sound annexed to it, as the sign of that precise determined collection, and no other. This is very necessary in names of modes, and especially moral words; which, having no settled objects in nature, from whence their ideas are taken, as from their original, are apt to be very confused. JUSTICE is a word in every man's mouth, but most commonly with a very undetermined, loose signification; which will always be so, unless a man has in his mind a distinct comprehension of the component parts that complex idea consists of and if it be decompounded, must be able to resolve it still only till he at last comes to the simple ideas that make it up: and unless this be done, a man makes an ill use of the word, let it be justice, for example, or any other. I do not say, a man needs stand to recollect, and make this analysis at large, every time the word justice comes in his way: but this at least is necessary, that he have so examined the signification of that name, and settled the idea of all its parts in his mind, that he can do it when he pleases. If any one who makes his complex idea of justice to be, such a treatment of the person or goods of another as is according to law, hath not a clear and distinct idea what LAW is, which makes a part of his complex idea of justice, it is plain his idea of justice itself will be confused and imperfect. This exactness will, perhaps, be judged very troublesome; and therefore most men will think they may be excused from settling the complex ideas of mixed modes so precisely in their minds. But yet I must say, till this be done, it must not be wondered, that they have a great deal of obscurity and confusion in their own minds, and a great deal of wrangling in their discourse with others.

10. And distinct and conformable ideas in Words that stand for Substances. In the names of substances, for a right use of them, something more is required than barely DETERMINED IDEAS. In these the names must also be CONFORMABLE TO THINGS AS THEY EXIST; but of this I shall have occasion to speak more at large by and by. This exactness is absolutely necessary in inquiries after philosophical knowledge, and in controversies about truth. And though it would be well, too, if it extended itself to common conversation and the ordinary affairs of life; yet I think that is scarce to be expected. Vulgar notions suit vulgar discourses: and both, though confused enough, yet serve pretty well the market and the wake. Merchants and lovers, cooks and tailors, have words wherewithal to dispatch their ordinary affairs: and so, I think, might philosophers and disputants too, if they had a mind to understand, and to clearly understood.

11. Third Remedy: To apply Words to such ideas as common use has annexed them to.

Thirdly, it is not enough that men have ideas, determined ideas, for which they make these signs stand; but they must also take care to apply their words as near as may be to such ideas as common use has annexed them to. For words, especially of languages already framed, being no man's private possession, but the common measure of commerce and communication, it is not for any one at pleasure to change the stamp they are current in, nor alter the ideas they are affixed to; or at least, when there is a necessity to do so, he is bound to give notice of it. Men's intentions in speaking are, or at least should be, to be understood; which cannot be without frequent explanations, demands, and other the like incommodious interruptions, where men do not follow common use. Propriety of speech is that which gives our thoughts entrance into other men's minds with the greatest ease and advantage: and therefore deserves some part of our care and study, especially in the names of moral words. The proper signification and use of terms is best to be learned from those who in their writings and discourses appear to have had the clearest notions, and applied to them their terms with the exactest choice and fitness. This way of using a man's words, according to the propriety of the language, though it have not always the good fortune to be understood; yet most commonly leaves the blame of it on him who is so unskilful in the language he speaks, as not to understand it when made use of as it ought to be.

12. Fourth Remedy: To declare the meaning in which we use them.

Fourthly, But, because common use has not so visibly annexed any signification to words, as to make men know always certainly what they precisely stand for: and because men, in the improvement of their knowledge, come to have ideas different from the vulgar and ordinary received ones, for which they must either make new words, (which men seldom venture to do, for fear of being thought guilty of affectation or novelty,) or else must use old ones in a new signification: therefore, after the observation of the foregoing rules, it is sometimes necessary, for the ascertaining the signification of words, to DECLARE THEIR MEANING; where either common use has left it uncertain and loose, (as it has in most names of very complex ideas;) or where the term, being very material in the discourse, and that upon which it chiefly turns, is liable to any doubtfulness or mistake.

13. And that in three Ways.

As the ideas men's words stand for are of different sorts, so the way of making known the ideas they stand for, when there is occasion, is also different. For though DEFINING be thought the proper way to make known the proper signification of words; yet there are some words that will not be defined, as there are others whose precise meaning cannot be made known but by definition: and perhaps a third, which partake somewhat of both the other, as we shall see in the names of simple ideas, modes, and substances.

14. In Simple Ideas, either by synonymous terms, or by showing examples.

I. First, when a man makes use of the name of any simple idea, which he perceives is not understood, or is in danger to be mistaken, he is obliged, by the laws of ingenuity and the end of speech, to declare his meaning, and make known what idea he makes it stand for. This, as has been shown, cannot be done by definition: and therefore, when a synonymous word fails to do it, there is but one of these ways left. First, Sometimes the NAMING the subject wherein that simple idea is to be found, will make its name to be understood by those who are acquainted with that subject, and know it by that name. So to make a countryman understand what FEUILLEMORTE colour signifies, it may suffice to tell him, it is the colour of withered leaves falling in autumn. Secondly, but the only sure way of making known the signification of the name of any simple idea, is BY PRESENTING TO HIS SENSES THAT SUBJECT WHICH MAY PRODUCE IT IN HIS MIND, and make him actually have the idea that word stands for.

15. In mixed Modes, by Definition.

II. Secondly, Mixed modes, especially those belonging to morality, being most of them such combinations of ideas as the mind puts together of its own choice, and whereof there are not always standing patterns to be found existing, the signification of their names cannot be made known, as those of simple ideas, by any showing: but, in recompense thereof, may be perfectly and exactly defined. For they being combinations of several ideas that the mind of man has arbitrarily put together, without reference to any archetypes, men may, if they please, exactly know the ideas that go to each composition, and so both use these words in a certain and undoubted signification, and perfectly declare, when there is occasion, what they stand for. This, if well considered, would lay great blame on those who make not their discourses about MORAL things very clear and distinct. For since the precise signification of the names of mixed modes, or, which is all one, the real essence of each species is to be known, they being not of nature's, but man's making, it is a great negligence and perverseness to discourse of moral things with uncertainty and obscurity; which is more pardonable in treating of natural substances, where doubtful terms are hardly to be avoided, for a quite contrary reason, as we shall see by and by.

16. Morality capable of Demonstration.

Upon this ground it is that I am bold to think that morality is capable of demonstration, as well as mathematics: since the precise real essence of the things moral words stand for may be perfectly known, and so the congruity and incongruity of the things themselves be certainly discovered; in which consists perfect knowledge. Nor let any one object, that the names of substances are often to be made use of in morality, as well as those of modes, from which will arise obscurity. For, as to substances, when concerned in moral discourses, their divers natures are not so much inquired into as supposed: v.g. when we say that man is subject to law, we mean nothing by man but a corporeal rational creature: what the real essence or other qualities of that creature are in this case is no way considered. And, therefore, whether a child or changeling be a man, in a physical sense, may amongst the naturalists be as disputable as it will, it concerns not at all the moral man, as I may call him, which is this immovable, unchangeable idea, a corporeal rational being. For, were there a monkey, or any other creature, to be found that had the use of reason to such a degree, as to be able to understand general signs, and to deduce consequences about general ideas, he would no doubt be subject to law, and in that sense be a MAN, how much soever he differed in shape from others of that name. The names of substances, if they be used in them as they should, can no more disturb moral than they do mathematical discourses; where, if the mathematician speaks of a cube or globe of gold, or of any other body, he has his clear, settled idea, which varies not, though it may by mistake be applied to a particular body to which it belongs not.

17. Definitions can make moral Discourse clear.

This I have here mentioned, by the by, to show of what consequence it is for men, in their names of mixed modes, and consequently in all their moral discourses, to define their words when there is occasion: since thereby moral knowledge may be brought to so great clearness and certainty. And it must be great want of ingenuousness (to say no worse of it) to refuse to do it: since a definition is the only way whereby the precise meaning of moral words can be known; and yet a way whereby their meaning may be known certainly, and without leaving any room for any contest about it. And therefore the negligence or perverseness of mankind cannot be excused, if their discourses in morality be not much more clear than those in natural philosophy: since they are about ideas in the mind, which are none of them false or disproportionate; they having no external beings for the archetypes which they are referred to and must correspond with. It is far easier for men to frame in their minds an idea, which shall be the standard to which they will give the name justice; with which pattern so made, all actions that agree shall pass under that denomination, than, having seen Aristides, to frame an idea that shall in all things be exactly like him; who is as he is, let men make what idea they please of him. For the one, they need but know the combination of ideas that are put together in their own minds; for the other, they must inquire into the whole nature, and abstruse hidden constitution, and various qualities of a thing existing without them.

18. And is the only way in which the meaning of mixed Modes can be made known.

Another reason that makes the defining of mixed modes so necessary, especially of moral words, is what I mentioned a little before, viz. that it is the only way whereby the signification of the most of them can be known with certainty. For the ideas they stand for, being for the most part such whose component parts nowhere exist together, but scattered and mingled with others, it is the mind alone that collects them, and gives them the union of one idea: and it is only by words enumerating the several simple ideas which the mind has united, that we can make known to others what their names stand for; the assistance of the senses in this case not helping us, by the proposal of sensible objects, to show the ideas which our names of this kind stand for, as it does often in the names of sensible simple ideas, and also to some degree in those of substances.

19. In Substances, both by showing and by defining.

III. Thirdly, for the explaining the signification of the names of substances, as they stand for the ideas we have of their distinct species, both the forementioned ways, viz. of showing and defining, are requisite, in many cases, to be made use of. For, there being ordinarily in each sort some leading qualities, to which we suppose the other ideas which make up our complex idea of that species annexed, we forwardly give the specific name to that thing wherein that characteristic mark is found, which we take to be the most distinguishing idea of that species. These leading or characteristical (as I may call them) ideas, in the sorts of animals and vegetables, are (as has been before remarked, ch vi. Section 29 and ch. ix. Section 15) mostly figure; and in inanimate bodies, colour; and in some, both together. Now,

20. Ideas of the leading Qualities of Substances are best got by showing.

These leading sensible qualities are those which make the chief ingredients of our specific ideas, and consequently the most observable and invariable part in the definitions of our specific names, as attributed to sorts of substances coming under our knowledge. For though the sound MAN, in its own nature, be as apt to signify a complex idea made up of animality and rationality, united in the same subject, as to signify any other combination; yet, used as a mark to stand for a sort of creatures we count of our own kind, perhaps the outward shape is as necessary to be taken into our complex idea, signified by the word man, as any other we find in it: and therefore, why Plato's ANIMAL IMPLUME BIPES LATIS UNGUIBUS should not be a good definition of the name man, standing for that sort of creatures, will not be easy to show: for it is the shape, as the leading quality, that seems more to determine that species, than a faculty of reasoning, which appears not at first, and in some never. And if this be not allowed to be so, I do not know how they can be excused from murder who kill monstrous births, (as we call them,) because of an unordinary shape, without knowing whether they have a rational soul or no; which can be no more discerned in a well-formed than ill-shaped infant, as soon as born. And who is it has informed us that a rational soul can inhabit no tenement, unless it has just such a sort of frontispiece; or can join itself to, and inform no sort of body, but one that is just of such an outward structure?

21. And can hardly be made known otherwise.

Now these leading qualities are best made known by showing, and can hardly be made known otherwise. For the shape of a horse or cassowary will be but rudely and imperfectly imprinted on the mind by words; the sight of the animals doth it a thousand times better. And the idea of the particular colour of gold is not to be got by any description of it, but only by the frequent exercise of the eyes about as is evident in those who are used to this metal, who frequently distinguish true from counterfeit, pure from adulterate, by the sight, where others (who have as good eyes, but yet by use have not got the precise nice idea of that peculiar yellow) shall not perceive any difference. The like may be said of those other simple ideas, peculiar in their kind to any substance; for which precise ideas there are no peculiar names. The particular ringing sound there is in gold, distinct from the sound of other bodies, has no particular name annexed to it, no more than the particular yellow that belongs to that metal.

22. The Ideas of the Powers of Substances are best known by Definition.

But because many of the simple ideas that make up our specific ideas of substances are powers which lie not obvious to our senses in the things as they ordinarily appear; therefore, in the signification of our names of substances, some part of the signification will be better made known by enumerating those simple ideas, than by showing the substance itself. For, he that to the yellow shining colour of gold, got by sight, shall, from my enumerating them, have the ideas of great ductility, fusibility, fixedness, and solubility, in aqua regia, will have a perfecter idea of gold than he can have by seeing a piece of gold, and thereby imprinting in his mind only its obvious qualities. But if the formal constitution of this shining, heavy, ductile thing, (from whence all these its properties flow,) lay open to our senses, as the formal constitution or essence of a triangle does, the signification of the word gold might as easily be ascertained as that of triangle.

23. A Reflection on the Knowledge of corporeal things possessed by Spirits separate from bodies.

Hence we may take notice, how much the foundation of all our knowledge of corporeal things lies in our senses. For how spirits, separate from bodies, (whose knowledge and ideas of these things are certainly much more perfect than ours,) know them, we have no notion, no idea at all. The whole extent of our knowledge or imagination reaches not beyond our own ideas limited to our ways of perception. Though yet it be not to be doubted that spirits of a higher rank than those immersed in flesh may have as clear ideas of the radical constitution of substances as we have of a triangle, and so perceive how all their properties and operations flow from thence: but the manner how they come by that knowledge exceeds our conceptions.

24. Ideas of Substances must also be conformable to Things.

Fourthly, But, though definitions will serve to explain the names of substances as they stand for our ideas, yet they leave them not without great imperfection as they stand for things. For our names of substances being not put barely for our ideas, but being made use of ultimately to represent things, and so are put in their place, their signification must agree with the truth of things as well as with men's ideas. And therefore, in substances, we are not always to rest in the ordinary complex idea commonly received as the signification of that word, but must go a little further, and inquire into the nature and properties of the things themselves, and thereby perfect, as much as we can, our ideas of their distinct species; or else learn them from such as are used to that sort of things, and are experienced in them. For, since it is intended their names should stand for such collections of simple ideas as do really exist in things themselves, as well as for the complex idea in other men's minds, which in their ordinary acceptation they stand for, therefore, to define their names right, natural history is to be inquired into, and their properties are, with care and examination, to be found out. For it is not enough, for the avoiding inconveniences in discourse and arguings about natural bodies and substantial things, to have learned, from the propriety of the language, the common, but confused, or very imperfect, idea to which each word is applied, and to keep them to that idea in our use of them; but we must, by acquainting ourselves with the history of that sort of things, rectify and settle our complex idea belonging to each specific name; and in discourse with others, (if we find them mistake us,) we ought to tell what the complex idea is that we make such a name stand for. This is the more necessary to be done by all those who search after knowledge and philosophical verity, in that children, being taught words, whilst they have but imperfect notions of things, apply them at random, and without much thinking, and seldom frame determined ideas to be signified by them. Which custom (it being easy, and serving well enough for the ordinary affairs of life and conversation) they are apt to continue when they are men: and so begin at the wrong end, learning words first and perfectly, but make the notions to which they apply those words afterwards very overtly. By this means it comes to pass, that men speaking the language of their country, i.e. according to grammar rules of that language, do yet speak very improperly of things themselves; and, by their arguing one with another, make but small progress in the discoveries of useful truths, and the knowledge of things, as they are to be found in themselves, and not in our imaginations; and it matters not much for the improvement of our knowledge how they are called.

25. Not easy to be made so.

It were therefore to be wished, That men versed in physical inquiries, and acquainted with the several sorts of natural bodies, would set down those simple ideas wherein they observe the individuals of each sort constantly to agree. This would remedy a great deal of that confusion which comes from several persons applying the same name to a collection of a smaller or greater number of sensible qualities, proportionably as they have been more or less acquainted with, or accurate in examining, the qualities of any sort of things which come under one denomination. But a dictionary of this sort, containing, as it were, a natural history, requires too many hands as well as too much time, cost, pains, and sagacity ever to be hoped for; and till that be done, we must content ourselves with such definitions of the names of substances as explain the sense men use them in. And it would be well, where there is occasion, if they would afford us so much. This yet is not usually done; but men talk to one another, and dispute in words, whose meaning is not agreed between them, out of a mistake that the significations of common words are certainly established, and the precise ideas they stand for perfectly known; and that it is a shame to be ignorant of them. Both which suppositions are false, no names of complex ideas having so settled determined significations, that they are constantly used for the same precise ideas. Nor is it a shame for a man to have a certain knowledge of anything, but by the necessary ways of attaining it; and so it is no discredit not to know what precise idea any sound stands for in another man's mind, without he declare it to me by some other way than barely using that sound, there being no other way, without such a declaration, certainly to know it. Indeed the necessity of communication by language brings men to an agreement in the signification of common words, within some tolerable latitude, that may serve for ordinary conversation: and so a man cannot be supposed wholly ignorant of the ideas which are annexed to words by common use, in a language familiar to him. But common use being but a very uncertain rule, which reduces itself at last to the ideas of particular men, proves often but a very variable standard. But though such a Dictionary as I have above mentioned will require too much time, cost, and pains to be hoped for in this age; yet methinks it is not unreasonable to propose, that words standing for things which are known and distinguished by their outward shapes should be expressed by little draughts and prints made of them. A vocabulary made after this fashion would perhaps with more ease, and in less time, teach the true signification of many terms, especially in languages of remote countries or ages, and settle truer ideas in men's minds of several things, whereof we read the names in ancient authors, than all the large and laborious comments of learned critics. Naturalists, that treat of plants and animals, have found the benefit of this way: and he that has had occasion to consult them will have reason to confess that he has a clearer idea of APIUM or IBEX, from a little print of that herb or beast, than he could have from a long definition of the names of either of them. And so no doubt he would have of STRIGIL and SISTRUM, if, instead of CURRYCOMB and CYMBAL, (which are the English names dictionaries render them by,) he could see stamped in the margin small pictures of these instruments, as they were in use amongst the ancients. TOGA, TUNICA, PALLIUM, are words easily translated by GOWN, COAT, and CLOAK; but we have thereby no more true ideas of the fashion of those habits amongst the Romans, than we have of the faces of the tailors who made them. Such things as these, which the eye distinguishes by their shapes, would be best let into the mind by draughts made of them, and more determine the signification of such words, than any other words set for them, or made use of to define them. But this is only by the bye.

26. V. Fifth Remedy: To use the same word constantly in the same sense. Fifthly, If men will not be at the pains to declare the meaning of their words, and definitions of their terms are not to be had, yet this is the least that can be expected, that, in all discourses wherein one man pretends to instruct or convince another, he should use the same word constantly in the same sense. If this were done, (which nobody can refuse without great disingenuity,) many of the books extant might be spared; many of the controversies in dispute would be at an end; several of those great volumes, swollen with ambiguous words, now used in one sense, and by and by in another, would shrink into a very narrow compass; and many of the philosophers (to mention no other) as well as poets works, might be contained in a nutshell.

27. When not so used, the Variation is to be explained.

But after all, the provision of words is so scanty in respect to that infinite variety of thoughts, that men, wanting terms to suit their precise notions, will, notwithstanding their utmost caution, be forced often to use the same word in somewhat different senses. And though in the continuation of a discourse, or the pursuit of an argument, there can be hardly room to digress into a particular definition, as often as a man varies the signification of any term; yet the import of the discourse will, for the most part, if there be no designed fallacy, sufficiently lead candid and intelligent readers into the true meaning of it; but where there is not sufficient to guide the reader, there it concerns the writer to explain his meaning, and show in what sense he there uses that term.

BOOK IV

OF KNOWLEDGE AND PROBABILITY SYNOPSIS OF THE FOURTH BOOK.

Locke's review of the different sorts of ideas, or appearances of what exists, that can be entertained in a human understanding, and of their relations to words, leads, in the Fourth Book, to an investigation of the extent and validity of the Knowledge that our ideas bring within our reach; and into the nature of faith in Probability, by which assent is extended beyond Knowledge, for the conduct of life. He finds (ch. i, ii) that Knowledge is either an intuitive, a demonstrative, or a sensuous perception of absolute certainty, in regard to one or other of four sorts of agreement or disagreement on the part of ideas:—(1) of each idea with itself, as identical, and different from every other; (2) in their abstract relations to one another; (3) in their necessary connexions, as qualities and powers coexisting in concrete substances; and (4) as revelations to us of the final realities of existence. The unconditional certainty that constitutes Knowledge is perceptible by man only in regard to the first, second, and fourth of these four sorts: in all general propositions only in regard to the first and second; that is to say, in identical propositions, and in those which express abstract relations of simple or mixed modes, in which nominal and real essences coincide, e. g. propositions in pure mathematics and abstract morality (chh. iii, v-viii). The fourth sort, which express certainty as to realities of existence, refer to any of three realities. For every man is able to perceive with absolute certainty that he himself exists, that God must exist, and that finite beings other than himself exist;—the first of these perceptions being awakened by all our ideas, the second as the consequence of perception of the first, and the last in the reception of our simple ideas of sense (chh. i. Section 7; ii. Section 14; iii. Section 21; iv, ix-xi). Agreement of the third sort, of necessary coexistence of simple ideas as qualities and powers in particular substances, with which all physical inquiry is concerned, lies beyond human Knowledge; for here the nominal and real essences are not coincident: general propositions of this sort are determined by analogies of experience, in judgments that are more or less probable: intellectually necessary science of nature presupposes Omniscience; man's interpretations of nature have to turn upon presumptions of Probability (chh. iii. Sections 9-17; iv. SectionS 11-17; vi, xiv-xvi). In forming their stock of Certainties and Probabilities men employ the faculty of reason, faith in divine revelation, and enthusiasm (chh. xvii-xix); much misled by the last, as well as by other causes of 'wrong assent' (ch. xx), when they are at work in 'the three great provinces of the intellectual world' (ch. xxi), concerned respectively with (1) 'things as knowable' (physica); (2) 'actions as they depend on us in order to happiness' (practica); and (3) methods for interpreting the signs of what is, and of what ought to be, that are presented in our ideas and words (logica).

CHAPTER I.

OF KNOWLEDGE IN GENERAL.

1. Our Knowledge conversant about our Ideas only.

Since the mind, in all its thoughts and reasonings, hath no other immediate object but its own ideas, which it alone does or can contemplate, it is evident that our knowledge is only conversant about them.

2. Knowledge is the Perception of the Agreement or Disagreement of two Ideas.

KNOWLEDGE then seems to me to be nothing but THE PERCEPTION OF THE
CONNEXION OF AND AGREEMENT, OR DISAGREEMENT AND REPUGNANCY OF ANY OF OUR
IDEAS. In this alone it consists.

Where this perception is, there is knowledge, and where it is not, there, though we may fancy, guess, or believe, yet we always come short of knowledge. For when we know that white is not black, what do we else but perceive, that these two ideas do not agree? When we possess ourselves with the utmost security of the demonstration, that the three angles of a triangle are equal to two right ones, what do we more but perceive, that equality to two right ones does necessarily agree to, and is inseparable from, the three angles of a triangle?

3. This Agreement or Disagreement may be any of four sorts.

But to understand a little more distinctly wherein this agreement or disagreement consists, I think we may reduce it all to these four sorts:
I. IDENTITY, or DIVERSITY. II. RELATION. III. CO-EXISTENCE, or NECESSARY
CONNEXION. IV. REAL EXISTENCE.

4. First, Of Identity, or Diversity in ideas.

FIRST, As to the first sort of agreement or disagreement, viz. IDENTITY or DIVERSITY. It is the first act of the mind, when it has any sentiments or ideas at all, to perceive its ideas; and so far as it perceives them, to know each what it is, and thereby also to perceive their difference, and that one is not another. This is so absolutely necessary, that without it there could be no knowledge, no reasoning, no imagination, no distinct thoughts at all. By this the mind clearly and infallibly perceives each idea to agree with itself, and to be what it is; and all distinct ideas to disagree, i. e. the one not to be the other: and this it does without pains, labour, or deduction; but at first view, by its natural power of perception and distinction. And though men of art have reduced this into those general rules, WHAT IS, IS, and IT IS IMPOSSIBLE FOR THE SAME THING TO BE AND NOT TO BE, for ready application in all cases, wherein there may be occasion to reflect on it: yet it is certain that the first exercise of this faculty is about particular ideas. A man infallibly knows, as soon as ever he has them in his mind, that the ideas he calls WHITE and ROUND are the very ideas they are; and that they are not other ideas which he calls RED or SQUARE. Nor can any maxim or proposition in the world make him know it clearer or surer than he did before, and without any such general rule. This then is the first agreement or disagreement which the mind perceives in its ideas; which it always perceives at first sight: and if there ever happen any doubt about it, it will always be found to be about the names, and not the ideas themselves, whose identity and diversity will always be perceived, as soon and clearly as the ideas themselves are; nor can it possibly be otherwise.

5. Secondly, Of abstract Relations between ideas.

SECONDLY, the next sort of agreement or disagreement the mind perceives in any of its ideas may, I think, be called RELATIVE, and is nothing but the perception of the RELATION between any two ideas, of what kind soever, whether substances, modes, or any other. For, since all distinct ideas must eternally be known not to be the same, and so be universally and constantly denied one of another, there could be no room for any positive knowledge at all, if we could not perceive any relation between our ideas, and find out the agreement or disagreement they have one with another, in several ways the mind takes of comparing them.

6. Thirdly, Of their necessary Co-existence in Substances.

THIRDLY, The third sort of agreement or disagreement to be found in our ideas, which the perception of the mind is employed about, is CO-EXISTENCE or NON-CO-EXISTENCE in the SAME SUBJECT; and this belongs particularly to substances. Thus when we pronounce concerning gold, that it is fixed, our knowledge of this truth amounts to no more but this, that fixedness, or a power to remain in the fire unconsumed, is an idea that always accompanies and is joined with that particular sort of yellowness, weight, fusibility, malleableness, and solubility in AQUA REGIA, which make our complex idea signified by the word gold.

7. Fourthly, Of real Existence agreeing to any idea.

FOURTHLY, The fourth and last sort is that of ACTUAL REAL EXISTENCE agreeing to any idea.

Within these four sorts of agreement or disagreement is, I suppose, contained all the knowledge we have, or are capable of. For all the inquiries we can make concerning any of our ideas, all that we know or can affirm concerning any of them, is, That it is, or is not, the same with some other; that it does or does not always co-exist with some other idea in the same subject; that it has this or that relation with some other idea; or that it has a real existence without the mind. Thus, 'blue is not yellow,' is of identity. 'Two triangles upon equal bases between two parallels are equal,' is of relation. 'Iron is susceptible of magnetical impressions,' is of co-existence. 'God is,' is of real existence. Though identity and co-existence are truly nothing but relations, yet they are such peculiar ways of agreement or disagreement of our ideas, that they deserve well to be considered as distinct heads, and not under relation in general; since they are so different grounds of affirmation and negation, as will easily appear to any one, who will but reflect on what is said in several places of this ESSAY.

I should now proceed to examine the several degrees of our knowledge, but that it is necessary first, to consider the different acceptations of the word KNOWLEDGE.

8. Knowledge is either actual or habitual.

There are several ways wherein the mind is possessed of truth; each of which is called knowledge.

I. There is ACTUAL KNOWLEDGE, which is the present view the mind has of the agreement or disagreement of any of its ideas, or of the relation they have one to another.

II. A man is said to know any proposition, which having been once laid before his thoughts, he evidently perceived the agreement or disagreement of the ideas whereof it consists; and so lodged it in his memory, that whenever that proposition comes again to be reflected on, he, without doubt or hesitation, embraces the right side, assents to, and is certain of the truth of it. This, I think, one may call HABITUAL KNOWLEDGE. And thus a man may be said to know all those truths which are lodged in his memory, by a foregoing clear and full perception, whereof the mind is assured past doubt as often as it has occasion to reflect on them. For our finite understandings being able to think clearly and distinctly but on one thing at once, if men had no knowledge of any more than what they actually thought on, they would all be very ignorant: and he that knew most, would know but one truth, that being all he was able to think on at one time.

9. Habitual Knowledge is of two degrees.

Of habitual knowledge there are, also, vulgarly speaking, two degrees:

First, The one is of such truths laid up in the memory as, whenever they occur to the mind, it ACTUALLY PERCEIVES THE RELATION is between those ideas. And this is in all those truths whereof we have an intuitive knowledge; where the ideas themselves, by an immediate view, discover their agreement or disagreement one with another.

Secondly, The other is of such truths whereof the mind having been convinced, it RETAINS THE MEMORY OF THE CONVICTION, WITHOUT THE PROOFS. Thus, a man that remembers certainly that he once perceived the demonstration, that the three angles of a triangle are equal to two right ones, is certain that he knows it, because he cannot doubt the truth of it. In his adherence to a truth, where the demonstration by which it was at first known is forgot, though a man may be thought rather to believe his memory than really to know, and this way of entertaining a truth seemed formerly to me like something between opinion and knowledge; a sort of assurance which exceeds bare belief, for that relies on the testimony of another;—yet upon a due examination I find it comes not short of perfect certainty, and is in effect true knowledge. That which is apt to mislead our first thoughts into a mistake in this matter is, that the agreement or disagreement of the ideas in this case is not perceived, as it was at first, by an actual view of all the intermediate ideas whereby the agreement or disagreement of those in the proposition was at first perceived; but by other intermediate ideas, that show the agreement or disagreement of the ideas contained in the proposition whose certainty we remember. For example: in this proposition, that 'the three angles of a triangle are equal to two right ones,' one who has seen and clearly perceived the demonstration of this truth knows it to be true, when that demonstration is gone out of his mind; so that at present it is not actually in view, and possibly cannot be recollected: but he knows it in a different way from what he did before. The agreement of the two ideas joined in that proposition is perceived; but it is by the intervention of other ideas than those which at first produced that perception. He remembers, i.e. he knows (for remembrance is but the reviving of some past knowledge) that he was once certain of the truth of this proposition, that the three angles of a triangle are equal to two right ones. The immutability of the same relations between the same immutable things is now the idea that shows him, that if the three angles of a triangle were once equal to two right ones, they will always be equal to two right ones. And hence he comes to be certain, that what was once true in the case, is always true; what ideas once agreed will always agree; and consequently what he once knew to be true, he will always know to be true; as long as he can remember that he once knew it. Upon this ground it is, that particular demonstrations in mathematics afford general knowledge. If then the perception, that the same ideas will ETERNALLY have the same habitudes and relations, be not a sufficient ground of knowledge, there could be no knowledge of general propositions in mathematics; for no mathematical demonstration would be any other than particular: and when a man had demonstrated any proposition concerning one triangle or circle, his knowledge would not reach beyond that particular diagram. If he would extend it further, he must renew his demonstration in another instance, before he could know it to be true in another like triangle, and so on: by which means one could never come to the knowledge of any general propositions. Nobody, I think, can deny, that Mr. Newton certainly knows any proposition that he now at any time reads in his book to be true; though he has not in actual view that admirable chain of intermediate ideas whereby he at first discovered it to be true. Such a memory as that, able to retain such a train of particulars, may be well thought beyond the reach of human faculties, when the very discovery, perception, and laying together that wonderful connexion of ideas, is found to surpass most readers' comprehension. But yet it is evident the author himself knows the proposition to be true, remembering he once saw the connexion of those ideas; as certainly as he knows such a man wounded another, remembering that he saw him run him through. But because the memory is not always so clear as actual perception, and does in all men more or less decay in length of time, this, amongst other differences, is one which shows that DEMONSTRATIVE knowledge is much more imperfect than INTUITIVE, as we shall see in the following chapter.

CHAPTER II.

OF THE DEGREES OF OUR KNOWLEDGE.

1. Of the degrees, or differences in clearness, of our Knowledge: I. Intuitive All our knowledge consisting, as I have said, in the view the mind has of its own ideas, which is the utmost light and greatest certainty we, with our faculties, and in our way of knowledge, are capable of, it may not be amiss to consider a little the degrees of its evidence. The different clearness of our knowledge seems to me to lie in the different way of perception the mind has of the agreement or disagreement of any of its ideas. For if we will reflect on our own ways of thinking, we will find, that sometimes the mind perceives the agreement or disagreement of two ideas IMMEDIATELY BY THEMSELVES, without the intervention of any other: and this I think we may call INTUITIVE KNOWLEDGE. For in this the mind is at no pains of proving or examining, but perceives the truth as the eye doth light, only by being directed towards it. Thus the mind perceives that WHITE is not BLACK, that a CIRCLE is not a TRIANGLE, that THREE are more than TWO and equal to ONE AND TWO. Such kinds of truths the mind perceives at the first sight of the ideas together, by bare intuition; without the intervention of any other idea: and this kind of knowledge is the clearest and most certain that human frailty is capable of. This part of knowledge is irresistible, and, like bright sunshine, forces itself immediately to be perceived, as soon as ever the mind turns its view that way; and leaves no room for hesitation, doubt, or examination, but the mind is presently filled with the clear light of it. IT IS ON THIS INTUITION THAT DEPENDS ALL THE CERTAINTY AND EVIDENCE OF ALL OUR KNOWLEDGE; which certainty every one finds to be so great, that he cannot imagine, and therefore not require a greater: for a man cannot conceive himself capable of a greater certainty than to know that any idea in his mind is such as he perceives it to be; and that two ideas, wherein he perceives a difference, are different and not precisely the same. He that demands a greater certainty than this, demands he knows not what, and shows only that he has a mind to be a sceptic, without being able to be so. Certainty depends so wholly on this intuition, that, in the next degree of knowledge which I call demonstrative, this intuition is necessary in all the connexions of the intermediate ideas, without which we cannot attain knowledge and certainty.

2. II. Demonstrative.

The next degree of knowledge is, where the mind perceives the agreement or disagreement of any ideas, but not immediately. Though wherever the mind perceives the agreement or disagreement of any of its ideas, there be certain knowledge; yet it does not always happen, that the mind sees that agreement or disagreement, which there is between them, even where it is discoverable; and in that case remains in ignorance, and at most gets no further than a probable conjecture. The reason why the mind cannot always perceive presently the agreement or disagreement of two ideas, is, because those ideas, concerning whose agreement or disagreement the inquiry is made, cannot by the mind be so put together as to show it. In this case then, when the mind cannot so bring its ideas together as by their immediate comparison, and as it were juxta-position or application one to another, to perceive their agreement or disagreement, it is fain, BY THE INTERVENTION OF OTHER IDEAS, (one or more, as it happens) to discover the agreement or disagreement which it searches; and this is that which we call REASONING. Thus, the mind being willing to know the agreement or disagreement in bigness between the three angles of a triangle and two right ones, cannot by an immediate view and comparing them do it: because the three angles of a triangle cannot be brought at once, and be compared with any other one, or two, angles; and so of this the mind has no immediate, no intuitive knowledge. In this case the mind is fain to find out some other angles, to which the three angles of a triangle have an equality; and, finding those equal to two right ones, comes to know their equality to two right ones.

3. Demonstration depends on clearly perceived proofs.

Those intervening ideas, which serve to show the agreement of any two others, are called PROOFS; and where the agreement and disagreement is by this means plainly and clearly perceived, it is called DEMONSTRATION; it being SHOWN to the understanding, and the mind made to see that it is so. A quickness in the mind to find out these intermediate ideas, (that shall discover the agreement or disagreement of any other,) and to apply them right, is, I suppose, that which is called SAGACITY.

4. As certain, but not so easy and ready as Intuitive Knowledge.

This knowledge, by intervening proofs, though it be certain, yet the evidence of it is not altogether so clear and bright, nor the assent so ready, as in intuitive knowledge. For, though in demonstration the mind does at last perceive the agreement or disagreement of the ideas it considers; yet it is not without pains and attention: there must be more than one transient view to find it. A steady application and pursuit are required to this discovery: and there must be a progression by steps and degrees, before the mind can in this way arrive at certainty, and come to perceive the agreement or repugnancy between two ideas that need proofs and the use of reason to show it.

5. The demonstrated conclusion not without Doubt, precedent to the demonstration.

Another difference between intuitive and demonstrative knowledge is, that, though in the latter all doubt be removed when, by the intervention of the intermediate ideas, the agreement or disagreement is perceived, yet before the demonstration there was a doubt; which in intuitive knowledge cannot happen to the mind that has its faculty of perception left to a degree capable of distinct ideas; no more than it can be a doubt to the eye (that can distinctly see white and black), Whether this ink and this paper be all of a colour. If there be sight in the eyes, it will, at first glimpse, without hesitation, perceive the words printed on this paper different from the colour of the paper: and so if the mind have the faculty of distinct perception, it will perceive the agreement or disagreement of those ideas that produce intuitive knowledge. If the eyes have lost the faculty of seeing, or the mind of perceiving, we in vain inquire after the quickness of sight in one, or clearness of perception in the other.

6. Not so clear as Intuitive Knowledge.

It is true, the perception produced by demonstration is also very clear; yet it is often with a great abatement of that evident lustre and full assurance that always accompany that which I call intuitive: like a face reflected by several mirrors one to another, where, as long as it retains the similitude and agreement with the object, it produces a knowledge; but it is still, in every successive reflection, with a lessening of that perfect clearness and distinctness which is in the first; till at last, after many removes, it has a great mixture of dimness, and is not at first sight so knowable, especially to weak eyes. Thus it is with knowledge made out by a long train of proof.

7. Each Step in Demonstrated Knowledge must have Intuitive Evidence.

Now, in every step reason makes in demonstrative knowledge, there is an intuitive knowledge of that agreement or disagreement it seeks with the next intermediate idea which it uses as a proof: for if it were not so, that yet would need a proof; since without the perception of such agreement or disagreement, there is no knowledge produced: if it be perceived by itself, it is intuitive knowledge: if it cannot be perceived by itself, there is need of some intervening idea, as a common measure, to show their agreement or disagreement. By which it is plain, that every step in reasoning that produces knowledge, has intuitive certainty; which when the mind perceives, there is no more required but to remember it, to make the agreement or disagreement of the ideas concerning which we inquire visible and certain. So that to make anything a demonstration, it is necessary to perceive the immediate agreement of the intervening ideas, whereby the agreement or disagreement of the two ideas under examination (whereof the one is always the first, and the other the last in the account) is found. This intuitive perception of the agreement or disagreement of the intermediate ideas, in each step and progression of the demonstration, must also be carried exactly in the mind, and a man must be sure that no part is left out: which, because in long deductions, and the use of many proofs, the memory does not always so readily and exactly retain; therefore it comes to pass, that this is more imperfect than intuitive knowledge, and men embrace often falsehood for demonstrations.

8. Hence the Mistake, ex praecognitis, et praeconcessis.

The necessity of this intuitive knowledge, in each step of scientifical or demonstrative reasoning, gave occasion, I imagine, to that mistaken axiom, That all reasoning was EX PRAECOGNITIS ET PRAECONCESSIS: which, how far it is a mistake, I shall have occasion to show more at large, when I come to consider propositions, and particularly those propositions which are called maxims, and to show that it is by a mistake that they are supposed to be the foundations of all our knowledge and reasonings.

9. Demonstration not limited to ideas of mathematical Quantity.

[It has been generally taken for granted, that mathematics alone are capable of demonstrative certainty: but to have such an agreement or disagreement as may intuitively be perceived, being, as I imagine, not the privilege of the ideas of number, extension, and figure alone, it may possibly be the want of due method and application in us, and not of sufficient evidence in things, that demonstration has been thought to have so little to do in other parts of knowledge, and been scarce so much as aimed at by any but mathematicians.] For whatever ideas we have wherein the mind can perceive the immediate agreement or disagreement that is between them, there the mind is capable of intuitive knowledge; and where it can perceive the agreement or disagreement of any two ideas, by an intuitive perception of the agreement or disagreement they have with any intermediate ideas, there the mind is capable of demonstration: which is not limited to ideas of extension, figure, number, and their modes.

10. Why it has been thought to be so limited.

The reason why it has been generally sought for, and supposed to be only in those, I imagine has been, not only the general usefulness of those sciences; but because, in comparing their equality or excess, the modes of numbers have every the least difference very clear and perceivable: and though in extension every the least excess is not so perceptible, yet the mind has found out ways to examine, and discover demonstratively, the just equality of two angles, or extensions, or figures: and both these, i. e. numbers and figures, can be set down by visible and lasting marks, wherein the ideas under consideration are perfectly determined; which for the most part they are not, where they are marked only by names and words.

11. Modes of Qualities not demonstrable like modes of Quantity.

But in other simple ideas, whose modes and differences are made and counted by degrees, and not quantity, we have not so nice and accurate a distinction of their differences as to perceive, or find ways to measure, their just equality, or the least differences. For those other simple ideas, being appearances of sensations produced in us, by the size, figure, number, and motion of minute corpuscles singly insensible; their different degrees also depend upon the variation of some or of all those causes: which, since it cannot be observed by us, in particles of matter whereof each is too subtile to be perceived, it is impossible for us to have any exact measures of the different degrees of these simple ideas. For, supposing the sensation or idea we name whiteness be produced in us by a certain number of globules, which, having a verticity about their own centres, strike upon the retina of the eye, with a certain degree of rotation, as well as progressive swiftness; it will hence easily follow, that the more the superficial parts of any body are so ordered as to reflect the greater number of globules of light, and to give them the proper rotation, which is fit to produce this sensation of white in us, the more white will that body appear, that from an equal space sends to the retina the greater number of such corpuscles, with that peculiar sort of motion. I do not say that the nature of light consists in very small round globules; nor of whiteness in such a texture of parts as gives a certain rotation to these globules when it reflects them: for I am not now treating physically of light or colours. But this I think I may say, that I cannot (and I would be glad any one would make intelligible that he did) conceive how bodies without us can any ways affect our senses, but by the immediate contact of the sensible bodies themselves, as in tasting and feeling, or the impulse of some sensible particles coming from them, as in seeing, hearing, and smelling; by the different impulse of which parts, caused by their different size, figure, and motion, the variety of sensations is produced in us.

12. Particles of light and simple ideas of colour.

Whether then they be globules or no; or whether they have a verticity about their own centres that produces the idea of whiteness in us; this is certain, that the more particles of light are reflected from a body, fitted to give them that peculiar motion which produces the sensation of whiteness in us; and possibly too, the quicker that peculiar motion is,—the whiter does the body appear from which the greatest number are reflected, as is evident in the same piece of paper put in the sunbeams, in the shade, and in a dark hole; in each of which it will produce in us the idea of whiteness in far different degrees.

13. The secondary Qualities of things not discovered by Demonstration.

Not knowing, therefore, what number of particles, nor what motion of them, is fit to produce any precise degree of whiteness, we cannot DEMONSTRATE the certain equality of any two degrees of whiteness; because we have no certain standard to measure them by, nor means to distinguish every the least real difference, the only help we have being from our senses, which in this point fail us. But where the difference is so great as to produce in the mind clearly distinct ideas, whose differences can be perfectly retained, there these ideas or colours, as we see in different kinds, as blue and red, are as capable of demonstration as ideas of number and extension. What I have here said of whiteness and colours, I think holds true in all secondary qualities and their modes.

14. III. Sensitive Knowledge of the particular Existence of finite beings without us.

These two, viz. intuition and demonstration, are the degrees of our KNOWLEDGE; whatever comes short of one of these, with what assurance soever embraced, is but FAITH or OPINION, but not knowledge, at least in all general truths. There is, indeed, another perception of the mind, employed about THE PARTICULAR EXISTENCE OF FINITE BEINGS WITHOUT US, which, going beyond bare probability, and yet not reaching perfectly to either of the foregoing degrees of certainty, passes under the name of KNOWLEDGE. There can be nothing more certain than that the idea we receive from an external object is in our minds: this is intuitive knowledge. But whether there be anything more than barely that idea in our minds; whether we can thence certainly infer the existence of anything without us, which corresponds to that idea, is that whereof some men think there may be a question made;

because men may have such ideas in their minds, when no such thing exists, no such object affects their senses. But yet here I think we are provided with an evidence that puts us past doubting. For I ask any one, Whether he be not invincibly conscious to himself of a different perception, when he looks on the sun by day, and thinks on it by night; when he actually tastes wormwood, or smells a rose, or only thinks on that savour or odour? We as plainly find the difference there is between any idea revived in our minds by our own memory, and actually coming into our minds by our senses, as we do between any two distinct ideas. If any one say, a dream may do the same thing, and all these ideas may be produced, in us without any external objects; he may please to dream that I make him this answer:—1. That it is no great matter, whether I remove his scruple or no: where all is but dream, reasoning and arguments are of no use, truth and knowledge nothing. 2. That I believe he will allow a very manifest difference between dreaming of being in the fire, and being actually in it. But yet if he be resolved to appear so sceptical as to maintain, that what I call being actually in the fire is nothing but a dream; and that we cannot thereby certainly know, that any such thing as fire actually exists without us: I answer, That we certainly finding that pleasure or pain follows upon the application of certain objects to us, whose existence we perceive, or dream that we perceive, by our senses; this certainty is as great as our happiness or misery, beyond which we have no concernment to know or to be. So that, I think, we may add to the two former sorts of knowledge this also, of the existence of particular external objects, by that perception and consciousness we have of the actual entrance of ideas from them, and allow these three degrees of knowledge, viz. INTUITIVE, DEMONSTRATIVE, and SENSITIVE; in each of which there are different degrees and ways of evidence and certainty.

15. Knowledge not always clear, where the Ideas that enter into it are clear. But since our knowledge is founded on and employed about our ideas only, will it not follow from thence that it is conformable to our ideas; and that where our ideas are clear and distinct, or obscure and confused, our knowledge will be so too? To which I answer, No: for our knowledge consisting in the perception of the agreement or disagreement of any two ideas, its clearness or obscurity consists in the clearness or obscurity of that perception, and not in the clearness or obscurity of the ideas themselves: v. g. a man that has as clear ideas of the angles of a triangle, and of equality to two right ones, as any mathematician in the world, may yet have but a very obscure perception of their AGREEMENT, and so have but a very

obscure knowledge of it. [But ideas which, by reason of their obscurity or otherwise, are confused, cannot produce any clear or distinct knowledge; because, as far as any ideas are confused, so far the mind cannot perceive clearly whether they agree or disagree. Or to express the same thing in a way less apt to be misunderstood: he that hath not determined ideas to the words he uses, cannot make propositions of them of whose truth he can be certain.]

CHAPTER III.

OF THE EXTENT OF HUMAN KNOWLEDGE.

1. Extent of our Knowledge.
Knowledge, as has been said, lying in the perception of the agreement or disagreement of any of our ideas, it follows from hence, That,
First, it extends no further than we have Ideas.
First, we can have knowledge no further than we have IDEAS.
2. Secondly, It extends no further than we can perceive their Agreement or Disagreement.
Secondly, That we can have no knowledge further than we can have PERCEPTION of that agreement or disagreement. Which perception being: 1. Either by INTUITION, or the immediate comparing any two ideas; or, 2. By REASON, examining the agreement or disagreement of two ideas, by the intervention of some others; or, 3. By SENSATION, perceiving the existence of particular things: hence it also follows:
3. Thirdly, Intuitive Knowledge extends itself not to all the relation of all our Ideas.
Thirdly, That we cannot have an INTUITIVE KNOWLEDGE that shall extend itself to all our ideas, and all that we would know about them; because we cannot examine and perceive all the relations they have one to another, by juxta-position, or an immediate comparison one with another. Thus, having the ideas of an obtuse and an acute angled triangle, both drawn from equal bases, and between parallels, I can, by intuitive knowledge, perceive the one not to be the other, but cannot that way know whether they be equal or no; because their agreement or disagreement in equality can never be perceived by an immediate comparing them: the difference of figure makes their parts incapable of an exact immediate application; and therefore there is need of some intervening qualities to measure them by, which is demonstration, or rational knowledge.
4. Fourthly, Nor does Demonstrative Knowledge.
Fourthly, It follows, also, from what is above observed, that our RATIONAL KNOWLEDGE cannot reach to the whole extent of our ideas: because between two different ideas we would examine, we cannot always find such mediums as we can connect one to another with an intuitive knowledge in all the parts of the deduction; and wherever that fails, we come short of knowledge and demonstration.
5. Fifthly, Sensitive Knowledge narrower than either.

Fifthly, SENSITIVE KNOWLEDGE reaching no further than the existence of things actually present to our senses, is yet much narrower than either of the former.

6. Sixthly, Our Knowledge, therefore narrower than our Ideas.

Sixthly, From all which it is evident, that the EXTENT OF OUR KNOWLEDGE comes not only short of the reality of things, but even of the extent of our own ideas. Though our knowledge be limited to our ideas, and cannot exceed them either in extent or perfection; and though these be very narrow bounds, in respect of the extent of All-being, and far short of what we may justly imagine to be in some even created understandings, not tied down to the dull and narrow information that is to be received from some few, and not very acute, ways of perception, such as are our senses; yet it would be well with us if our knowledge were but as large as our ideas, and there were not many doubts and inquiries CONCERNING THE IDEAS WE HAVE, whereof we are not, nor I believe ever shall be in this world resolved. Nevertheless, I do not question but that human knowledge, under the present circumstances of our beings and constitutions, may be carried much further than it has hitherto been, if men would sincerely, and with freedom of mind, employ all that industry and labour of thought, in improving the means of discovering truth, which they do for the colouring or support of falsehood, to maintain a system, interest, or party they are once engaged in. But yet after all, I think I may, without injury to human perfection, be confident, that our knowledge would never reach to all we might desire to know concerning those ideas we have; nor be able to surmount all the difficulties, and resolve all the questions that might arise concerning any of them. We have the ideas of a SQUARE, a CIRCLE, and EQUALITY; and yet, perhaps, shall never be able to find a circle equal to a square, and certainly know that it is so. We have the ideas of MATTER and THINKING, but possibly shall never be able to know whether [any mere material being] thinks or no; it being impossible for us, by the contemplation of our own ideas, without revelation, to discover whether Omnipotency has not given to some systems of matter, fitly disposed, a power to perceive and think, or else joined and fixed to matter, so disposed, a thinking immaterial substance: it being, in respect of our notions, not much more remote from our comprehension to conceive that GOD can, if he pleases, superadd to matter A FACULTY OF THINKING, than that he should superadd to it ANOTHER SUBSTANCE WITH A FACULTY OF THINKING; since we know not wherein thinking consists, nor to what sort of substances the Almighty has been pleased to give that power, which cannot be in any created being, but merely by the good pleasure and bounty of the Creator. For I see no contradiction in it, that the first Eternal thinking Being, or Omnipotent Spirit, should, if he pleased, give to certain systems of created senseless matter, put together as he thinks fit, some degrees of sense, perception, and thought: though, as I think I have proved, lib. iv. ch. 10, Section 14, &c., it is no less than a contradiction to suppose matter (which is evidently in its own nature void of sense and thought) should be that Eternal first-thinking Being. What certainty of knowledge can any one have, that some perceptions, such as, v. g., pleasure and pain, should not be in some bodies themselves, after a certain manner modified and moved, as well as that they should be in an immaterial substance, upon the motion of the parts of body: Body, as far as we can conceive, being able only to strike and affect body, and motion, according to the utmost reach of our ideas, being able to produce nothing but motion; so that when we allow it to produce pleasure or pain, or the idea of a colour or sound, we are fain to quit our reason, go beyond our ideas, and attribute it wholly to the good pleasure of our Maker. For, since we must allow He has annexed effects to motion which we can no way conceive motion able to produce, what reason have we to conclude that He could not order them as well to be produced in a subject we cannot conceive capable of them, as well as in a subject we cannot conceive the motion of matter can any way operate upon? I say not this, that I would any way lessen the belief of the soul's immateriality: I am not here speaking of probability, but knowledge, and I think not only that it becomes the modesty of philosophy not to pronounce magisterially, where we want that evidence that can produce knowledge; but also, that it is of use to us to discern how far our knowledge does reach; for the state we are at present in, not being that of vision, we must in many things content ourselves with faith and probability: and in the present question, about the Immateriality of the Soul, if our faculties cannot arrive at demonstrative certainty, we need not think it strange. All the great ends of morality and religion are well enough secured, without philosophical proofs of the soul's immateriality; since it is evident, that he who made us at the beginning to subsist here, sensible intelligent beings, and for several years continued us in such a state, can and will restore us to the like state of sensibility in another world, and make us capable there to receive the retribution he has designed to men, according to their doings in this life. [And therefore it is not of such mighty necessity to determine one way or the other, as some, over-zealous for or against the immateriality of the soul, have been forward to make the world believe. Who, either on the one side, indulging too much their thoughts immersed altogether in matter, can allow no existence to what is not material: or who, on the other side, finding not COGITATION within the natural powers of matter, examined over and over again by the utmost intention of mind, have the confidence to conclude—That Omnipotency itself cannot give perception and thought to a substance which has the modification of solidity. He that considers how hardly sensation is, in our thoughts, reconcilable to extended matter; or existence to anything that has no extension at all, will confess that he is very far from certainly knowing what his soul is. It is a point which seems to me to be put out of the reach of our knowledge: and he who will give himself leave to consider freely, and look into the dark and intricate part of each hypothesis, will scarce find his reason able to determine him fixedly for or against the soul's materiality. Since, on which side soever he views it, either as an UNEXTENDED SUBSTANCE, or as a THINKING EXTENDED MATTER, the difficulty to conceive either will, whilst either alone is in his thoughts, still drive him to the contrary side. An unfair way which some men take with themselves: who, because of the inconceivableness of something they find in one, throw themselves violently into the contrary hypothesis, though altogether as unintelligible to an unbiassed understanding. This serves not only to show the weakness and the scantiness of our knowledge, but the insignificant triumph of such sort of arguments; which, drawn from our own views, may satisfy us that we can find no certainty on one side of the question: but do not at all thereby help us to truth by running into the opposite opinion; which, on examination, will be found clogged with equal difficulties. For what safety, what advantage to any one is it, for the avoiding the seeming absurdities, and to him unsurmountable rubs, he meets with in one opinion, to take refuge in the contrary, which is built on something altogether as inexplicable, and as far remote from his comprehension? It is past controversy, that we have in us SOMETHING that thinks; our very doubts about what it is, confirm the certainty of its being, though we must content ourselves in the ignorance of what KIND of being it is: and it is in vain to go about to be sceptical in this, as it is unreasonable in most other cases to be positive against the being of anything, because we cannot comprehend its nature. For I would fain know what substance exists, that has not something in it which manifestly baffles our understandings. Other spirits, who see and know the nature and inward constitution of things, how much must they exceed us in knowledge? To which, if we add larger comprehension, which enables them at one glance to see the connexion and agreement of very many ideas, and readily supplies to them the intermediate proofs, which we by single and slow steps, and long poring in the dark, hardly at last find out, and are often ready to forget one before we have hunted out another; we may guess at some part of the happiness of superior ranks of spirits, who have a quicker and more penetrating sight, as well as a larger field of knowledge.]

But to return to the argument in hand: our knowledge, I say, is not only limited to the paucity and imperfections of the ideas we have, and which we employ it about, but even comes short of that too: but how far it reaches, let us now inquire.

7. How far our Knowledge reaches.

The affirmations or negations we make concerning the ideas we have, may, as I have before intimated in general, be reduced to these four sorts, viz. identity, co-existence, relation, and real existence. I shall examine how far our knowledge extends in each of these:

8. Firstly, Our Knowledge of Identity and Diversity in ideas extends as far as our Ideas themselves.

FIRST, as to IDENTITY and DIVERSITY. In this way of agreement or disagreement of our ideas, our intuitive knowledge is as far extended as our ideas themselves: and there can be no idea in the mind, which it does not, presently, by an intuitive knowledge, perceive to be what it is, and to be different from any other.

9. Secondly, Of their Co-existence, extends only a very little way.

SECONDLY, as to the second sort, which is the agreement or disagreement of our ideas in CO-EXISTENCE, in this our knowledge is very short; though in this consists the greatest and most material part of our knowledge concerning substances. For our ideas of the species of substances being, as I have showed, nothing but certain collections of simple ideas united in one subject, and so co-existing together; v.g. our idea of flame is a body hot, luminous, and moving upward; of gold, a body heavy to a certain degree, yellow, malleable, and fusible: for these, or some such complex ideas as these, in men's minds, do these two names of the different substances, flame and gold, stand for. When we would know anything further concerning these, or any other sort of substances, what do we inquire, but what OTHER qualities or powers these substances have or have not? Which is nothing else but to know what OTHER simple ideas do, or do not co-exist with those that make up that complex idea?

10. Because the Connexion between simple Ideas in substances is for the most part unknown.

This, how weighty and considerable a part soever of human science, is yet very narrow, and scarce any at all. The reason whereof is, that the simple ideas whereof our complex ideas of substances are made up are, for the most part, such as carry with them, in their own nature, no VISIBLE NECESSARY connexion or inconsistency with any other simple ideas, whose co-existence with them we would inform ourselves about.

11. Especially of the secondary Qualities of Bodies.

The ideas that our complex ones of substances are made up of, and about which our knowledge concerning substances is most employed, are those of their secondary qualities; which depending all (as has been shown) upon the primary qualities of their minute and insensible parts; or, if not upon them, upon something yet more remote from our comprehension; it is impossible we should know which have a NECESSARY union or inconsistency one with another. For, not knowing the root they spring from, not knowing what size, figure, and texture of parts they are, on which depend, and from which result those qualities which make our complex idea of gold, it is impossible we should know what OTHER qualities result from, or are incompatible with, the same constitution of the insensible parts of gold; and so consequently must always co-exist with that complex idea we have of it, or else are inconsistent with it.

12. Because necessary Connexion between any secondary and the primary Qualities is undiscoverable by us.

Besides this ignorance of the primary qualities of the insensible parts of bodies, on which depend all their secondary qualities, there is yet another and more incurable part of ignorance, which sets us more remote from a certain knowledge of the co-existence or INCO-EXISTENCE (if I may so say) of different ideas in the same subject; and that is, that there is no discoverable connexion between any secondary quality and those primary qualities which it depends on.

13. We have no perfect knowledge of their Primary Qualities.

That the size, figure, and motion of one body should cause a change in the size, figure, and motion of another body, is not beyond our conception; the separation of the parts of one body upon the intrusion of another; and the change from rest to motion upon impulse; these and the like seem to have SOME CONNEXION one with another. And if we knew these primary qualities of bodies, we might have reason to hope we might be able to know a great deal more of these operations of them one upon another: but our minds not being able to discover any connexion betwixt these primary qualities of bodies and the sensations that are produced in us by them, we can never be able to establish certain and undoubted rules of the CONSEQUENCE or CO-EXISTENCE of any secondary qualities, though we could discover the size, figure, or motion of those invisible parts which immediately produce them. We are so far from knowing WHAT figure, size, or motion of parts produce a yellow colour, a sweet taste, or a sharp sound, that we can by no means conceive how ANY size, figure, or motion of any particles, can possibly produce in us the idea of any colour, taste, or sound whatsoever: there is no conceivable connexion between the one and the other.

14. And seek in vain for certain and universal knowledge of unperceived qualities in substances.

In vain, therefore, shall we endeavour to discover by our ideas (the only true way of certain and universal knowledge) what other ideas are to be found constantly joined with that of OUR complex idea of any substance: since we neither know the real constitution of the minute parts on which their qualities do depend; nor, did we know them, could we discover any necessary connexion between them and any of the secondary qualities: which is necessary to be done before we can certainly know their necessary co-existence. So, that, let our complex idea of any species of substances be what it will, we can hardly, from the simple ideas contained in it, certainly determine the necessary co-existence of any other quality whatsoever. Our knowledge in all these inquiries reaches very little further than our experience. Indeed some few of the primary qualities have a necessary dependence and visible connexion one with another, as figure necessarily supposes extension; receiving or communicating motion by impulse, supposes solidity. But though these, and perhaps some others of our ideas have: yet there are so few of them that have a visible connexion one with another, that we can by intuition or demonstration discover the co-existence of very few of the qualities that are to be found united in substances: and we are left only to the assistance of our senses to make known to us what qualities they contain. For of all the qualities that are co-existent in any subject, without this dependence and evident connexion of their ideas one with another, we cannot know certainly any two to co-exist, any further than experience, by our senses, informs us. Thus, though we see the yellow colour, and, upon trial, find the weight, malleableness, fusibility, and fixedness that are united in a piece of gold; yet, because no one of these ideas has any evident dependence or necessary connexion with the other, we cannot certainly know that where any four of these are, the fifth will be there also, how highly probable soever it may be; because the highest probability amounts not to certainty, without which there can be no true knowledge. For this co-existence can be no further known than it is perceived; and it cannot be perceived but either in particular subjects, by the observation of our senses, or, in general, by the necessary connexion of the ideas themselves.

15. Of Repugnancy to co-exist, our knowledge is larger.

As to the incompatibility or repugnancy to co-existence, we may know that any subject may have of each sort of primary qualities but one particular at once: v.g. each particular extension, figure, number of parts, motion, excludes all other of each kind. The like also is certain of all sensible ideas peculiar to each sense; for whatever of each kind is present in any subject, excludes all other of that sort: v.g. no one subject can have two smells or two colours at the same time. To this, perhaps will be said, Has not an opal, or the infusion of LIGNUM NEPHRITICUM, two colours at the same time? To which I answer, that these bodies, to eyes differently, placed, may at the same time afford different colours: but I take liberty also to say, that, to eyes differently placed, it is different parts of the object that reflect the particles of light: and therefore it is not the same part of the object, and so not the very same subject, which at the same time appears both yellow and azure. For, it is as impossible that the very same particle of any body should at the same time differently modify or reflect the rays of light, as that it should have two different figures and textures at the same time.

16. Our Knowledge of the Co-existence of Power in Bodies extends but a very little Way.

But as to the powers of substances to change the sensible qualities of other bodies, which make a great part of our inquiries about them, and is no inconsiderable branch of our knowledge; I doubt as to these, whether our knowledge reaches much further than our experience; or whether we can come to the discovery of most of these powers, and be certain that they are in any subject, by the connexion with any of those ideas which to us make its essence. Because the active and passive powers of bodies, and their ways of operating, consisting in a texture and motion of parts which we cannot by any means come to discover; it is but in very few cases we can be able to perceive their dependence on, or repugnance to, any of those ideas which make our complex one of that sort of things. I have here instanced in the corpuscularian hypothesis, as that which is thought to go furthest in an intelligible explication of those qualities of bodies; and I fear the weakness of human understanding is scarce able to substitute another, which will afford us a fuller and clearer discovery of the necessary connexion and co-existence of the powers which are to be observed united in several sorts of them. This at least is certain, that, whichever hypothesis be clearest and truest, (for of that it is not my business to determine,) our knowledge concerning corporeal substances will be very little advanced by any of them, till we are made to see what qualities and powers of bodies have a NECESSARY connexion or repugnancy one with another; which in the present state of philosophy I think we know but to a very small degree: and I doubt whether, with those faculties we have, we shall ever be able to carry our general knowledge (I say not particular experience) in this part much further. Experience is that which in this part we must depend on. And it were to be wished that it were more improved. We find the advantages some men's generous pains have this way brought to the stock of natural knowledge. And if others, especially the philosophers by fire, who pretend to it, had been so wary in their observations, and sincere in their reports as those who call themselves philosophers ought to have been, our acquaintance with the bodies here about us, and our insight into their powers and operations had been yet much greater.

17. Of the Powers that co-exist in Spirits yet narrower.

If we are at a loss in respect of the powers and operations of bodies, I think it is easy to conclude we are much more in the dark in reference to spirits; whereof we naturally have no ideas but what we draw from that of our own, by reflecting on the operations of our own souls within us, as far as they can come within our observation. But how inconsiderable a rank the spirits that inhabit our bodies hold amongst those various and possibly innumerable kinds of nobler beings; and how far short they come of the endowments and perfections of cherubim and seraphim, and infinite sorts of spirits above us, is what by a transient hint in another place I have offered to my reader's consideration.

18. Thirdly, Of Relations between abstracted ideas it is not easy to say how far our knowledge extends.

THIRDLY, As to the third sort of our knowledge, viz. the agreement or disagreement of any of our ideas in any other relation: this, as it is the largest field of our knowledge, so it is hard to determine how far it may extend: because the advances that are made in this part of knowledge, depending on our sagacity in finding intermediate ideas, that may show the relations and habitudes of ideas whose co-existence is not considered, it is a hard matter to tell when we are at an end of such discoveries; and when reason has all the helps it is capable of, for the finding of proofs, or examining the agreement or disagreement of remote ideas. They that are ignorant of Algebra cannot imagine the wonders in this kind are to be done by it: and what further improvements and helps advantageous to other parts of knowledge the sagacious mind of man may yet find out, it is not easy to determine. This at least I believe, that the IDEAS OF QUANTITY are not those alone that are capable of demonstration and knowledge; and that other, and perhaps more useful, parts of contemplation, would afford us certainty, if vices, passions, and domineering interest did not oppose or menace such endeavours.

Morality capable of Demonstration

The idea of a supreme Being, infinite in power, goodness, and wisdom, whose workmanship we are, and on whom we depend; and the idea of ourselves, as understanding, rational creatures, being such as are clear in us, would, I suppose, if duly considered and pursued, afford such foundations of our duty and rules of action as might place MORALITY amongst the SCIENCES CAPABLE OF DEMONSTRATION: wherein I doubt not but from self-evident propositions, by necessary consequences, as incontestible as those in mathematics, the measures of right and wrong might be made out, to any one that will apply himself with the same indifferency and attention to the one as he does to the other of these sciences. The RELATION of other MODES may certainly be perceived, as well as those of number and extension: and I cannot see why they should not also be capable of demonstration, if due methods were thought on to examine or pursue their agreement or disagreement. 'Where there is no property there is no injustice,' is a proposition as certain as any demonstration in Euclid: for the idea of property being a right to anything, and the idea of which the name 'injustice' is given being the invasion or violation of that right, it is evident that these ideas, being thus established, and these names annexed to them, I can as certainly know this proposition to be true, as that a triangle has three angles equal to two right ones. Again: 'No government allows absolute liberty.' The idea of government being the establishment of society upon certain rules or laws which require conformity to them; and the idea of absolute liberty being for any one to do whatever he pleases; I am as capable of being certain of the truth of this proposition as of any in the mathematics.

19. Two things have made moral Ideas to be thought incapable of Demonstration: their unfitness for sensible representation, and their complexedness.

That which in this respect has given the advantage to the ideas of quantity, and made them thought more capable of certainty and demonstration, is,

First, That they can be set down and represented by sensible marks, which have a greater and nearer correspondence with them than any words or sounds whatsoever. Diagrams drawn on paper are copies of the ideas in the mind, and not liable to the uncertainty that words carry in their signification. An angle, circle, or square, drawn in lines, lies open to the view, and cannot be mistaken: it remains unchangeable, and may at leisure be considered and examined, and the demonstration be revised, and all the parts of it may be gone over more than once, without any danger of the least change in the ideas. This cannot be thus done in moral ideas: we have no sensible marks that resemble them, whereby we can set them down; we have nothing but words to express them by; which, though when written they remain the same, yet the ideas they stand for may change in the same man; and it is very seldom that they are not different in different persons. Secondly, Another thing that makes the greater difficulty in ethics is, That moral ideas are commonly more complex than those of the figures ordinarily considered in mathematics. From whence these two inconveniences follow:—First, that their names are of more uncertain signification, the precise collection of simple ideas they stand for not being so easily agreed on; and so the sign that is used for them in communication always, and in thinking often, does not steadily carry with it the same idea. Upon which the same disorder, confusion, and error follow, as would if a man, going to demonstrate something of an heptagon, should, in the diagram he took to do it, leave out one of the angles, or by oversight make the figure with one angle more than the name ordinarily imported, or he intended it should when at first he thought of his demonstration. This often happens, and is hardly avoidable in very complex moral ideas, where the same name being retained, one angle, i.e. one simple idea, is left out, or put in the complex one (still called by the same name) more at one time than another. Secondly, From the complexedness of these moral ideas there follows another inconvenience, viz. that the mind cannot easily retain those precise combinations so exactly and perfectly as is necessary in the examination of the habitudes and correspondences, agreements or disagreements, of several of them one with another; especially where it is to be judged of by long deductions, and the intervention of several other complex ideas to show the agreement or disagreement of two remote ones. The great help against this which mathematicians find in diagrams and figures, which remain unalterable in their draughts, is very apparent, and the memory would often have great difficulty otherwise to retain them so exactly, whilst the mind went over the parts of them step by step to examine their several correspondences. And though in casting up a long sum either in addition, multiplication, or division, every part be only a progression of the mind taking a view of its own ideas, and considering their agreement or disagreement, and the resolution of the question be nothing but the result of the whole, made up of such particulars, whereof the mind has a clear perception: yet, without setting down the several parts by marks, whose precise significations are known, and by marks that last, and remain in view when the memory had let them go, it would be almost impossible to carry so many different ideas in the mind, without confounding or letting slip some parts of the reckoning, and thereby making all our reasonings about it useless. In which case the cyphers or marks help not the mind at all to perceive the agreement of any two or more numbers, their equalities or proportions; that the mind has only by intuition of its own ideas of the numbers themselves. But the numerical characters are helps to the memory, to record and retain the several ideas about which the demonstration is made, whereby a man may know how far his intuitive knowledge in surveying several of the particulars has proceeded; that so he may without confusion go on to what is yet unknown; and at last have in one view before him the result of all his perceptions and reasonings.

20. Remedies of our Difficulties in dealing demonstratively with moral ideas.

One part of these disadvantages in moral ideas which has made them be thought not capable of demonstration, may in a good measure be remedied by definitions, setting down that collection of simple ideas, which every term shall stand for; and then using the terms steadily and constantly for that precise collection. And what methods algebra, or something of that kind, may hereafter suggest, to remove the other difficulties, it is not easy to foretell. Confident I am, that, if men would in the same method, and with the same indifferency, search after moral as they do mathematical truths, they would find them have a stronger connexion one with another, and a more necessary consequence from our clear and distinct ideas, and to come nearer perfect demonstration than is commonly imagined. But much of this is not to be expected, whilst the desire of esteem, riches, or power makes men espouse the well-endowed opinions in fashion, and then seek arguments either to make good their beauty, or varnish over and cover their deformity. Nothing being so beautiful to the eye as truth is to the mind; nothing so deformed and irreconcilable to the understanding as a lie. For though many a man can with satisfaction enough own a no very handsome wife in his bosom; yet who is bold enough openly to avow that he has espoused a falsehood, and received into his breast so ugly a thing as a lie? Whilst the parties of men cram their tenets down all men's throats whom they can get into their power, without permitting them to examine their truth or falsehood; and will not let truth have fair play in the world, nor men the liberty to search after it; what improvements can be expected of this kind? What greater light can be hoped for in the moral sciences? The subject part of mankind in most places might, instead thereof, with Egyptian bondage, expect Egyptian darkness, were not the candle of the Lord set up by himself in men's minds, which it is impossible for the breath or power of man wholly to extinguish.

21. Fourthly, Of the three real Existences of which we have certain knowledge.

FOURTHLY, As to the fourth sort of our knowledge, viz. of the REAL ACTUAL EXISTENCE OF THINGS, we have an intuitive knowledge of OUR OWN EXISTENCE, and a demonstrative knowledge of the existence of a GOD: of the existence of ANYTHING ELSE, we have no other but a sensitive knowledge; which extends not beyond the objects present to our senses.

22. Our Ignorance great.

Our knowledge being so narrow, as I have shown, it will perhaps give us some light into the present state of our minds if we look a little into the dark side, and take a view of OUR IGNORANCE; which, being infinitely larger than our knowledge, may serve much to the quieting of disputes, and improvement of useful knowledge; if, discovering how far we have clear and distinct ideas, we confine our thoughts within the contemplation of those things that are within the reach of our understandings, and launch not out into that abyss of darkness, (where we have not eyes to see, nor faculties to perceive anything), out of a presumption that nothing is beyond our comprehension. But to be satisfied of the folly of such a conceit, we need not go far. He that knows anything, knows this, in the first place, that he need not seek long for instances of his ignorance. The meanest and most obvious things that come in our way have dark sides, that the quickest sight cannot penetrate into. The clearest and most enlarged understandings of thinking men find themselves puzzled and at a loss in every particle of matter. We shall the less wonder to find it so, when we consider the CAUSES OF OUR IGNORANCE; which, from what has been said, I suppose will be found to be these three:—

First, Want of ideas. Its causes.

Secondly, Want of a discoverable connexion between the ideas we have.

Thirdly, Want of tracing and examining our ideas.

23. First, One Cause of our ignorance Want of Ideas.

I. Want of simple ideas that other creatures in other parts of the universe may have.

FIRST, There are some things, and those not a few, that we are ignorant of, for want of ideas.

First, all the simple ideas we have are confined (as I have shown) to those we receive from corporeal objects by sensation, and from the operations of our own minds as the objects of reflection. But how much these few and narrow inlets are disproportionate to the vast whole extent of all beings, will not be hard to persuade those who are not so foolish as to think their span the measure of all things. What other simple ideas it is possible the creatures in other parts of the universe may have, by the assistance of senses and faculties more or perfecter than we have, or different from ours, it is not for us to determine. But to say or think there are no such, because we conceive nothing of them, is no better an argument than if a blind man should be positive in it, that there was no such thing as sight and colours, because he had no manner of idea of any such thing, nor could by any means frame to himself any notions about seeing. The ignorance and darkness that is in us no more hinders nor confines the knowledge that is in others, than the blindness of a mole is an argument against the quicksightedness of an eagle. He that will consider the infinite power, wisdom, and goodness of the Creator of all things will find reason to think it was not all laid out upon so inconsiderable, mean, and impotent a creature as he will find man to be; who in all probability is one of the lowest of all intellectual beings. What faculties, therefore, other species of creatures have to penetrate into the nature and inmost constitutions of things; what ideas they may receive of them far different from ours, we know not. This we know and certainly find, that we want several other views of them besides those we have, to make discoveries of them more perfect. And we may be convinced that the ideas we can attain to by our faculties are very disproportionate to things themselves, when a positive, clear, distinct one of substance itself, which is the foundation of all the rest, is concealed from us. But want of ideas of this kind, being a part as well as cause of our ignorance, cannot be described. Only this I think I may confidently say of it, That the intellectual and sensible world are in this perfectly alike: that that part which we see of either of them holds no proportion with what we see not; and whatsoever we can reach with our eyes or our thoughts of either of them is but a point, almost nothing in comparison of the the rest.

24. Want of simple ideas that men are capable of having, but having not,(1) Because their remoteness, or,

Secondly, Another great cause of ignorance is the want of ideas we are capable of. As the want of ideas which our faculties are not able to give us shuts us wholly from those views of things which it is reasonable to think other beings, perfecter than we, have, of which we know nothing; so the want of ideas I now speak of keeps us in ignorance of things we conceive capable of being known to us. Bulk, figure, and motion we have ideas of. But though we are not without ideas of these primary qualities of bodies in general, yet not knowing what is the particular bulk, figure, and motion, of the greatest part of the bodies of the universe, we are ignorant of the several powers, efficacies, and ways of operation, whereby the effects which we daily see are produced. These are hid from us, in some things by being too remote, and in others by being too minute. When we consider the vast distance of the known and visible parts of the world, and the reasons we have to think that what lies within our ken is but a small part of the universe, we shall then discover a huge abyss of ignorance. What are the particular fabrics of the great masses of matter which make up the whole stupendous frame of corporeal beings; how far they are extended; what is their motion, and how continued or communicated; and what influence they have one upon another, are contemplations that at first glimpse our thoughts lose themselves in. If we narrow our contemplations, and confine our thoughts to this little canton—I mean this system of our sun, and the grosser masses of matter that visibly move about it, What several sorts of vegetables, animals, and intellectual corporeal beings, infinitely different from those of our little spot of earth, may there probably be in the other planets, to the knowledge of which, even of their outward figures and parts, we can no way attain whilst we are confined to this earth; there being no natural means, either by sensation or reflection, to convey their certain ideas into our minds? They are out of the reach of those inlets of all our knowledge: and what sorts of furniture and inhabitants those mansions contain in them we cannot so much as guess, much less have clear and distinct ideas of them.

25. (2) Because of their Minuteness.

If a great, nay, far the greatest part of the several ranks of bodies in the universe escape our notice by their remoteness, there are others that are no less concealed from us by their minuteness. These INSENSIBLE

CORPUSCLES, being the active parts of matter, and the great instruments of nature, on which depend not only all their secondary qualities, but also most of their natural operations, our want of precise distinct ideas of their primary qualities keeps us in an incurable ignorance of what we desire to know about them. I doubt not but if we could discover the figure, size, texture, and motion of the minute constituent parts of any two bodies, we should know without trial several of their operations one upon another; as we do now the properties of a square or a triangle. Did we know the mechanical affections of the particles of rhubarb, hemlock, opium, and a man, as a watchmaker does those of a watch, whereby it performs its operations; and of a file, which by rubbing on them will alter the figure of any of the wheels; we should be able to tell beforehand that rhubarb will purge, hemlock kill, and opium make a man sleep: as well as a watchmaker can, that a little piece of paper laid on the balance will keep the watch from going till it be removed; or that, some small part of it being rubbed by a file, the machine would quite lose its motion, and the watch go no more. The dissolving of silver in AQUA FORTIS, and gold in AQUA REGIA, and not VICE VERSA, would be then perhaps no more difficult to know than it is to a smith to understand why the turning of one key will open a lock, and not the turning of another. But whilst we are destitute of senses acute enough to discover the minute particles of bodies, and to give us ideas of their mechanical affections, we must be content to be ignorant of their properties and ways of operation; nor can we be assured about them any further than some few trials we make are able to reach. But whether they will succeed again another time, we cannot be certain. This hinders our certain knowledge of universal truths concerning natural bodies: and our reason carries us herein very little beyond particular matter of fact.

26. Hence no Science of Bodies within our reach.

And therefore I am apt to doubt that, how far soever human industry may advance useful and experimental philosophy in physical things, SCIENTIFICAL will still be out of our reach: because we want perfect and adequate ideas of those very bodies which are nearest to us, and most under our command. Those which we have ranked into classes under names, and we think ourselves best acquainted with, we have but very imperfect and incomplete ideas of. Distinct ideas of the several sorts of bodies that fall under the examination of our senses perhaps we may have: but adequate ideas, I suspect, we have not of any one amongst them. And though the former of these will serve us for common use and discourse, yet whilst we want the latter, we are not capable of scientific knowledge; nor shall ever be able to discover general, instructive, unquestionable truths concerning them. CERTAINTY and DEMONSTRATION are things we must not, in these matters, pretend to. By the colour, figure, taste, and smell, and other sensible qualities, we have as clear and distinct ideas of sage and hemlock, as we have of a circle and a triangle: but having no ideas of the particular primary qualities of the minute parts of either of these plants, nor of other bodies which we would apply them to, we cannot tell what effects they will produce; nor when we see those effects can we so much as guess, much less know, their manner of production. Thus, having no ideas of the particular mechanical affections of the minute parts of bodies that are within our view and reach, we are ignorant of their constitutions, powers, and operations: and of bodies more remote we are yet more ignorant, not knowing so much as their very outward shapes, or the sensible and grosser parts of their constitutions.

27. Much less a science of unembodied Spirits.

This at first will show us how disproportionate our knowledge is to the whole extent even of material beings; to which if we add the consideration of that infinite number of spirits that may be, and probably are, which are yet more remote from our knowledge, whereof we have no cognizance, nor can frame to ourselves any distinct ideas of their several ranks and sorts, we shall find this cause of ignorance conceal from us, in an impenetrable obscurity, almost the whole intellectual world; a greater certainly, and more beautiful world than the material. For, bating some very few, and those, if I may so call them, superficial ideas of spirit, which by reflection we get of our own, and from thence the best we can collect of the Father of all spirits, the eternal independent Author of them, and us, and all things, we have no certain information, so much as of the existence of other spirits, but by revelation. Angels of all sorts are naturally beyond our discovery; and all those intelligences, whereof it is likely there are more orders than of corporeal substances, are things whereof our natural faculties give us no certain account at all. That there are minds and thinking beings in other men as well as himself, every man has a reason, from their words and actions, to be satisfied: and the knowledge of his own mind cannot suffer a man that considers, to be ignorant that there is a God. But that there are degrees of spiritual beings between us and the great God, who is there, that, by his own search and ability, can come to know? Much less have we distinct ideas of their different natures, conditions, states, powers, and several constitutions wherein they agree or differ from one another and from us. And, therefore, in what concerns their different species and properties we are in absolute ignorance.

28. Secondly, Another cause, Want of a discoverable Connexion between Ideas we have.

SECONDLY, What a small part of the substantial beings that are in the universe the want of ideas leaves open to our knowledge, we have seen. In the next place, another cause of ignorance, of no less moment, is a want of a discoverable connection between those ideas we have. For wherever we want that, we are utterly incapable of universal and certain knowledge; and are, in the former case, left only to observation and experiment: which, how narrow and confined it is, how far from general knowledge we need not be told. I shall give some few instances of this cause of our ignorance, and so leave it. It is evident that the bulk, figure, and motion of several bodies about us produce in us several sensations, as of colours, sounds, tastes, smells, pleasure, and pain, &c. These mechanical affections of bodies having no affinity at all with those ideas they produce in us, (there being no conceivable connexion between any impulse of any sort of body and any perception of a colour or smell which we find in our minds,) we can have no distinct knowledge of such operations beyond our experience; and can reason no otherwise about them, than as effects produced by the appointment of an infinitely Wise Agent, which perfectly surpass our comprehensions. As the ideas of sensible secondary qualities which we have in our minds, can by us be no way deduced from bodily causes, nor any correspondence or connexion be found between them and those primary qualities which (experience shows us) produce them in us; so, on the other side, the operation of our minds upon our bodies is as inconceivable. How any thought should produce a motion in body is as remote from the nature of our ideas, as how any body should produce any thought in the mind. That it is so, if experience did not convince us, the consideration of the things themselves would never be able in the least to discover to us. These, and the like, though they have a constant and regular connexion in the ordinary course of things; yet that connexion being not discoverable in the ideas themselves, which appearing to have no necessary dependence one on another, we can attribute their connexion to nothing else but the arbitrary determination of that All-wise Agent who has made them to be, and to operate as they do, in a way wholly above our weak understandings to conceive.

29. Instances

In some of our ideas there are certain relations, habitudes, and connexions, so visibly included in the nature of the ideas themselves, that we cannot conceive them separable from them by any power whatsoever. And in these only we are capable of certain and universal knowledge. Thus the idea of a right-lined triangle necessarily carries with it an equality of its angles to two right ones. Nor can we conceive this relation, this connexion of these two ideas, to be possibly mutable, or to depend on any arbitrary power, which of choice made it thus, or could make it otherwise. But the coherence and continuity of the parts of matter; the production of sensation in us of colours and sounds, &c., by impulse and motion; nay, the original rules and communication of motion being such, wherein we can discover no natural connexion with any ideas we have, we cannot but ascribe them to the arbitrary will and good pleasure of the Wise Architect. I need not, I think, here mention the resurrection of the dead, the future state of this globe of earth, and such other things, which are by every one acknowledged to depend wholly on the determination of a free agent. The things that, as far as our observation reaches, we constantly find to proceed regularly, we may conclude do act by a law set them; but yet by a law that we know not: whereby, though causes work steadily, and effects constantly flow from them, yet their connexions and dependencies being not discoverable in our ideas, we can have but an experimental knowledge of them. From all which it is easy to perceive what a darkness we are involved in, how little it is of Being, and the things that are, that we are capable to know. And therefore we shall do no injury to our knowledge, when we modestly think with ourselves, that we are so far from being able to comprehend the whole nature of the universe, and all the things contained in it, that we are not capable of a philosophical knowledge of the bodies that are about us, and make a part of us: concerning their secondary qualities, powers, and operations, we can have no universal certainty. Several effects come every day within the notice of our senses, of which we have so far sensitive knowledge: but the causes, manner, and certainty of their production, for the two foregoing reasons, we must be content to be very ignorant of. In these we can go no further than particular experience informs us of matter of fact, and by analogy to guess what effects the like bodies are, upon other trials, like to produce. But as to a PERFECT SCIENCE of natural bodies, (not to mention spiritual beings,) we are, I think, so far from being capable of any such thing, that I conclude it lost labour to seek after it.

30. Thirdly A third cause, Want of Tracing our ideas.

THIRDLY, Where we have adequate ideas, and where there is a certain and discoverable connexion between them, yet we are often ignorant, for want of tracing those ideas which we have or may have; and for want of finding out those intermediate ideas, which may show us what habitude of agreement or disagreement they have one with another. And thus many are ignorant of mathematical truths, not out of any imperfection of their faculties, or uncertainty in the things themselves, but for want of application in acquiring, examining, and by due ways comparing those ideas. That which has most contributed to hinder the due tracing of our ideas, and finding out their relations, and agreements or disagreements, one with another, has been, I suppose, the ill use of words. It is impossible that men should ever truly seek or certainly discover the agreement or disagreement of ideas themselves, whilst their thoughts flutter about, or stick only in sounds of doubtful and uncertain significations. Mathematicians abstracting their thoughts from names, and accustoming themselves to set before their minds the ideas themselves that they would consider, and not sounds instead of them, have avoided thereby a great part of that perplexity, puddering, and confusion, which has so much hindered men's progress in other parts of knowledge. For whilst they stick in words of undetermined and uncertain signification, they are unable to distinguish true from false, certain from probable, consistent from inconsistent, in their own opinions. This having been the fate or misfortune of a great part of men of letters, the increase brought into the stock of real knowledge has been very little, in proportion to the schools disputes, and writings, the world has been filled with; whilst students, being lost in the great wood of words, knew not whereabouts they were, how far their discoveries were advanced, or what was wanting in their own, or the general stock of knowledge. Had men, in the discoveries of the material, done as they have in those of the intellectual world, involved all in the obscurity of uncertain and doubtful ways of talking, volumes writ of navigation and voyages, theories and stories of zones and tides, multiplied and disputed; nay, ships built, and fleets sent out, would never have taught us the way beyond the line; and the Antipodes would be still as much unknown, as when it was declared heresy to hold there were any. But having spoken sufficiently of words, and the ill or careless use that is commonly made of them, I shall not say anything more of it here.

31. Extent of Human Knowledge in respect to its Universality.

Hitherto we have examined the extent of our knowledge, in respect of the several sorts of beings that are. There is another extent of it, in respect of

UNIVERSALITY, which will also deserve to be considered; and in this regard, our knowledge follows the nature of our ideas. If the ideas are abstract, whose agreement or disagreement we perceive, our knowledge is universal. For what is known of such general ideas, will be true of every particular thing in whom that essence, i.e. that abstract idea, is to be found: and what is once known of such ideas, will be perpetually and for ever true. So that as to all GENERAL KNOWLEDGE we must search and find it only in our minds; and it is only the examining of our own ideas that furnisheth us with that. Truths belonging to essences of things (that is, to abstract ideas) are eternal; and are to be found out by the contemplation only of those essences: as the existence of things is to be known only from experience. But having more to say of this in the chapters where I shall speak of general and real knowledge, this may here suffice as to the universality of our knowledge in general.

CHAPTER IV. OF THE REALITY OF KNOWLEDGE.

1. Objection. 'Knowledge placed in our Ideas may be all unreal or chimerical'
I DOUBT not but my reader, by this time, may be apt to think that I have been all this while only building a castle in the air; and be ready to say to me:—
'To what purpose all this stir? Knowledge, say you, is only the perception of the agreement or disagreement of our own ideas: but who knows what those ideas may be? Is there anything so extravagant as the imaginations of men's brains? Where is the head that has no chimeras in it? Or if there be a sober and a wise man, what difference will there be, by your rules, between his knowledge and that of the most extravagant fancy in the world? They both have their ideas, and perceive their agreement and disagreement one with another. If there be any difference between them, the advantage will be on the warm-headed man's side, as having the more ideas, and the more lively. And so, by your rules, he will be the more knowing. If it be true, that all knowledge lies only in the perception of the agreement or disagreement of our own ideas, the visions of an enthusiast and the reasonings of a sober man will be equally certain. It is no matter how things are: so a man observe but the agreement of his own imaginations, and talk conformably, it is all truth, all certainty. Such castles in the air will be as strongholds of truth, as the demonstrations of Euclid. That an harpy is not a centaur is by this way as certain knowledge, and as much a truth, as that a square is not a circle.
'But of what use is all this fine knowledge of MEN'S OWN IMAGINATIONS, to a man that inquires after the reality of things? It matters not what men's fancies are, it is the knowledge of things that is only to be prized: it is this alone gives a value to our reasonings, and preference to one man's knowledge over another's, that it is of things as they really are, and not of dreams and fancies.'
2. Answer Not so, where Ideas agree with Things.
To which I answer, That if our knowledge of our ideas terminate in them, and reach no further, where there is something further intended, our most serious thoughts will be of little more use than the reveries of a crazy brain; and the truths built thereon of no more weight than the discourses of a man who sees things clearly in a dream, and with great assurance utters them. But I hope, before I have done, to make it evident, that this way of certainty, by the knowledge of our own ideas, goes a little further than bare

imagination: and I believe it will appear that all the certainty of general truths a man has lies in nothing else.

3. But what shall be the criterion of this agreement?

It is evident the mind knows not things immediately, but only by the intervention of the ideas it has of them. Our knowledge, therefore, is real only so far as there is a CONFORMITY between our ideas and the reality of things. But what shall be here the criterion? How shall the mind, when it perceives nothing but its own ideas, know that they agree with things themselves? This, though it seems not to want difficulty, yet, I think, there be two sorts of ideas that we may be assured agree with things.

4. As, First All Simple Ideas are really conformed to Things.

FIRST, The first are simple ideas, which since the mind, as has been showed, can by no means make to itself, must necessarily be the product of things operating on the mind, in a natural way, and producing therein those perceptions which by the Wisdom and Will of our Maker they are ordained and adapted to. From whence it follows, that simple ideas are not fictions of our fancies, but the natural and regular productions of things without us, really operating upon us; and so carry with them all the conformity which is intended; or which our state requires: for they represent to us things under those appearances which they are fitted to produce in us: whereby we are enabled to distinguish the sorts of particular substances, to discern the states they are in, and so to take them for our necessities, and apply them to our uses. Thus the idea of whiteness, or bitterness, as it is in the mind, exactly answering that power which is in any body to produce it there, has all the real conformity it can or ought to have, with things without us. And this conformity between our simple ideas and the existence of things, is sufficient for real knowledge.

5. Secondly, All Complex Ideas, except ideas of Substances, are their own archetypes.

Secondly, All our complex ideas, EXCEPT THOSE OF SUBSTANCES, being archetypes of the mind's own making, not intended to be the copies of anything, nor referred to the existence of anything, as to their originals, cannot want any conformity necessary to real knowledge. For that which is not designed to represent anything but itself, can never be capable of a wrong representation, nor mislead us from the true apprehension of anything, by its dislikeness to it: and such, excepting those of substances, are all our complex ideas. Which, as I have showed in another place, are combinations of ideas, which the mind, by its free choice, puts together, without considering any connexion they have in nature. And hence it is, that in all these sorts the ideas themselves are considered as the archetypes, and things no otherwise regarded, but as they are conformable to them. So that we cannot but be infallibly certain, that all the knowledge we attain concerning these ideas is real, and reaches things themselves. Because in all our thoughts, reasonings, and discourses of this kind, we intend things no further than as they are conformable to our ideas. So that in these we cannot miss of a certain and undoubted reality.

6. Hence the reality of Mathematical Knowledge

I doubt not but it will be easily granted, that the knowledge we have of mathematical truths is not only certain, but real knowledge; and not the bare empty vision of vain, insignificant chimeras of the brain: and yet, if we will consider, we shall find that it is only of our own ideas. The mathematician considers the truth and properties belonging to a rectangle or circle only as they are in idea in his own mind. For it is possible he never found either of them existing mathematically, i.e. precisely true, in his life. But yet the knowledge he has of any truths or properties belonging to a circle, or any other mathematical figure, are nevertheless true and certain, even of real things existing: because real things are no further concerned, nor intended to be meant by any such propositions, than as things really agree to those archetypes in his mind. Is it true of the IDEA of a triangle, that its three angles are equal to two right ones? It is true also of a triangle, wherever it REALLY EXISTS. Whatever other figure exists, that it is not exactly answerable to that idea of a triangle in his mind, is not at all concerned in that proposition. And therefore he is certain all his knowledge concerning such ideas is real knowledge: because, intending things no further than they agree with those his ideas, he is sure what he knows concerning those figures, when they have BARELY AN IDEAL EXISTENCE in his mind, will hold true of them also when they have A REAL EXISTANCE in matter: his consideration being barely of those figures, which are the same wherever or however they exist.

7. And of Moral.

And hence it follows that moral knowledge is as capable of real certainty as mathematics. For certainty being but the perception of the agreement or disagreement of our ideas, and demonstration nothing but the perception of such agreement, by the intervention of other ideas or mediums; our moral ideas, as well as mathematical, being archetypes themselves, and so adequate and complete ideas; all the agreement or disagreement which we shall find in them will produce real knowledge, as well as in mathematical figures.

8. Existence not required to make Abstract Knowledge real.

[For the attaining of knowledge and certainty, it is requisite that we have determined ideas:] and, to make our knowledge real, it is requisite that the ideas answer their archetypes. Nor let it be wondered, that I place the certainty of our knowledge in the consideration of our ideas, with so little care and regard (as it may seem) to the real existence of things: since most of those discourses which take up the thoughts and engage the disputes of those who pretend to make it their business to inquire after truth and certainty, will, I presume, upon examination, be found to be general propositions, and notions in which existence is not at all concerned. All the discourses of the mathematicians about the squaring of a circle, conic sections, or any other part of mathematics, concern not the existence of any of those figures: but their demonstrations, which depend on their ideas, are the same, whether there be any square or circle existing in the world or no. In the same manner, the truth and certainty of moral discourses abstracts from the lives of men, and the existence of those virtues in the world whereof they treat: nor are Tully's Offices less true, because there is nobody in the world that exactly practises his rules, and lives up to that pattern of a virtuous man which he has given us, and which existed nowhere when he writ but in idea. If it be true in speculation, i.e. in idea, that murder deserves death, it will also be true in reality of any action that exists conformable to that idea of murder. As for other actions, the truth of that proposition concerns them not. And thus it is of all other species of things, which have no other essences but those ideas which are in the minds of men.

9. Nor will it be less true or certain, because Moral Ideas are of our own making and naming.

But it will here be said, that if moral knowledge be placed in the contemplation of our own moral ideas, and those, as other modes, be of our own making, What strange notions will there be of justice and temperance? What confusion of virtues and vices, if every one may make what ideas of them he pleases? No confusion or disorder in the things themselves, nor the reasonings about them; no more than (in mathematics) there would be a disturbance in the demonstration, or a change in the properties of figures, and their relations one to another, if a man should make a triangle with four corners, or a trapezium with four right angles: that is, in plain English, change the names of the figures, and call that by one name, which mathematicians call ordinarily by another. For, let a man make to himself the idea of a figure with three angles, whereof one is a right one, and call it, if he please, EQUILATERUM or TRAPEZIUM, or anything else; the properties of, and demonstrations about that idea will be the same as if he called it a rectangular triangle. I confess the change of the name, by the impropriety of speech, will at first disturb him who knows not what idea it stands for: but as soon as the figure is drawn, the consequences and demonstrations are plain and clear. Just the same is it in moral knowledge: let a man have the idea of taking from others, without their consent, what their honest industry has possessed them of, and call this JUSTICE if he please. He that takes the name here without the idea put to it will be mistaken, by joining another idea of his own to that name: but strip the idea of that name, or take it such as it is in the speaker's mind, and the same things will agree to it, as if you called it INJUSTICE. Indeed, wrong names in moral discourses breed usually more disorder, because they are not so easily rectified as in mathematics, where the figure, once drawn and seen, makes the name useless and of no force. For what need of a sign, when the thing signified is present and in view? But in moral names, that cannot be so easily and shortly done, because of the many decompositions that go to the making up the complex ideas of those modes. But yet for all this, the miscalling of any of those ideas, contrary to the usual signification of the words of that language, hinders not but that we may have certain and demonstrative knowledge of their several agreements and disagreements, if we will carefully, as in mathematics, keep to the same precise ideas, and trace THEM in their several relations one to another, without being led away by their names. If we but separate the idea under consideration from the sign that stands for it, our knowledge goes equally on in the discovery of real truth and certainty, whatever sounds we make use of.

10. Misnaming disturbs not the certainty of the Knowledge

One thing more we are to take notice of, That where God or any other law-maker, hath defined any moral names, there they have made the essence of that species to which that name belongs; and there it is not safe to apply or use them otherwise: but in other cases it is bare impropriety of speech to apply them contrary to the common usage of the country. But yet even this too disturbs not the certainty of that knowledge, which is still to be had by a due contemplation and comparing of those even nick-named ideas.

11. Thirdly, Our complex Ideas of Substances have their Archetypes without us; and here knowledge comes short.

THIRDLY, There is another sort of complex ideas, which, being referred to archetypes without us, may differ from them, and so our knowledge about them may come short of being real. Such are our ideas of substances, which, consisting of a collection of simple ideas, supposed taken from the works of nature, may yet vary from them; by having more or different ideas united in them than are to be found united in the things themselves. From whence it comes to pass, that they may, and often do, fail of being exactly conformable to things themselves.

12. So far as our complex ideas agree with those Archetypes without us, so far our Knowledge concerning Substances is real.

I say, then, that to have ideas of SUBSTANCES which, by being conformable to things, may afford us real knowledge, it is not enough, as in MODES, to put together such ideas as have no inconsistence, though they did never before so exist: v.g. the ideas of sacrilege or perjury, &c., were as real and true ideas before, as after the existence of any such fact. But our ideas of substances, being supposed copies, and referred to archetypes without us, must still be taken from something that does or has existed: they must not consist of ideas put together at the pleasure of our thoughts, without any real pattern they were taken from, though we can perceive no inconsistence in such a combination. The reason whereof is because we, knowing not what real constitution it is of substances whereon our simple ideas depend, and which really is the cause of the strict union of some of them one with another, and the exclusion of others; there are very few of them that we can be sure are or are not inconsistent in nature: any further than experience and sensible observation reach Herein, therefore, is founded the reality of our knowledge concerning substances— That all our complex ideas of them must be such, and such only, as are made up of such simple ones as have been discovered to co-exist in nature. And our ideas being thus true, though not perhaps very exact copies, are yet the subjects of real (as far as we have any) knowledge of them. Which (as has been already shown) will not be found to reach very far: but so far as it does, it will still be real knowledge. Whatever ideas we have, the agreement we find they have with others will still be knowledge. If those ideas be abstract, it will be general knowledge. But to make it real concerning substances, the ideas must be taken from the real existence of things. Whatever simple ideas have been found to co-exist in any substance, these we may with confidence join together again, and so make abstract ideas of substances. For whatever have once had an union in nature, may be united again.

13. In our inquiries about Substances, we must consider Ideas, and not confine our Thoughts to Names, or Species supposed set out by Names.

This, if we rightly consider, and confine not our thoughts and abstract ideas to names, as if there were, or could be no other SORTS of things than what known names had already determined, and, as it were, set out, we should think of things with greater freedom and less confusion than perhaps we do. It would possibly be thought a bold paradox, if not a very dangerous falsehood, if I should say that some CHANGELINGS, who have lived forty years together, without any appearance of reason, are something between a man and a beast: which prejudice is founded upon nothing else but a false supposition, that these two names, man and beast, stand for distinct species so set out by real essences, that there can come no other species between them: whereas if we will abstract from those names, and the supposition of such specific essences made by nature, wherein all things of the same denominations did exactly and equally partake; if we would not fancy that there were a certain number of these essences, wherein all things, as in moulds, were cast and formed; we should find that the idea of the shape, motion, and life of a man without reason, is as much a distinct idea, and makes as much a distinct sort of things from man and beast, as the idea of the shape of an ass with reason would be different from either that of man or beast, and be a species of an animal between, or distinct from both.

14. Objection against a Changeling being something between a Man and Beast, answered.

Here everybody will be ready to ask, If changelings may be supposed something between man and beast, pray what are they? I answer, CHANGELINGS; which is as good a word to signify something different from the signification of MAN or BEAST, as the names man and beast are to have significations different one from the other. This, well considered, would resolve this matter, and show my meaning without any more ado. But I am not so unacquainted with the zeal of some men, which enables them to spin consequences, and to see religion threatened, whenever any one ventures to quit their forms of speaking, as not to foresee what names such a proposition as this is like to be charged with: and without doubt it will be asked, If changelings are something between man and beast, what will become of them in the other world? To which I answer, I. It concerns me not to know or inquire. To their own master they stand or fall. It will make their state neither better nor worse, whether we determine anything of it or no. They are in the hands of a faithful Creator and a bountiful Father, who disposes not of his creatures according to our narrow thoughts or opinions, nor distinguishes them according to names and species of our contrivance. And we that know so little of this present world we are in, may, I think, content ourselves without being peremptory in defining the different states which creatures shall come into when they go off this stage. It may suffice us, that He hath made known to all those who are capable of instruction, discoursing, and reasoning, that they shall come to an account, and receive according to what they have done in this body.

15. What will become of Changelings in a future state?

But, Secondly, I answer, The force of these men's question (viz. Will you deprive changelings of a future state?) is founded on one of these two suppositions, which are both false. The first is, That all things that have the outward shape and appearance of a man must necessarily be designed to an immortal future being after this life: or, secondly, That whatever is of human birth must be so. Take away these imaginations, and such questions will be groundless and ridiculous. I desire then those who think there is no more but an accidental difference between themselves and changelings, the essence in both being exactly the same, to consider, whether they can imagine immortality annexed to any outward shape of the body; the very proposing it is, I suppose, enough to make them disown it. No one yet, that ever I heard of, how much soever immersed in matter, allowed that excellency to any figure of the gross sensible outward consequence of it; or that any mass of matter should, after its dissolution here, be again restored hereafter to an everlasting state of sense, perception, and knowledge, only because it was moulded into this or that figure, and had such a particular frame of its visible parts. Such an opinion as this, placing immortality in a certain superficial figure, turns out of doors all consideration of soul or spirit; upon whose account alone some corporeal beings have hitherto been concluded immortal, and others not. This is to attribute more to the outside than inside of things; and to place the excellency of a man more in the external shape of his body, than internal perfections of his soul: which is but little better than to annex the great and inestimable advantage of immortality and life everlasting, which he has above other material beings, to annex it, I say, to the cut of his beard, or the fashion of his coat. For this or that outward mark of our bodies no more carries with it the hope of an eternal duration, than the fashion of a man's suit gives him reasonable grounds to imagine it will never wear out, or that it will make him immortal. It will perhaps be said, that nobody thinks that the shape makes anything immortal, but it is the shape that is the sign of a rational soul within, which is immortal. I wonder who made it the sign of any such thing: for barely saying it, will not make it so. It would require some proofs to persuade one of it. No figure that I know speaks any such language. For it may as rationally be concluded, that the dead body of a man, wherein there is to be found no more appearance or action of life than there is in a statue, has yet nevertheless a living soul in it, because of its shape; as that there is a rational soul in a changeling, because he has the outside of a rational creature, when his actions carry far less marks of reason with them, in the whole course of his life than what are to be found in many a beast.

16. Monsters

But it is the issue of rational parents, and must therefore be concluded to have a rational soul. I know not by what logic you must so conclude. I am sure this is a conclusion that men nowhere allow of. For if they did, they would not make bold, as everywhere they do to destroy ill-formed and mis-shaped productions. Ay, but these are MONSTERS. Let them be so: what will your drivelling, unintelligent, intractable changeling be? Shall a defect in the body make a monster; a defect in the mind (the far more noble, and, in the common phrase, the far more essential part) not? Shall the want of a nose, or a neck, make a monster, and put such issue out of the rank of men; the want of reason and understanding, not? This is to bring all back again to what was exploded just now: this is to place all in the shape, and to take the measure of a man only by his outside. To show that according to the ordinary way of reasoning in this matter, people do lay the whole stress on the figure, and resolve the whole essence of the species of man (as they make it) into the outward shape, how unreasonable soever it be, and how much soever they disown it, we need but trace their thoughts and practice a little further, and then it will plainly appear. The well-shaped changeling is a man, has a rational soul, though it appear not: this is past doubt, say you: make the ears a little longer, and more pointed, and the nose a little flatter than ordinary, and then you begin to boggle: make the face yet narrower, flatter, and longer, and then you are at a stand: add still more and more of the likeness of a brute to it, and let the head be perfectly that of some other animal, then presently it is a monster; and it is demonstration with you that it hath no rational soul, and must be destroyed. Where now (I ask) shall be the just measure; which the utmost bounds of that shape, that carries with it a rational soul? For, since there have been human foetuses produced, half beast and half man; and others three parts one, and one part the other; and so it is possible they may be in all the variety of approaches to the one or the other shape, and may have several degrees of mixture of the likeness of a man, or a brute;—I would gladly know what are those precise lineaments, which, according to this hypothesis, are or are not capable of a rational soul to be joined to them. What sort of outside is the certain sign that there is or is not such an inhabitant within? For till that be done, we talk at random of MAN: and shall always, I fear, do so, as long as we give ourselves up to certain sounds, and the imaginations of settled and fixed species in nature, we know not what. But, after all, I desire it may be considered, that those who think they have answered the difficulty, by telling us, that a mis-shaped foetus is a MONSTER, run into the same fault they are arguing against; by constituting a species between man and beast. For what else, I pray, is their monster in the case, (if the word monster signifies anything at all,) but something neither man nor beast, but partaking somewhat of either? And just so is the CHANGELING before mentioned. So necessary is it to quit the common notion of species and essences, if we will truly look into the nature of things, and examine them by what our faculties can discover in them as they exist, and not by groundless fancies that have been taken up about them.

17. Words and Species.

I have mentioned this here, because I think we cannot be too cautious that words and species, in the ordinary notions which we have been used to of them, impose not on us. For I am apt to think therein lies one great obstacle to our clear and distinct knowledge, especially in reference to substances: and from thence has rose a great part of the difficulties about truth and certainty. Would we accustom ourselves to separate our contemplations and reasonings from words, we might in a great measure remedy this inconvenience within our own thoughts: but yet it would still disturb us in our discourse with others, as long as we retained the opinion, that SPECIES and their ESSENCES were anything else but our abstract ideas (such as they are) with names annexed to them, to be the signs of them.

18. Recapitulation.

Wherever we perceive the agreement or disagreement of any of our ideas, there is certain knowledge: and wherever we are sure those ideas agree with the reality of things, there is certain real knowledge. Of which agreement of our ideas with the reality of things, having here given the marks, I think, I have shown WHEREIN IT IS THAT CERTAINTY, REAL CERTAINTY, CONSISTS. Which, whatever it was to others, was, I confess, to me heretofore, one of those desiderata which I found great want of.

CHAPTER V. OF TRUTH IN GENERAL.

1. What Truth is.

WHAT is truth? was an inquiry many ages since; and it being that which all mankind either do, or pretend to search after, it cannot but be worth our while carefully to examine wherein it consists; and so acquaint ourselves with the nature of it, as to observe how the mind distinguishes it from falsehood.

2. A right joining or separating of signs, i.e. either Ideas or Words.

Truth, then, seems to me, in the proper import of the word, to signify nothing but THE JOINING OR SEPERATING OF SIGNS, AS THE THINGS SIGNIFIED BY THEM DO AGREE OR DISAGREE ONE WITH ANOTHER. The joining or separating of signs here meant, is what by another name we call PROPOSITION. So that truth properly belongs only to propositions: whereof there are two sorts, viz. mental and verbal; as there are two sorts of signs commonly made use of, viz. ideas and words.

3. Which make mental or verbal Propositions.

To form a clear notion of truth, it is very necessary to consider truth of thought, and truth of words, distinctly one from another: but yet it is very difficult to treat of them asunder. Because it is unavoidable, in treating of mental propositions, to make use of words: and then the instances given of mental propositions cease immediately to be barely mental, and become verbal. For a MENTAL PROPOSITION being nothing but a bare consideration of the ideas, as they are in our minds, stripped of names, they lose the nature of purely mental propositions as soon as they are put into words.

4. Mental Propositions are very hard to be treated of.

And that which makes it yet harder to treat of mental and verbal propositions separately is, that most men, if not all, in their thinking and reasonings within themselves, make use of words instead of ideas; at least when the subject of their meditation contains in it complex ideas. Which is a great evidence of the imperfection and uncertainty of our ideas of that kind, and may, if attentively made use of, serve for a mark to show us what are those things we have clear and perfect established ideas of, and what not. For if we will curiously observe the way our mind takes in thinking and reasoning, we shall find, I suppose, that when we make any propositions within our own thoughts about WHITE or BLACK, SWEET or BITTER, a TRIANGLE or a CIRCLE, we can and often do frame in our minds the ideas themselves, without reflecting on the names. But when we would consider, or make propositions about the more complex ideas, as of a MAN, VITRIOL, FORTITUDE, GLORY, we usually put the name for the idea: because the ideas these names stand for, being for the most part imperfect, confused, and undetermined, we reflect on the names themselves, because they are more clear, certain, and distinct, and readier occur to our thoughts than the pure ideas: and so we make use of these words instead of the ideas themselves, even when we would meditate and reason within ourselves, and make tacit mental propositions. In substances, as has been already noticed, this is occasioned by the imperfections of our ideas: we making the name stand for the real essence, of which we have no idea at all. In modes, it is occasioned by the great number of simple ideas that go to the making them up. For many of them being compounded, the name occurs much easier than the complex idea itself, which requires time and attention to be recollected, and exactly represented to the mind, even in those men who have formerly been at the pains to do it; and is utterly impossible to be done by those who, though they have ready in their memory the greatest part of the common words of that language, yet perhaps never troubled themselves in all their lives to consider what precise ideas the most of them stood for. Some confused or obscure notions have served their turns; and many who talk very much of RELIGION and CONSCIENCE, of CHURCH and FAITH, of POWER and RIGHT, of OBSTRUCTIONS and HUMOURS, MELANCHOLY and CHOLER, would perhaps have little left in their thoughts and meditations, if one should desire them to think only of the things themselves, and lay by those words with which they so often confound others, and not seldom themselves also.

5. Mental and Verbal Propositions contrasted.

But to return to the consideration of truth: we must, I say, observe two sorts of propositions that we are capable of making:—

First, MENTAL, wherein the ideas in our understandings are without the use of words put together, or separated, by the mind perceiving or judging of their agreement or disagreement.

Secondly, VERBAL propositions, which are words, the signs of our ideas, put together or separated in affirmative or negative sentences. By which way of affirming or denying, these signs, made by sounds, are, as it were, put together or separated from another. So that proposition consists in joining or separating signs; and truth consists in the putting together or separating those signs, according as the things which they stand for agree or disagree.

6. When Mental Propositions contain real Truth, and when Verbal.
Every one's experience will satisfy him, that the mind, either by perceiving, or supposing, the agreement or disagreement of any of its ideas, does tacitly within itself put them into a kind of proposition affirmative or negative; which I have endeavoured to express by the terms putting together and separating. But this action of the mind, which is so familiar to every thinking and reasoning man, is easier to be conceived by reflecting on what passes in us when we affirm or deny, than to be explained by words. When a man has in his head the idea of two lines, viz. the side and diagonal of a square, whereof the diagonal is an inch long, he may have the idea also of the division of that line into a certain number of equal parts; v.g. into five, ten, a hundred, a thousand, or any other number, and may have the idea of that inch line being divisible, or not divisible, into such equal parts, as a certain number of them will be equal to the sideline. Now, whenever he perceives, believes, or supposes such a kind of divisibility to agree or disagree to his idea of that line, he, as it were, joins or separates those two ideas, viz. the idea of that line, and the idea of that kind of divisibility; and so makes a mental proposition, which is true or false, according as such a kind of divisibility, a divisibility into such ALIQUOT parts, does really agree to that line or no. When ideas are so put together, or separated in the mind, as they or the things they stand for do agree or not, that is, as I may call it, MENTAL TRUTH. But TRUTH OF WORDS is something more; and that is the affirming or denying of words one of another, as the ideas they stand for agree or disagree: and this again is two-fold; either purely verbal and trifling, which I shall speak of, (chap. viii.,) or real and instructive; which is the object of that real knowledge which we have spoken of already.

7. Objection against verbal Truth, that thus it may all be chimerical.
But here again will be apt to occur the same doubt about truth, that did about knowledge: and it will be objected, that if truth be nothing but the joining and separating of words in propositions, as the ideas they stand for agree or disagree in men's minds, the knowledge of truth is not so valuable a thing as it is taken to be, nor worth the pains and time men employ in the search of it: since by this account it amounts to no more than the conformity of words to the chimeras of men's brains. Who knows not what odd notions many men's heads are filled with, and what strange ideas all men's brains are capable of? But if we rest here, we know the truth of nothing by this rule, but of the visionary words in our own imaginations; nor have other truth, but what as much concerns harpies and centaurs, as

men and horses. For those, and the like, may be ideas in our heads, and have their agreement or disagreement there, as well as the ideas of real beings, and so have as true propositions made about them. And it will be altogether as true a proposition to say ALL CENTAURS ARE ANIMALS, as that ALL MEN ARE ANIMALS; and the certainty of one as great as the other. For in both the propositions, the words are put together according to the agreement of the ideas in our minds: and the agreement of the idea of animal with that of centaur is as clear and visable to the mind, as the agreement of the idea of animal with that of man; and so these two propositions are equally true, equally certain. But of what use is all such truth to us?

8. Answered, Real Truth is about Ideas agreeing to things.

Though what has been said in the foregoing chapter to distinguish real from imaginary knowledge might suffice here, in answer to this doubt, to distinguish real truth from chimerical, or (if you please) barely nominal, they depending both on the same foundation; yet it may not be amiss here again to consider, that though our words signify things, the truth they contain when put into propositions will be only verbal, when they stand for ideas in the mind that have not an agreement with the reality of things. And therefore truth as well as knowledge may well come under the distinction of verbal and real; that being only verbal truth, wherein terms are joined according to the agreement or disagreement of the ideas they stand for; without regarding whether our ideas are such as really have, or are capable of having, an existence in nature. But then it is they contain REAL TRUTH, when these signs are joined, as our ideas agree; and when our ideas are such as we know are capable of having an existence in nature: which in substances we cannot know, but by knowing that such have existed.

9. Truth and Falsehood in general.

Truth is the marking down in words the agreement or disagreement of ideas as it is. Falsehood is the marking down in words the agreement or disagreement of ideas otherwise than it is. And so far as these ideas, thus marked by sounds, agree to their archetypes, so far only is the truth real. The knowledge of this truth consists in knowing what ideas the words stand for, and the perception of the agreement or disagreement of those ideas, according as it is marked by those words.

10. General Propositions to be treated of more at large.

But because words are looked on as the great conduits of truth and knowledge, and that in conveying and receiving of truth, and commonly in reasoning about it, we make use of words and propositions, I shall more at large inquire wherein the certainty of real truths contained in propositions consists, and where it is to be had; and endeavour to show in what sort of universal propositions we are capable of being certain of their real truth or falsehood.

I shall begin with GENERAL propositions, as those which most employ our thoughts, and exercise our contemplation. General truths are most looked after by the mind as those that most enlarge our knowledge; and by their comprehensiveness satisfying us at once of many particulars, enlarge our view, and shorten our way to knowledge.

11. Moral and Metaphysical Truth.

Besides truth taken in the strict sense before mentioned, there are other sorts of truths: As, 1. Moral truth, which is speaking of things according to the persuasion of our own minds, though the proposition we speak agree not to the reality of things; 2. Metaphysical truth, which is nothing but the real existence of things, conformable to the ideas to which we have annexed their names. This, though it seems to consist in the very beings of things, yet, when considered a little nearly, will appear to include a tacit proposition, whereby the mind joins that particular thing to the idea it had before settled with the name to it. But these considerations of truth, either having been before taken notice of, or not being much to our present purpose, it may suffice here only to have mentioned them.

CHAPTER VI. OF UNIVERSAL PROPOSITIONS: THEIR TRUTH AND CERTAINTY.

1. Treating of Words necessary to Knowledge.
THOUGH the examining and judging of ideas by themselves, their names being quite laid aside, be the best and surest way to clear and distinct knowledge: yet, through the prevailing custom of using sounds for ideas, I think it is very seldom practised. Every one may observe how common it is for names to be made use of, instead of the ideas themselves, even when men think and reason within their own breasts; especially if the ideas be very complex, and made up of a great collection of simple ones. This makes the consideration of WORDS and PROPOSITIONS so necessary a part of the Treatise of Knowledge, that it is very hard to speak intelligibly of the one, without explaining the other.

2. General Truths hardly to be understood, but in verbal Propositions.
All the knowledge we have, being only of particular or general truths, it is evident that whatever may be done in the former of these, the latter, which is that which with reason is most sought after, can never be well made known, and is very seldom apprehended, but as conceived and expressed in words. It is not, therefore, out of our way, in the examination of our knowledge, to inquire into the truth and certainty of universal propositions.

3. Certainty twofold—of Truth and of Knowledge.
But that we may not be misled in this case by that which is the danger everywhere, I mean by the doubtfulness of terms, it is fit to observe that certainty is twofold: CERTAINTY OF TRUTH and CERTAINTY OF KNOWLEDGE. Certainty of truth is, when words are so put together in propositions as exactly to express the agreement or disagreement of the ideas they stand for, as really it is. Certainty of knowledge is to perceive the agreement or disagreement of ideas, as expressed in any proposition. This we usually call knowing, or being certain of the truth of any proposition.

4. No Proposition can be certainly known to be true, where the real Essence of each Species mentioned is not known.
Now, because we cannot be certain of the truth of any general proposition, unless we know the precise bounds and extent of the species its terms stand for, it is necessary we should know the essence of each species, which is that which constitutes and bounds it.
This, in all simple ideas and modes, is not hard to do. For in these the real and nominal essence being the same, or, which is all one, the abstract idea

which the general term stands for being the sole essence and boundary that is or can be supposed of the species, there can be no doubt how far the species extends, or what things are comprehended under each term; which, it is evident, are all that have an exact conformity with the idea it stands for, and no other. But in substances, wherein a real essence, distinct from the nominal, is supposed to constitute, determine, and bound the species, the extent of the general word is very uncertain; because, not knowing this real essence, we cannot know what is, or what is not of that species; and, consequently, what may or may not with certainty be affirmed of it. And thus, speaking of a MAN, or GOLD, or any other species of natural substances, as supposed constituted by a precise and real essence which nature regularly imparts to every individual of that kind, whereby it is made to be of that species, we cannot be certain of the truth of any affirmation or negation made of it. For man or gold, taken in this sense, and used for species of things constituted by real essences, different from the complex idea in the mind of the speaker, stand for we know not what; and the extent of these species, with such boundaries, are so unknown and undetermined, that it is impossible with any certainty to affirm, that all men are rational, or that all gold is yellow. But where the nominal essence is kept to, as the boundary of each species, and men extend the application of any general term no further than to the particular things in which the complex idea it stands for is to be found, there they are in no danger to mistake the bounds of each species, nor can be in doubt, on this account, whether any proposition be true or not. I have chosen to explain this uncertainty of propositions in this scholastic way, and have made use of the terms of ESSENCES, and SPECIES, on purpose to show the absurdity and inconvenience there is to think of them as of any other sort of realities, than barely abstract ideas with names to them. To suppose that the species of things are anything but the sorting of them under general names, according as they agree to several abstract ideas of which we make those names signs, is to confound truth, and introduce uncertainty into all general propositions that can be made about them. Though therefore these things might, to people not possessed with scholastic learning, be treated of in a better and clearer way yet those wrong notions of essences or species having got root in most people's minds who have received any tincture from the learning which has prevailed in this part of the world, are to be discovered and removed, to make way for that use of words which should convey certainty with it.

5. This more particularly concerns Substances.

The names of substances, then, whenever made to stand for species which are supposed to be constituted by real essences which we know not, are not capable to convey certainty to the understanding. Of the truth general propositions made up of such terms we cannot be sure. [The reason whereof is plain: for how can we be sure that this or that quality is in gold, when we know not what is or is not gold? Since in this way of speaking, nothing is gold but what partakes of an essence, which we, not knowing, cannot know where it is or is not, and so cannot be sure that any parcel of matter in the world is or is not in this sense gold; being incurably ignorant whether IT has or has not that which makes anything to be called gold; i. e. that real essence of gold whereof we have no idea at all. This being as impossible for us to know as it is for a blind man to tell in what flower the colour of a pansy is or is not to be found, whilst he has no idea of the colour of a pansy at all. Or if we could (which is impossible) certainly know where a real essence, which we know not, is, v.g. in what parcels of matter the real essence of gold is, yet could we not be sure that this or that quality could with truth be affirmed of gold; since it is impossible for us to know that this or that quality or idea has a necessary connexion with a real essence of which we have no idea at all, whatever species that supposed real essence may be imagined to constitute.]

6.

On the other side, the names of substances, when made use of as they should be, for the ideas men have in their minds, though they carry a clear and determinate signification with them, will not yet serve us to make many universal propositions of whose truth we can be certain. Not because in this use of them we are uncertain what things are signified by them, but because the complex ideas they stand for are such combinations of simple ones as carry not with them any discoverable connexion or repugnancy, but with a very few other ideas.

7.

The complex ideas that our names of the species of substances properly stand for, are collections of such qualities as have been observed to co-exist in an unknown substratum, which we call substance; but what other qualities necessarily co-exist with such combinations, we cannot certainly know, unless we can discover their natural dependence; which, in their primary qualities, we can go but a very little way in; and in all their secondary qualities we can discover no connexion at all: for the reasons mentioned, chap. iii. Viz. 1. Because we know not the real constitutions of substances, on which each secondary quality particularly depends. 2. Did we know that, it would serve us only for experimental (not universal) knowledge; and reach with certainty no further than that bare instance: because our understandings can discover no conceivable connexion between any secondary quality and any modification whatsoever of any of the primary ones. And therefore there are very few general propositions to be made concerning substances, which can carry with them undoubted certainty.

8. Instance in Gold.

'All gold is fixed,' is a proposition whose truth we cannot be certain of, how universally soever it be believed. For if, according to the useless imagination of the Schools, any one supposes the term gold to stand for a species of things set out by nature, by a real essence belonging to it, it is evident he knows not what particular substances are of that species; and so cannot with certainty affirm anything universally of gold. But if he makes gold stand for a species determined by its nominal essence, let the nominal essence, for example, be the complex idea of a body of a certain yellow colour, malleable, fusible, and heavier than any other known;—in this proper use of the word gold, there is no difficulty to know what is or is not gold. But yet no other quality can with certainty be universally affirmed or denied of gold, but what hath a DISCOVERABLE connexion or inconsistency with that nominal essence. Fixedness, for example, having no necessary connexion that we can discover, with the colour, weight, or any other simple idea of our complex one, or with the whole combination together; it is impossible that we should certainly know the truth of this proposition, that all gold is fixed.

9. No discoverable necessary connexion between nominal essence gold, and other simple ideas.

As there is no discoverable connexion between fixedness and the colour, weight, and other simple ideas of that nominal essence of gold; so, if we make our complex idea of gold, a body yellow, fusable, ductile, weighty, and fixed, we shall be at the same uncertainty concerning solubility in AQUA REGIA, and for the same reason. Since we can never, from consideration of the ideas themselves, with certainty affirm or deny of a body whose complex idea is made up of yellow, very weighty, ductile, fusible, and fixed, that it is soluble in AQUA REGIA: and so on of the rest of its qualities. I would gladly meet with one general affirmation concerning any will, no doubt, be presently objected, Is not this an universal proposition, ALL GOLD IS MALLEABLE? To which I answer, It is a very complex idea the word gold stands for. But then here is nothing affirmed of gold, but that that sound stands for an idea in which malleableness is contained: and such a sort of truth and certainty as this it is, to say a centaur is four-footed. But if malleableness make not a part of the specific essence the name of gold stands for, it is plain, ALL GOLD IS MALLEABLE, is not a certain proposition. Because, let the complex idea of gold be made up of whichsoever of its other qualities you please, malleableness will not appear to depend on that complex idea, nor follow from any simple one contained in it: the connexion that malleableness has (if it has any) with those other qualities being only by the intervention of the real constitution of its insensible parts; which, since we know not, it is impossible we should perceive that connexion, unless we could discover that which ties them together.

10. As far as any such Co-existence can be known, so far Universal Propositions maybe certain. But this will go but a little way.

The more, indeed, of these co-existing qualities we unite into one complex idea, under one name, the more precise and determinate we make the signification of that word; but never yet make it thereby more capable of universal certainty, IN RESPECT OF OTHER QUALITIES NOT CONTAINED IN OUR COMPLEX IDEA: since we perceive not their connexion or dependence on one another; being ignorant both of that real constitution in which they are all founded, and also how they flow from it. For the chief part of our knowledge concerning substances is not, as in other things, barely of the relation of two ideas that may exist separately; but is of the necessary connexion and co-existence of several distinct ideas in the same subject, or of their repugnancy so to co-exist. Could we begin at the other end, and discover what it was wherein that colour consisted, what made a body lighter or heavier, what texture of parts made it malleable, fusible, and fixed, and fit to be dissolved in this sort of liquor, and not in another;—if, I say, we had such an idea as this of bodies, and could perceive wherein all sensible qualities originally consist, and how they are produced; we might frame such abstract ideas of them as would furnish us with matter of more general knowledge, and enable us to make universal propositions, that should carry general truth and certainty with them. But whilst our complex ideas of the sorts of substances are so remote from that internal real constitution on which their sensible qualities depend, and are made up of nothing but an imperfect collection of those apparent qualities our senses can discover, there can be few general propositions concerning substances of whose real truth we can be certainly assured; since there are but few simple ideas of whose connexion and necessary co-existence we can have certain and undoubted knowledge. I imagine, amongst all the secondary qualities of substances, and the powers relating to them, there cannot any two be named, whose necessary co-existence, or repugnance to co-exist, can certainly be known; unless in those of the same sense, which necessarily exclude one another, as I have elsewhere showed. No one, I think, by the colour that is in any body, can certainly know what smell, taste, sound, or tangible qualities it has, nor what alterations it is capable to make or receive on or from other bodies. The same may be said of the sound or taste, &c. Our specific names of substances standing for any collections of such ideas, it is not to be wondered that we can with them make very few general propositions of undoubted real certainty. But yet so far as any complex idea of any sort of substances contains in it any simple idea, whose NECESSARY co-existence with any other MAY be discovered, so far universal propositions may with certainty be made concerning it: v.g. could any one discover a necessary connexion between malleableness and the colour or weight of gold, or any other part of the complex idea signified by that name, he might make a certain universal proposition concerning gold in this respect; and the real truth of this proposition, that ALL GOLD IS MALLIABLE, would be as certain as of this, THE THREE ANGLES OF ALL RIGHT-LINED TRIANGLES ARE ALL EQUAL TO TWO RIGHT ONES.

11. The Qualities which make our complex Ideas of Substances depend mostly on external, remote, and unperceived Causes.

Had we such ideas of substances as to know what real constitutions produce those sensible qualities we find in them, and how those qualities flowed from thence, we could, by the specific ideas of their real essences in our own minds, more certainly find out their properties, and discover what qualities they had or had not, than we can now by our senses: and to know the properties of gold, it would be no more necessary that gold should exist, and that we should make experiments upon it, than it is necessary for the knowing the properties of a triangle, that a triangle should exist in any matter, the idea in our minds would serve for the one as well as the other. But we are so far from being admitted into the secrets of nature, that we scarce so much as ever approach the first entrance towards them. For we are wont to consider the substances we meet with, each of them, as an entire thing by itself, having all its qualities in itself, and independent of other things; overlooking, for the most part, the operations of those invisible fluids they are encompassed with, and upon whose motions and operations depend the greatest part of those qualities which are taken notice of in them, and are made by us the inherent marks of distinction whereby we know and denominate them. Put a piece of gold anywhere by itself, separate from the reach and influence of all other bodies, it will immediately lose all its colour and weight, and perhaps malleableness too; which, for aught I know, would be changed into a perfect friability. Water, in which to us fluidity is an essential quality, left to itself, would cease to be fluid. But if inanimate bodies owe so much of their present state to other bodies without them, that they would not be what they appear to us were those bodies that environ them removed; it is yet more so in vegetables, which are nourished, grow, and produce leaves, flowers, and seeds, in a constant succession. And if we look a little nearer into the state of animals, we shall find that their dependence, as to life, motion, and the most considerable qualities to be observed in them, is so wholly on extrinsical causes and qualities of other bodies that make no part of them, that they cannot subsist a moment without them: though yet those bodies on which they depend are little taken notice of, and make no part of the complex ideas we frame of those animals. Take the air but for a minute from the greatest part of living creatures, and they presently lose sense, life, and motion. This the necessity of breathing has forced into our knowledge. But how many other extrinsical and possibly very remote bodies do the springs of these admirable machines depend on, which are not vulgarly observed, or so much as thought on; and how many are there which the severest inquiry can never discover? The inhabitants of this spot of the universe, though removed so many millions of miles from the sun, yet depend so much on the duly tempered motion of particles coming from or agitated by it, that were this earth removed but a small part of the distance out of its present situation, and placed a little further or nearer that source of heat, it is more than probable that the greatest part of the animals in it would immediately perish: since we find them so often destroyed by an excess or defect of the sun's warmth, which an accidental position in some parts of this our little globe exposes them to. The qualities observed in a loadstone must needs have their source far beyond the confines of that body; and the ravage made often on several sorts of animals by invisible causes, the certain death (as we are told) of some of them, by barely passing the line, or, as it is certain of other, by being removed into a neighbouring country; evidently show that the concurrence and operations of several bodies, with which they are seldom thought to have anything to do, is absolutely necessary to make them be what they appear to us, and to preserve those qualities by which we know and distinguish them. We are then quite out of the way, when we think that things contain WITHIN THEMSELVES the qualities that appear to us in them; and we in vain search for that constitution within the body of a fly or an elephant, upon which depend those qualities and powers we observe in them. For which, perhaps, to understand them aright, we ought to look not only beyond this our earth and atmosphere, but even beyond the sun or remotest star our eyes have yet discovered. For how much the being and operation of particular substances in this our globe depends on causes utterly beyond our view, is impossible for us to determine. We see and perceive some of the motions and grosser operations of things here about us; but whence the streams come that keep all these curious machines in motion and repair, how conveyed and modified, is beyond our notice and apprehension: and the great parts and wheels, as I may so say, of this stupendous structure of the universe, may, for aught we know, have such a connexion and dependence in their influences and operations one upon another, that perhaps things in this our mansion would put on quite another face, and cease to be what they are, if some one of the stars or great bodies incomprehensibly remote from us, should cease to be or move as it does. This is certain: things, however absolute and entire they seem in themselves, are but retainers to other parts of nature, for that which they are most taken notice of by us. Their observable qualities, actions, and powers are owing to something without them; and there is not so complete and perfect a part that we know of nature, which does not owe the being it has, and the excellences of it, to its neighbours; and we must not confine our thoughts within the surface of any body, but look a great deal further, to comprehend perfectly those qualities that are in it.

12. Our nominal essences of Substances furnish few universal propositions about them that are certain.

If this be so, it is not to be wondered that we have very imperfect ideas of substances, and that the real essences, on which depend their properties and operations, are unknown to us. We cannot discover so much as that size, figure, and texture of their minute and active parts, which is really in much less the different motions and impulses made in and upon them by bodies from without, upon which depends, and by which is formed the greatest and most remarkable part of those qualities we observe in them, and of which our complex ideas of them are made up. This consideration alone is enough to put an end to all our hopes of ever having the ideas of their real essences; which whilst we want, the nominal essences we make

use of instead of them will be able to furnish us but very sparingly with any general knowledge, or universal propositions capable of real certainty.
13. Judgment of Probability concerning Substances may reach further: but that is not Knowledge.
We are not therefore to wonder, if certainty be to be found in very few general propositions made concerning substances: our knowledge of their qualities and properties goes very seldom further than our senses reach and inform us. Possibly inquisitive and observing men may, by strength of judgment, penetrate further, and, on probabilities taken from wary observation, and hints well laid together, often guess right at what experience has not yet discovered to them. But this is but guessing still; it amounts only to opinion, and has not that certainty which is requisite to knowledge. For all general knowledge lies only in our own thoughts, and consists barely in the contemplation of our own abstract ideas. Wherever we perceive any agreement or disagreement amongst them, there we have general knowledge; and by putting the names of those ideas together accordingly in propositions, can with certainty pronounce general truths. But because the abstract ideas of substances, for which their specific names stand, whenever they have any distinct and determinate signification, have a discoverable connexion or inconsistency with but a very few other ideas, the certainty of universal propositions concerning substances is very narrow and scanty, in that part which is our principal inquiry concerning them; and there are scarce any of the names of substances, let the idea it is applied to be what it will, of which we can generally, and with certainty, pronounce, that it has or has not this or that other quality belonging to it, and constantly co-existing or inconsistent with that idea, wherever it is to be found.
14. What is requisite for our Knowledge of Substances.
Before we can have any tolerable knowledge of this kind, we must First know what changes the primary qualities of one body do regularly produce in the primary qualities of another, and how. Secondly, We must know what primary qualities of any body produce certain sensations or ideas in us. This is in truth no less than to know ALL the effects of matter, under its divers modifications of bulk, figure, cohesion of parts, motion and rest. Which, I think every body will allow, is utterly impossible to be known by us without revelation. Nor if it were revealed to us what sort of figure, bulk, and motion of corpuscles would produce in us the sensation of a yellow colour, and what sort of figure, bulk, and texture of parts in the superficies of any body were fit to give such corpuscles their due motion to produce

that colour; would that be enough to make universal propositions with certainty, concerning the several sorts of them; unless we had faculties acute enough to perceive the precise bulk, figure, texture, and motion of bodies, in those minute parts, by which they operate on our senses, so that we might by those frame our abstract ideas of them. I have mentioned here only corporeal substances, whose operations seem to lie more level to our understandings. For as to the operations of spirits, both their thinking and moving of bodies, we at first sight find ourselves at a loss; though perhaps, when we have applied our thoughts a little nearer to the consideration of bodies and their operations, and examined how far our notions, even in these, reach with any clearness beyond sensible matter of fact, we shall be bound to confess that, even in these too, our discoveries amount to very little beyond perfect ignorance and incapacity.

15. Whilst our complex Ideas of Substances contain not ideas of their real Constitutions, we can make but few general Propositions concerning them. This is evident, the abstract complex ideas of substances, for which their general names stand, not comprehending their real constitutions, can afford us very little universal certainty. Because our ideas of them are not made up of that on which those qualities we observe in them, and would inform ourselves about, do depend, or with which they have any certain connexion: v.g. let the ideas to which we give the name MAN be, as it commonly is, a body of the ordinary shape, with sense, voluntary motion, and reason joined to it. This being the abstract idea, and consequently the essence of OUR species, man, we can make but very few general certain propositions concerning man, standing for such an idea. Because, not knowing the real constitution on which sensation, power of motion, and reasoning, with that peculiar shape, depend, and whereby they are united together in the same subject, there are very few other qualities with which we can perceive them to have a necessary connexion: and therefore we cannot with certainty affirm: That all men sleep by intervals; That no man can be nourished by wood or stones; That all men will be poisoned by hemlock: because these ideas have no connexion nor repugnancy with this our nominal essence of man, with this abstract idea that name stands for. We must, in these and the like, appeal to trial in particular subjects, which can reach but a little way. We must content ourselves with probability in the rest: but can have no general certainty, whilst our specific idea of man contains not that real constitution which is the root wherein all his inseparable qualities are united, and from whence they flow. Whilst our idea the word MAN stands for is only an imperfect collection of some

sensible qualities and powers in him, there is no discernible connexion or repugnance between our specific idea, and the operation of either the parts of hemlock or stones upon his constitution. There are animals that safely eat hemlock, and others that are nourished by wood and stones: but as long as we want ideas of those real constitutions of different sorts of animals whereon these and the like qualities and powers depend, we must not hope to reach certainty in universal propositions concerning them. Those few ideas only which have a discernible connexion with our nominal essence, or any part of it, can afford us such propositions. But these are so few, and of so little moment, that we may justly look on our certain general knowledge of substances as almost none at all.

16. Wherein lies the general Certainty of Propositions.

To conclude: general propositions, of what kind soever, are then only capable of certainty, when the terms used in them stand for such ideas, whose agreement or disagreement, as there expressed, is capable to be discovered by us. And we are then certain of their truth or falsehood, when we perceive the ideas the terms stand for to agree or not agree, according as they are affirmed or denied one of another. Whence we may take notice, that general certainty is never to be found but in our ideas. Whenever we go to seek it elsewhere, in experiment or observations without us, our knowledge goes not beyond particulars. It is the contemplation of our own abstract ideas that alone is able to afford us general knowledge.

CHAPTER VII. OF MAXIMS

1. Maxims or Axioms are Self-evident Propositions.
THERE are a sort of propositions, which, under the name of MAXIMS and AXIOMS, have passed for principles of science: and because they are SELF-EVIDENT, have been supposed innate, without that anybody (that I know) ever went about to show the reason and foundation of their clearness or cogency. It may, however, be worth while to inquire into the reason of their evidence, and see whether it be peculiar to them alone; and also to examine how far they influence and govern our other knowledge.
2. Where in that Self-evidence consists.
Knowledge, as has been shown, consists in the perception of the agreement or disagreement of ideas. Now, where that agreement or disagreement is perceived immediately by itself, without the intervention or help of any other, there our knowledge is self-evident. This will appear to be so to any who will but consider any of those propositions which, without any proof, he assents to at first sight: for in all of them he will find that the reason of his assent is from that agreement or disagreement which the mind, by an immediate comparing them, finds in those ideas answering the affirmation or negation in the proposition.
3. Self evidence not peculiar to received Axioms.
This being so, in the next place, let us consider whether this self-evidence be peculiar only to those propositions which commonly pass under the name of maxims, and have the dignity of axioms allowed them. And here it is plain, that several other truths, not allowed to be axioms, partake equally with them in this self-evidence. This we shall see, if we go over these several sorts of agreement or disagreement of ideas which I have above mentioned, viz. identity, relation, co-existence, and real existence; which will discover to us, that not only those few propositions which have had the credit of maxims are self-evident, but a great many, even almost an infinite number of other propositions are such.
4. As to Identity and Diversity all Propositions are equally self-evident.
I. For, FIRST, The immediate perception of the agreement or disagreement of IDENTITY being founded in the mind's having distinct ideas, this affords us as many self-evident propositions as we have distinct ideas. Every one that has any knowledge at all, has, as the foundation of it, various and distinct ideas: and it is the first act of the mind (without which it can never be capable of any knowledge) to know every one of its ideas by itself, and distinguish it from others. Every one finds in himself, that he

knows the ideas he has; that he knows also, when any one is in his understanding, and what it is; and that when more than one are there, he knows them distinctly and unconfusedly one from another; which always being so, (it being impossible but that he should perceive what he perceives,) he can never be in doubt when any idea is in his mind, that it is there, and is that idea it is; and that two distinct ideas, when they are in his mind, are there, and are not one and the same idea. So that all such affirmations and negations are made without any possibility of doubt, uncertainty, or hesitation, and must necessarily be assented to as soon as understood; that is, as soon as we have in our minds [determined ideas,] which the terms in the proposition stand for. [And, therefore, whenever the mind with attention considers any proposition, so as to perceive the two ideas signified by the terms, and affirmed or denied one of the other to be the same or different; it is presently and infallibly certain of the truth of such a proposition; and this equally whether these propositions be in terms standing for more general ideas, or such as are less so: v.g. whether the general idea of Being be affirmed of itself, as in this proposition, 'whatsoever is, is'; or a more particular idea be affirmed of itself, as 'a man is a man'; or, 'whatsoever is white is white'; or whether the idea of being in general be denied of not-Being, which is the only (if I may so call it) idea different from it, as in this other proposition, 'it is impossible for the same thing to be and not to be': or any idea of any particular being be denied of another different from it, as 'a man is not a horse'; 'red is not blue.' The difference of the ideas, as soon as the terms are understood, makes the truth of the proposition presently visible, and that with an equal certainty and easiness in the less as well as the more general propositions; and all for the same reason, viz. because the mind perceives, in any ideas that it has, the same idea to be the same with itself; and two different ideas to be different, and not the same; and this it is equally certain of, whether these ideas be more or less general, abstract, and comprehensive.] It is not, therefore, alone to these two general propositions—'whatsoever is, is'; and 'it is impossible for the same thing to be and not to be'—that this sort of self-evidence belongs by any peculiar right. The perception of being, or not being, belongs no more to these vague ideas, signified by the terms WHATSOEVER, and THING, than it does to any other ideas. [These two general maxims, amounting to no more, in short, but this, that THE SAME IS THE SAME, and THE SAME IS NOT DIFFERENT, are truths known in more particular instances, as well as in those general maxims; and known also in particular instances, before these general maxims are ever thought on; and draw all their force from the discernment of the mind employed about particular ideas. There is nothing more visible than that] the mind, without the help of any proof, [or reflection on either of these general propositions,] perceives so clearly, and knows so certainly, that the idea of white is the idea of white, and not the idea of blue; and that the idea of white, when it is in the mind, is there, and is not absent; [that the consideration of these axioms can add nothing to the evidence or certainty of its knowledge.] [Just so it is (as every one may experiment in himself) in all the ideas a man has in his mind: he knows each to be itself, and not to be another; and to be in his mind, and not away when it is there, with a certainty that cannot be greater; and, therefore, the truth of no general proposition can be known with a greater certainty, nor add anything to this.] So that, in respect of identity, our intuitive knowledge reaches as far as our ideas. And we are capable of making as many self-evident propositions, as we have names for distinct ideas. And I appeal to every one's own mind, whether this proposition, 'a circle is a circle,' be not as self-evident a proposition as that consisting of more general terms, 'whatsoever is, is'; and again, whether this proposition, 'blue is not red,' be not a proposition that the mind can no more doubt of, as soon as it understands the words, than it does of that axiom, 'it is impossible for the same thing to be and not to be?' And so of all the like.

5. In Co-existance we have few self-evident Propositions.

II. SECONDLY, as to CO-EXISTANCE, or such a necessary connexion between two ideas that, in the subject where one of them is supposed, there the other must necessarily be also: of such agreement or disagreement as this, the mind has an immediate perception but in very few of them. And therefore in this sort we have but very little intuitive knowledge: nor are there to be found very many propositions that are self-evident, though some there are: v.g. the idea of filling a place equal to the contents of its superficies, being annexed to our idea of body, I think it is a self-evident proposition, that two bodies cannot be in the same place.

6. III. In other Relations we may have many.

THIRDLY, As to the RELATIONS OF MODES, mathematicians have framed many axioms concerning that one relation of equality. As, 'equals taken from equals, the remainder will be equal'; which, with the rest of that kind, however they are received for maxims by the mathematicians, and are unquestionable truths, yet, I think, that any one who considers them will not find that they have a clearer self-evidence than these,—that 'one and one are equal to two', that 'if you take from the five fingers of one hand two, and from the five fingers of the other hand two, the remaining numbers will be equal.' These and a thousand other such propositions may be found in numbers, which, at the very first hearing, force the assent, and carry with them an equal if not greater clearness, than those mathematical axioms.

7. IV. Concerning real Existence, we have none.

FOURTHLY, as to REAL EXISTANCE, since that has no connexion with any other of our ideas, but that of ourselves, and of a First Being, we have in that, concerning the real existence of all other beings, not so much as demonstrative, much less a self-evident knowledge: and, therefore, concerning those, there are no maxims.

8. These Axioms do not much influence our other Knowledge.

In the next place let us consider, what influence these received maxims have upon the other parts of our knowledge. The rules established in the schools, that all reasonings are EX PRAECOGNITIS ET PRAECONCESSIS, seem to lay the foundation of all other knowledge in these maxims, and to suppose them to be PRAECOGNITA. Whereby, I think, are meant these two things: first, that these axioms are those truths that are first known to the mind; and, secondly, that upon them the other parts of our knowledge depend.

9. Because Maxims or Axioms are not the Truths we first knew.

FIRST, That they are not the truths first known to the mind is evident to experience, as we have shown in another place. (Book I. chap, 1.) Who perceives not that a child certainly knows that a stranger is not its mother; that its sucking-bottle is not the rod, long before he knows that 'it is impossible for the same thing to be and not to be?' And how many truths are there about numbers, which it is obvious to observe that the mind is perfectly acquainted with, and fully convinced of, before it ever thought on these general maxims, to which mathematicians, in their arguings, do sometimes refer them? Whereof the reason is very plain: for that which makes the mind assent to such propositions, being nothing else but the perception it has of the agreement or disagreement of its ideas, according as it finds them affirmed or denied one of another in words it understands; and every idea being known to be what it is, and every two distinct ideas being known not to be the same; it must necessarily follow that such self-evident truths must be first known which consist of ideas that are first in the mind. And the ideas first in the mind, it is evident, are those of particular things, from whence by slow degrees, the understanding proceeds to some few general ones; which being taken from the ordinary and familiar objects of sense, are settled in the mind, with general names to them. Thus PARTICULAR IDEAS are first received and distinguished, and so knowledge got about them; and next to them, the less general or specific, which are next to particular. For abstract ideas are not so obvious or easy to children, or the yet unexercised mind, as particular ones. If they seem so to grown men, it is only because by constant and familiar use they are made so. For, when we nicely reflect upon them, we shall find that GENERAL IDEAS are fictions and contrivances of the mind, that carry difficulty with them and do not so easily offer themselves as we are apt to imagine. For example, does it not require some pains and skill to form the general idea of a triangle,(which is yet none of the more abstract, comprehensive, and difficult,) for it must be neither oblique nor rectangle, neither equilateral, equicrural, nor scalinon; but all and none of these at once. In effect, it is something imperfect, that cannot exist; an idea wherein some part of several different and inconsistant ideas are put together. It is true, the mind, in this imperfect state, has need of such ideas, and makes all the haste to them it can, for the conveniency of communication and enlargement of knowledge; to both which it is naturally very much inclined. But yet one has reason to suspect such ideas are marks of our imperfection; at least, this is enough to show that the most abstract and general ideas are not those that the mind is first and most easily acquainted with, nor such as its earliest knowledge is conversant about.

10. Because on perception of them the other Parts of our Knowledge do not depend.

Secondly, from what has been said it plainly follows, that these magnified maxims are not the principles and foundations of all our other knowledge. For if there be a great many other truths, which have as much self-evidence as they, and a great many that we know before them, it is impossible they should be the principles from which we deduce all other truths. Is it impossible to know that one and two are equal to three, but by virtue of this, or some such axiom, viz. 'the whole is equal to all its parts taken together?' Many a one knows that one and two are equal to three, without having heard, or thought on, that or any other axiom by which it might be proved; and knows it as certainly as any other man knows, that 'the whole is equal to all its parts,' or any other maxim; and all from the same reason of self-evidence: the equality of those ideas being as visible and certain to him without that or any other axiom as with it, it needing no proof to make it perceived. Nor after the knowledge, that the whole is equal to all its parts, does he know that one and two are equal to three, better or more certainly than he did before. For if there be any odds in those ideas, the whole and parts are more obscure, or at least more difficult to be settled in the mind than those of one, two, and three. And indeed, I think, I may ask these men, who will needs have all knowledge, besides those general principles themselves, to depend on general, innate, and self-evident principles. What principle is requisite to prove that one and one are two, that two and two are four, that three times two are six? Which being known without any proof, do evince, That either all knowledge does not depend on certain PRAECOGNITA or general maxims, called principles; or else that these are principles: and if these are to be counted principles, a great part of numeration will be so. To which, if we add all the self-evident propositions which may be made about all our distinct ideas, principles will be almost infinite, at least innumerable, which men arrive to the knowledge of, at different ages; and a great many of these innate principles they never come to know all their lives. But whether they come in view of the mind earlier or later, this is true of them, that they are all known by their native evidence; are wholly independent; receive no light, nor are capable of any proof one from another; much less the more particular from the more general, or the more simple from the more compounded; the more simple and less abstract being the most familiar, and the easier and earlier apprehended. But whichever be the clearest ideas, the evidence and certainty of all such propositions is in this, That a man sees the same idea to be the same idea, and infallibly perceives two different ideas to be different ideas. For when a man has in his understanding the ideas of one and of two, the idea of yellow, and the idea of blue, he cannot but certainly know that the idea of one is the idea of one, and not the idea of two; and that the idea of yellow is the idea of yellow, and not the idea of blue. For a man cannot confound the ideas in his mind, which he has distinct: that would be to have them confused and distinct at the same time, which is a contradiction: and to have none distinct, is to have no use of our faculties, to have no knowledge at all. And, therefore, what idea soever is affirmed of itself, or whatsoever two entire distinct ideas are denied one of another, the mind cannot but assent to such a proposition as infallibly true, as soon as it understands the terms, without hesitation or need of proof, or regarding those made in more general terms and called maxims.

11. What use these general Maxims or Axioms have.

[What shall we then say? Are these general maxims of no use? By no means; though perhaps their use is not that which it is commonly taken to be. But, since doubting in the least of what hath been by some men ascribed to these maxims may be apt to be cried out against, as overturning the foundations of all the sciences; it may be worth while to consider them with respect to other parts of our knowledge, and examine more particularly to what purposes they serve, and to what not.

{Of no use to prove less general propositions, nor as foundations on consideration of which any science has been built.}

(1) It is evident from what has been already said, that they are of no use to prove or confirm less general self-evident propositions. (2) It is as plain that they are not, nor have been the foundations whereon any science hath been built. There is, I know, a great deal of talk, propagated from scholastic men, of sciences and the maxims on which they are built: but it has been my ill-luck never to meet with any such sciences; much less any one built upon these two maxims, WHAT IS, IS; and IT IS IMPOSSIBLE FOR THE SAME THING TO BE AND NOT TO BE. And I would be glad to be shown where any such science, erected upon these or any other general axioms is to be found: and should be obliged to any one who would lay before me the frame and system of any science so built on these or any such like maxims, that could not be shown to stand as firm without any consideration of them. I ask, Whether these general maxims have not the same use in the study of divinity, and in theological questions, that they have in other sciences? They serve here, too, to silence wranglers, and put an end to dispute. But I think that nobody will therefore say, that the Christian religion is built upon these maxims, or that the knowledge we have of it is derived from these principles. It is from revelation we have received it, and without revelation these maxims had never been able to help us to it. When we find out an idea by whose intervention we discover the connexion of two others, this is a revelation from God to us by the voice of reason: for we then come to know a truth that we did not know before. When God declares any truth to us, this is a revelation to us by the voice of his Spirit, and we are advanced in our knowledge. But in neither of these do we receive our light or knowledge from maxims. But in the one, the things themselves afford it: and we see the truth in them by perceiving their agreement or disagreement. In the other, God himself affords it immediately to us: and we see the truth of what he says in his unerring veracity.

(3) Nor as helps in the discovery of yet unknown truths.

They are not of use to help men forward in the advancement of sciences, or new discoveries of yet unknown truths. Mr. Newton, in his never enough to be admired book, has demonstrated several propositions, which are so many new truths, before unknown to the world, and are further advances in mathematical knowledge: but, for the discovery of these, it was not the general maxims, 'what is, is;' or, 'the whole is bigger than a part,' or the like, that helped him. These were not the clues that led him into the discovery of the truth and certainty of those propositions. Nor was it by them that he got the knowledge of those demonstrations, but by finding out intermediate ideas that showed the agreement or disagreement of the ideas, as expressed in the propositions he demonstrated. This is the greatest exercise and improvement of human understanding in the enlarging of knowledge, and advancing the sciences; wherein they are far enough from receiving any help from the contemplation of these or the like magnified maxims. Would those who have this traditional admiration of these propositions, that they think no step can be made in knowledge without the support of an axiom, no stone laid in the building of the sciences without a general maxim, but distinguish between the method of acquiring knowledge, and of communicating it; between the method of raising any science, and that of teaching it to others, as far as it is advanced—they would see that those general maxims were not the foundations on which the first discoverers raised their admirable structures, nor the keys that unlocked and opened those secrets of knowledge. Though afterwards, when schools were erected, and sciences had their professors to teach what others had found out, they often made use of maxims, i.e. laid down certain propositions which were self-evident, or to be received for true; which being settled in the minds of their scholars as unquestionable verities, they on occasion made use of, to convince them of truths in particular instances, that were not so familiar to their minds as those general axioms which had before been inculcated to them, and carefully settled in their minds. Though these particular instances, when well reflected on, are no less self-evident to the understanding than the general maxims brought to confirm them: and it was in those particular instances that the first discoverer found the truth, without the help of the general maxims: and so may any one else do, who with attention considers them.

{Maxims of use in the exposition of what has been discovered, and in silencing obstinate wranglers.}

To come, therefore, to the use that is made of maxims. (1) They are of use, as has been observed, in the ordinary methods of teaching sciences as far as they are advanced: but of little or none in advancing them further. (2) They are of use in disputes, for the silencing of obstinate wranglers, and bringing those contests to some conclusion. Whether a need of them to that end came not in the manner following, I crave leave to inquire. The Schools having made disputation the touchstone of men's abilities, and the criterion of knowledge, adjudged victory to him that kept the field: and he that had the last word was concluded to have the better of the argument, if not of the cause. But because by this means there was like to be no decision between skilful combatants, whilst one never failed of a MEDIUS TERMINUS to prove any proposition; and the other could as constantly, without or with a distinction, deny the major or minor; to prevent, as much as could be, running out of disputes into an endless train of syllogisms, certain general propositions—most of them, indeed, self-evident—were introduced into the Schools: which being such as all men allowed and agreed in, were looked on as general measures of truth, and served instead of principles (where the disputants had not lain down any other between them) beyond which there was no going, and which must not be receded from by either side. And thus these maxims, getting the name of principles, beyond which men in dispute could not retreat, were by mistake taken to be the originals and sources from whence all knowledge began, and the foundations whereon the sciences were built. Because when in their disputes they came to any of these, they stopped there, and went no further; the matter was determined. But how much this is a mistake, hath been already shown.

{How Maxims came to be so much in vogue.}

This method of the Schools, which have been thought the fountains of knowledge, introduced, as I suppose, the like use of these maxims into a great part of conversation out of the Schools, to stop the mouths of cavillers, whom any one is excused from arguing any longer with, when they deny these general self-evident principles received by all reasonable men who have once thought of them: but yet their use herein is but to put an end to wrangling. They in truth, when urged in such cases, teach nothing: that is already done by the intermediate ideas made use of in the debate, whose connexion may be seen without the help of those maxims, and so the truth known before the maxim is produced, and the argument brought to a first principle. Men would give off a wrong argument before it came to that, if in their disputes they proposed to themselves the finding and embracing of truth, and not a contest for victory. And thus maxims have their use to put a stop to their perverseness, whose ingenuity should have yielded sooner. But the method of the Schools having allowed and encouraged men to oppose and resist evident truth till they are baffled, i.e. till they are reduced to contradict themselves, or some established principles: it is no wonder that they should not in civil conversation be ashamed of that which in the Schools is counted a virtue and a glory, viz. obstinately to maintain that side of the question they have chosen, whether true or false, to the last extremity; even after conviction. A strange way to attain truth and knowledge: and that which I think the rational part of mankind, not corrupted by education, could scare believe should ever be admitted amongst the lovers of truth, and students of religion or nature, or introduced into the seminaries of those who are to propegate the truths of religion or philosophy amongst the ignorant and unconvinced. How much such a way of learning is like to turn young men's minds from the sincere search and love of truth; nay, and to make them doubt whether there is any such thing, or, at least, worth the adhering to, I shall not now inquire. This I think, that, bating those places, which brought the Peripatetic Philosophy into their schools, where it continued many ages, without teaching the world anything but the art of wrangling, these maxims were nowhere thought the foundations on which the sciences were built, nor the great helps to the advancement of knowledge.]

{Of great use to stop wranglers in disputes, but of little use to the discovery of truths.}

As to these general maxims, therefore, they are, as I have said, of great use in disputes, to stop the mouths of wranglers; but not of much use to the discovery of unknown truths, or to help the mind forwards in its search after knowledge. For who ever began to build his knowledge on this general proposition, WHAT IS, IS; or, IT IS IMPOSSIBLE FOR THE SAME THING TO BE AND NOT TO BE: and from either of these, as from a principle of science, deduced a system of useful knowledge? Wrong opinions often involving contradictions, one of these maxims, as a touchstone, may serve well to show whither they lead. But yet, however fit to lay open the absurdity or mistake of a man's reasoning or opinion, they are of very little use for enlightening the understanding: and it will not be found that the mind receives much help from them in its progress in knowledge; which would be neither less, nor less certain, were these two general propositions never thought on. It is true, as I have said, they sometimes serve in argumentation to stop a wrangler's mouth, by showing the absurdity of what he saith, [and by exposing him to the shame of contradicting what all the world knows, and he himself cannot but own to be true.] But it is one thing to show a man that he is in an error, and another to put him in possession of truth, and I would fain know what truths these two propositions are able to teach, and by their influence make us know which we did not know before, or could not know without them. Let us reason from them as well as we can, they are only about identical predications, and influence, if any at all, none but such. Each particular proposition concerning identity or diversity is as clearly and certainly known in itself, if attended to, as either of these general ones: [only these general ones, as serving in all cases, are therefore more inculcated and insisted on.] As to other less general maxims, many of them are no more than bare verbal propositions, and teach us nothing but the respect and import of names one to another. 'The whole is equal to all its parts:' what real truth, I beseech you, does it teach us? What more is contained in that maxim, than what the signification of the word TOTUM, or the WHOLE, does of itself import? And he that knows that the WORD whole stands for what is made up of all its parts, knows very little less than that the whole is equal to all its parts. And, upon the same ground, I think that this proposition, 'A hill is higher than a valley', and several the like, may also pass for maxims. But yet [masters of mathematics, when they would, as teachers of what they know, initiate others in that science do not] without reason place this and some other such maxims [at the entrance of their systems]; that their scholars, having in the beginning perfectly acquainted their thoughts with these propositions, made in such general terms, may be used to make such reflections, and have these more general propositions, as formed rules and sayings, ready to apply to all particular cases. Not that if they be equally weighed, they are more clear and evident than the particular instances they are brought to confirm; but that, being more familiar to the mind, the very naming them is enough to satisfy the understanding. But this, I say, is more from our custom of using them, and the establishment they have got in our minds by our often thinking of them, than from the different evidence of the things. But before custom has settled methods of thinking and reasoning in our minds, I am apt to imagine it is quite otherwise; and that the child, when a part of his apple is taken away, knows it better in that particular instance, than by this general proposition, 'The whole is equal to all its parts;' and that, if one of these have need to be confirmed to him by the other, the general has more need to be let into his mind by the particular, than the particular by the general. For in *particulars* our knowledge begins, and so spreads itself, by degrees, to *generals* [Footnote: This is the order in time of the conscious acquistion of knowledge that is human. The *Essay* might be regarded as a commentary on this one sentence. Our intellectual progress is from particulars and involuntary recipiency, through reactive doubt and criticism, into what is at last reasoned faith.]. Though afterwards the mind takes the quite contrary course, and having drawn its knowledge into as general propositions as it can, makes those familiar to its thoughts, and accustoms itself to have recourse to them, as to the standards of truth and falsehood. [Footnote: This is the philosophic attitude. Therein one consciously apprehends the intellectual necessities that were UNCONCIOUSLY PRESUPPOSED, its previous intellectual progress. In philosophy we 'draw our knowledge into as general propositions as it can' be made to assume, and thus either learn to see it as an organic while in a speculative unity, or learn that it cannot be so seen in a finite intelligence, and that even at the last it must remain 'broken' and mysterious in the human understanding.] By which familiar use of them, as rules to measure the truth of other propositions, it comes in time to be thought, that more particular propositions have their truth and evidence from their conformity to these more general ones, which, in discourse and argumentation, are so frequently urged, and constantly admitted. And this I think to be the reason why, amongst so many self-evident propositions, the MOST GENERAL ONLY have had the title of MAXIMS.

12. Maxims, if care be not taken in the Use of Words, may prove Contradictions.

One thing further, I think, it may not be amiss to observe concerning these general maxims, That they are so far from improving or establishing our minds in true knowledge that if our notions be wrong, loose, or unsteady, and we resign up our thoughts to the sound of words, rather than [fix them on settled, determined] ideas of things; I say these general maxims will serve to confirm us in mistakes; and in such a way of use of words, which is most common, will serve to prove contradictions: v.g. he that with Descartes shall frame in his mind an idea of what he calls body to be nothing but extension, may easily demonstrate that there is no vacuum, i.e. no space void of body, by this maxim, WHAT IS, IS. For the idea to which he annexes the name body, being bare extension, his knowledge that space cannot be without body, is certain. For he knows his own idea of extension clearly and distinctly, and knows that it is what it is, and not another idea, though it be called by these three names,—extension, body, space. Which three words, standing for one and the same idea, may, no doubt, with the same evidence and certainty be affirmed one of another, as each of itself: and it is as certain, that, whilst I use them all to stand for one and the same idea, this predication is as true and identical in its signification, that 'space is body,' as this predication is true and identical, that 'body is body,' both in signification and sound.

13. Instance in Vacuum.

But if another should come and make to himself another idea, different from Descartes's, of the thing, which yet with Descartes he calls by the same name body, and make his idea, which he expresses by the word body, to be of a thing that hath both extension and solidity together; he will as easily demonstrate, that there may be a vacuum or space without a body, as Descartes demonstrated the contrary. Because the idea to which he gives the name space being barely the simple one of extension, and the idea to which he gives the name body being the complex idea of extension and resistibility or solidity, together in the same subject, these two ideas are not exactly one and the same, but in the understanding as distinct as the ideas of one and two, white and black, or as of CORPOREITY and HUMANITY, if I may use those barbarous terms: and therefore the predication of them in our minds, or in words standing for them, is not identical, but the negation of them one of another; [viz. this proposition: 'Extension or space is not body,' is] as true and evidently certain as this maxim, IT IS IMPOSSIBLE FOR THE SAME THING TO BE AND NOT TO BE, [can make any proposition.]

14. But they prove not the Existance of things without us.

But yet, though both these propositions (as you see) may be equally demonstrated, viz. that there may be a vacuum, and that there cannot be a vacuum, by these two certain principles, viz. WHAT IS, IS, and THE SAME THING CANNOT BE AND NOT BE: yet neither of these principles will serve to prove to us, that any, or what bodies do exist: for that we are left to our senses to discover to us as far as they can. Those universal and self-evident principles being only our constant, clear, and distinct knowledge of our own ideas, more general or comprehensive, can assure us of nothing that passes without the mind: their certainty is founded only upon the knowledge we have of each idea by itself, and of its distinction from others, about which we cannot be mistaken whilst they are in our minds; though we may be and often are mistaken when we retain the names without the ideas; or use them confusedly, sometimes for one and sometimes for another idea. In which cases the force of these axioms, reaching only to the sound, and not the signification of the words, serves only to lead us into confusion, mistake, and error. [It is to show men that these maxims, however cried up for the great guards of truth, will not secure them from error in a careless loose use of their words, that I have made this remark. In all that is here suggested concerning their little use for the improvement of knowledge, or dangerous use in undetermined ideas, I have been far enough from saying or intending they should be laid aside; as some have been too forward to charge me. I affirm them to be truths, self-evident truths; and so cannot be laid aside. As far as their influence will reach, it is in vain to endeavour, nor will I attempt, to abridge it. But yet, without any injury to truth or knowledge, I may have reason to think their use is not answerable to the great stress which seems to be laid on them; and I may warn men not to make an ill use of them, for the confirming themselves in errors.]

15. They cannot add to our knowledge of Substances, and their Application to complex Ideas is dangerous.

But let them be of what use they will in verbal propositions, they cannot discover or prove to us the least knowledge of the nature of substances, as they are found and exist without us, any further than grounded on experience. And though the consequence of these two propositions, called principles, be very clear, and their use not dangerous or hurtful, in the probation of such things wherein there is no need at all of them for proof, but such as are clear by themselves without them, viz. where our ideas are [determined] and known by the names that stand for them: yet when these principles, viz. WHAT IS, IS, and IT IS IMPOSSIBLE FOR THE SAME THING TO BE AND NOT TO BE, are made use of in the probation of propositions wherein are words standing for complex ideas, v.g. man, horse, gold, virtue; there they are of infinite danger, and most commonly make men receive and retain falsehood for manifest truth, and uncertainty for demonstration: upon which follow error, obstinacy, and all the mischiefs that can happen from wrong reasoning. The reason whereof is not, that these principles are less true [or of less force] in proving propositions made of terms standing for complex ideas, than where the propositions are about simple ideas. [But because men mistake generally,—thinking that where the same terms are preserved, the propositions are about the same things, though the ideas they stand for are in truth different, therefore these maxims are made use of to support those which in sound and appearance are contradictory propositions; and is clear in the demonstrations above mentioned about a vacuum. So that whilst men take words for things, as usually they do, these maxims may and do commonly serve to prove contradictory propositions; as shall yet be further made manifest]

16. Instance in demonstrations about Man which can only be verbal.

For instance: let MAN be that concerning which you would by these first principles demonstrate anything, and we shall see, that so far as demonstration is by these principles, it is only verbal, and gives us no certain, universal, true proposition, or knowledge, of any being existing without us. First, a child having framed the idea of a man, it is probable that his idea is just like that picture which the painter makes of the visible appearances joined together; and such a complication of ideas together in his understanding makes up the single complex idea which he calls man, whereof white or flesh-colour in England being one, the child can demonstrate to you that a negro is not a man, because white colour was one of the constant simple ideas of the complex idea he calls man; and therefore he can demonstrate, by the principle, IT IS IMPOSSIBLE FOR THE SAME THING TO BE AND NOT TO BE, that a negro is NOT a man; the foundation of his certainty being not that universal proposition, which perhaps he never heard nor thought of, but the clear, distinct perception he hath of his own simple ideas of black and white, which he cannot be persuaded to take, nor can ever mistake one for another, whether he knows that maxim or no. And to this child, or any one who hath such an idea, which he calls man, can you never demonstrate that a man hath a soul, because his idea of man includes no such notion or idea in it. And therefore, to him, the principle of WHAT IS, IS, proves not this matter; but it depends upon collection and observation, by which he is to make his complex idea called man.

17. Another instance.

Secondly, Another that hath gone further in framing and collecting the idea he calls MAN, and to the outward shape adds laughter and rational discourse, may demonstrate that infants and changelings are no men, by this maxim, IT IS IMPOSSIBLE FOR THE SAME THING TO BE AND NOT TO BE; and I have discoursed with very rational men, who have actually denied that they are men.

18. A third instance.

Thirdly, Perhaps another makes up the complex idea which he calls MAN, only out of the ideas of body in general, and the powers of language and reason, and leaves out the shape wholly: this man is able to demonstrate that a man may have no hands, but be QUADRUPES, neither of those being included in his idea of man: and in whatever body or shape he found speech and reason joined, that was a man; because, having a clear knowledge of such a complex idea, it is certain that WHAT IS, IS.

19. Little use of these Maxims in Proofs where we have clear and distinct Ideas.

So that, if rightly considered, I think we may say, That where our ideas are determined in our minds, and have annexed to them by us known and steady names under those settled determinations, there is little need, or no use at all of these maxims, to prove the agreement or disagreement of any of them. He that cannot discern the truth or falsehood of such propositions, without the help of these and the like maxims, will not be helped by these maxims to do it: since he cannot be supposed to know the truth of these maxims themselves without proof, if he cannot know the truth of others without proof, which are as self-evident as these. Upon this ground it is that intuitive knowledge neither requires nor admits any proof, one part of it more than another. He that will suppose it does, takes away the foundation of all knowledge and certainty; and he that needs any proof to make him certain, and give his assent to this proposition, that two are equal to two, will also have need of a proof to make him admit, that what is, is. He that needs a probation to convince him that two are not three, that white is not black, that a triangle is not a circle, &c., or any other two [determined] distinct ideas are not one and the same, will need also a demonstration to convince him that IT IS IMPOSSIBLE FOR THE SAME THING TO BE AND NOT TO BE.

20. Their Use dangerous where our Ideas are not determined

And as these maxims are of little use where we have determined ideas, so they are, as I have showed, of dangerous use where [our ideas are not determined; and where] we use words that are not annexed to determined ideas, but such as are of a loose and wandering signification, sometimes standing for one, and sometimes for another idea: from which follow mistake and error, which these maxims (brought as proofs to establish propositions, wherein the terms stand for undetermined ideas) do by their authority confirm and rivet.

CHAPTER VIII. OF TRIFLING PROPOSITIONS.

1. Some Propositions bring no Increase to our Knowledge.
WHETHER the maxims treated of in the foregoing chapter be of that use to real knowledge as is generally supposed, I leave to be considered. This, I think, may confidently be affirmed, That there ARE universal propositions, which, though they be certainly true, yet they add no light to our understanding; bring no increase to our knowledge. Such are—
2. As, First, identical Propositions.
First, All purely IDENTICAL PROPOSITIONS. These obviously and at first blush appear to contain no instruction in them; for when we affirm the said term of itself, whether it be barely verbal, or whether it contains any clear and real idea, it shows us nothing but what we must certainly know before, whether such a proposition be either made by, or proposed to us. Indeed, that most general one, WHAT IS, IS, may serve sometimes to show a man the absurdity he is guilty of, when, by circumlocution or equivocal terms, he would in particular instances deny the same thing of itself; because nobody will so openly bid defiance to common sense, as to affirm visible and direct contradictions in plain words; or, if he does, a man is excused if he breaks off any further discourse with him. But yet I think I may say, that neither that received maxim, nor any other identical proposition, teaches us anything; and though in such kind of propositions this great and magnified maxim, boasted to be the foundation of demonstration, may be and often is made use of to confirm them, yet all it proves amounts to no more than this, That the same word may with great certainty be affirmed of itself, without any doubt of the truth of any such proposition; and let me add, also, without any real knowledge.
3. Examples.
For, at this rate, any very ignorant person, who can but make a proposition, and knows what he means when he says ay or no, may make a million of propositions of whose truth he may be infallibly certain, and yet not know one thing in the world thereby; v.g. 'what is a soul, is a soul;' or, 'a soul is a soul;' 'a spirit is a spirit;' 'a fetiche is a fetiche,' &c. These all being equivalent to this proposition, viz. WHAT IS, IS; i.e. what hath existence, hath existence; or, who hath a soul, hath a soul. What is this more than trifling with words? It is but like a monkey shifting his oyster from one hand to the other: and had he but words, might no doubt have said, 'Oyster in right hand is subject, and oyster in left hand is predicate:' and so might have made a self-evident proposition of oyster, i.e. oyster is oyster; and

yet, with all this, not have been one whit the wiser or more knowing: and that way of handling the matter would much at one have satisfied the monkey's hunger, or a man's understanding, and they would have improved in knowledge and bulk together.

4. Secondly, Propositions in which a part of any complex Idea is predicated of the Whole.

II. Another sort of trifling propositions is, WHEN A PART OF THE COMPLEX IDEA IS PREDICATED OF THE NAME OF THE WHOLE; a part of the definition of the word defined. Such are all propositions wherein the genus is predicated of the species, or more comprehensive of less comprehensive terms. For what information, what knowledge, carries this proposition in it, viz. 'Lead is a metal' to a man who knows the complex idea the name lead stands for? All the simple ideas that go to the complex one signified by the term metal, being nothing but what he before comprehended and signified by the name lead. Indeed, to a man that knows the signification of the word metal, and not of the word lead, it is a shorter way to explain the signification of the word lead, by saying it is a metal, which at once expresses several of its simple ideas, than to enumerate them one by one, telling him it is a body very heavy, fusible, and malleable.

5. As part of the Definition of the Term Defined.

Alike trifling it is to predicate any other part of the definition of the term defined, or to affirm anyone of the simple ideas of a complex one of the name of the whole complex idea; as, 'All gold is fusible.' For fusibility being one of the simple ideas that goes to the making up the complex one the sound gold stands for, what can it be but playing with sounds, to affirm that of the name gold, which is comprehended in its received signification? It would be thought little better than ridiculous to affirm gravely, as a truth of moment, that gold is yellow; and I see not how it is any jot more material to say it is fusible, unless that quality be left out of the complex idea, of which the sound gold is the mark in ordinary speech. What instruction can it carry with it, to tell one that which he hath been told already, or he is supposed to know before? For I am supposed to know the signification of the word another uses to me, or else he is to tell me. And if I know that the name gold stands for this complex idea of body, yellow, heavy, fusible, malleable, it will not much instruct me to put it solemnly afterwards in a proposition, and gravely say, all gold is fusible. Such propositions can only serve to show the disingenuity of one who will go from the definition of his own terms, by reminding him sometimes of it; but carry no knowledge with them, but of the signification of words, however certain they be.

6. Instance, Man and Palfrey.

'Every man is an animal, or living body,' is as certain a proposition as can be; but no more conducing to the knowledge of things than to say, a palfrey is an ambling horse, or a neighing, ambling animal, both being only about the signification of words, and make me know but this—That body, sense, and motion, or power of sensation and moving, are three of those ideas that I always comprehend and signify by the word man: and where they are not to be found together, the NAME MAN belongs not to that thing: and so of the other—That body, sense, and a certain way of going, with a certain kind of voice, are some of those ideas which I always comprehend and signify by the WORD PALFREY; and when they are not to be found together, the name palfrey belongs not to that thing. It is just the same, and to the same purpose, when any term standing for any one or more of the simple ideas, that altogether make up that complex idea which is called man, is affirmed of the term man:—v.g. suppose a Roman signified by the word HOMO all these distinct ideas united in one subject, CORPORIETAS, SENSIBILITAS, POTENTIA SE MOVENDI, RATIONALITAS, RISIBILITAS; he might, no doubt, with great certainty, universally affirm one, more, or all of these together of the word HOMO, but did no more than say that the word HOMO, in his country, comprehended in its signification all these ideas. Much like a romance knight, who by the word PALFREY signified these ideas:—body of a certain figure, four-legged, with sense, motion, ambling, neighing, white, used to have a woman on his back—might with the same certainty universally affirm also any or all of these of the WORD palfrey: but did thereby teach no more, but that the word palfrey, in his or romance language, stood for all these, and was not to be applied to anything where any of these was wanting But he that shall tell me, that in whatever thing sense, motion, reason, and laughter, were united, that thing had actually a notion of God, or would be cast into a sleep by opium, made indeed an instructive proposition: because neither having the notion of God, nor being cast into sleep by opium, being contained in the idea signified by the word man, we are by such propositions taught something more than barely what the word MAN stands for: and therefore the knowledge contained in it is more than verbal.

7. For this teaches but the Signification of Words.

Before a man makes any proposition, he is supposed to understand the terms he uses in it, or else he talks like a parrot, only making a noise by imitation, and framing certain sounds, which he has learnt of others; but not as a rational creature, using them for signs of ideas which he has in his mind. The hearer also is supposed to understand the terms as the speaker uses them, or else he talks jargon, and makes an unintelligible noise. And therefore he trifles with words who makes such a proposition, which, when it is made, contains no more than one of the terms does, and which a man was supposed to know before: v.g. a triangle hath three sides, or saffron is yellow. And this is no further tolerable than where a man goes to explain his terms to one who is supposed or declares himself not to understand him; and then it teaches only the signification of that word, and the use of that sign.

8. But adds no real Knowledge.

We can know then the truth of two sorts of propositions with perfect certainty. The one is, of those trifling propositions which have a certainty in them, but it is only a verbal certainty, but not instructive. And, secondly, we can know the truth, and so may be certain in propositions, which affirm something of another, which is a necessary consequence of its precise complex idea, but not contained in it: as that, the external angle of all triangles is bigger than either of the opposite internal angles. Which relation of the outward angle to either of the opposite internal angles, making no part of the complex idea signified by the name triangle, this is a real truth, and conveys with it instructive real knowledge.

9. General Propositions concerning Substances are often trifling.

We having little or no knowledge of what combinations there be of simple ideas existing together in substances, but by our senses, we cannot make any universal certain propositions concerning them, any further than our nominal essences lead us. Which being to a very few and inconsiderable truths, in respect of those which depend on their real constitutions, the general propositions that are made about substances, if they are certain, are for the most part but trifling; and if they are instructive, are uncertain, and such as we can have no knowledge of their real truth, how much soever constant observation and analogy may assist our judgment in guessing. Hence it comes to pass, that one may often meet with very clear and coherent discourses, that amount yet to nothing. For it is plain that names of substantial beings, as well as others, as far as they have relative significations affixed to them, may, with great truth, be joined negatively and affirmatively in propositions, as their relative definitions make them fit to be so joined; and propositions consisting of such terms, may, with the same clearness, be deduced one from another, as those that convey the most real truths: and all this without any knowledge of the nature or reality of things existing without us. By this method one may make demonstrations and undoubted propositions in words, and yet thereby advance not one jot in the knowledge of the truth of things: v. g. he that having learnt these following words, with their ordinary mutual relative acceptations annexed to them; v. g. SUBSTANCE, MAN, ANIMAL, FORM, SOUL, VEGETATIVE, SENSITIVE, RATIONAL, may make several undoubted propositions about the soul, without knowing at all what the soul really is: and of this sort, a man may find an infinite number of propositions, reasonings, and conclusions, in books of metaphysics, school-divinity, and some sort of natural philosophy; and, after all, know as little of God, spirits, or bodies, as he did before he set out.

10. And why.

He that hath liberty to define, i.e. to determine the signification of his names of substances (as certainly every one does in effect, who makes them stand for his own ideas), and makes their significations at a venture, taking them from his own or other men's fancies, and not from an examination or inquiry into the nature of things themselves; may with little trouble demonstrate them one of another, according to those several respects and mutual relations he has given them one to another; wherein, however things agree or disagree in their own nature, he needs mind nothing but his own notions, with the names he hath bestowed upon them: but thereby no more increases his own knowledge than he does his riches, who, taking a bag of counters, calls one in a certain place a pound, another in another place a shilling, and a third in a third place a penny; and so proceeding, may undoubtedly reckon right, and cast up a great sum, according to his counters so placed, and standing for more or less as he pleases, without being one jot the richer, or without even knowing how much a pound, shilling, or penny is, but only that one is contained in the other twenty times, and contains the other twelve: which a man may also do in the signification of words, by making them, in respect of one another, more or less, or equally comprehensive.

11. Thirdly, using Words variously is trifling with them.

Though yet concerning most words used in discourses, equally argumentative and controversial, there is this more to be complained of, which is the worst sort of trifling, and which sets us yet further from the certainty of knowledge we hope to attain by them, or find in them; viz. that most writers are so far from instructing us in the nature and knowledge of things, that they use their words loosely and uncertainly, and do not, by using them constantly and steadily in the same significations make plain and clear deductions of words one from another, and make their discourses coherent and clear, (how little soever they were instructive); which were not difficult to do, did they not find it convenient to shelter their ignorance or obstinacy under the obscurity and perplexedness of their terms: to which, perhaps, inadvertency and ill custom do in many men much contribute.

12. Marks of verbal Propositions. First, Predication in Abstract.

To conclude. Barely verbal propositions may be known by these following marks:

First, All propositions wherein two abstract terms are affirmed one of another, are barely about the signification of sounds. For since no abstract idea can be the same with any other but itself, when its abstract name is affirmed of any other term, it can signify no more but this, that it may, or ought to be called by that name; or that these two names signify the same idea. Thus, should any one say that parsimony is frugality, that gratitude is justice, that this or that action is or is not temperate: however specious these and the like propositions may at first sight seem, yet when we come to press them, and examine nicely what they contain, we shall find that it all amounts to nothing but the signification of those terms.

13. Secondly, A part of the Definition predicated of any Term.

Secondly, All propositions wherein a part of the complex idea which any term stands for is predicated of that term, are only verbal: v.g. to say that gold is a metal, or heavy. And thus all propositions wherein more comprehensive words, called genera, are affirmed of subordinate or less comprehensive, called species, or individuals, are barely verbal.

When by these two rules we have examined the propositions that make up the discourses we ordinarily meet with, both in and out of books, we shall perhaps find that a greater part of them than is usually suspected are purely about the signification of words, and contain nothing in them but the use and application of these signs.

This I think I may lay down for an infallible rule, That, wherever the distinct idea any word stands for is not known and considered, and something not contained in the idea is not affirmed or denied of it, there our thoughts stick wholly in sounds, and are able to attain no real truth or falsehood. This, perhaps, if well heeded, might save us a great deal of useless amusement and dispute; and very much shorten our trouble and wandering in the search of real and true knowledge.

CHAPTER IX. OF OUR THREEFOLD KNOWLEDGE OF EXISTENCE.

1. General Propositions that are certain concern not Existence.
HITHERTO we have only considered the essences of things; which being only abstract ideas, and thereby removed in our thoughts from particular existence, (that being the proper operation of the mind, in abstraction, to consider an idea under no other existence but what it has in the understandings,) gives us no knowledge of real existence at all. Where, by the way, we may take notice, that universal propositions of whose truth or falsehood we can have certain knowledge concern not existence: and further, that all particular affirmations or negations that would not be certain if they were made general, are only concerning existence; they declaring only the accidental union or separation of ideas in things existing, which, in their abstract natures, have no known necessary union or repugnancy.

2. A threefold Knowledge of Existence.
But, leaving the nature of propositions, and different ways of predication to be considered more at large in another place, let us proceed now to inquire concerning our knowledge of the EXISTANCE OF THINGS, and how we come by it. I say, then, that we have the knowledge of OUR OWN existence by intuition; of the existence of GOD by demonstration; and of OTHER THINGS by sensation.

3. Our Knowledge of our own Existence is Intuitive.
As for OUR OWN EXISTENCE, we perceive it so plainly and so certainly, that it neither needs nor is capable of any proof for nothing can be more evident to us than our own existence. I think, I reason, I feel pleasure and pain: can any of these be more evident to me than my own existence? If I doubt of all other things, that very doubt makes me perceive my own existence, and will not suffer me to doubt of that. For if I know I feel pain, it is evident I have as certain perception of my own existence, as of the existence of the pain I feel: or if I know I doubt, I have as certain perception of the existence of the thing doubting, as of that thought which I CALL DOUBT. Experience then convinces us, that we have an INTUITIVE KNOWLEDGE of our own existence, and an internal infallible perception that we are. In every act of sensation, reasoning, or thinking, we are conscious to ourselves of our own being; and, in this matter, come not short of the highest degree of certainty.

CHAPTER X. OF OUR KNOWLEDGE OF THE EXISTENCE OF A GOD.

1. We are capable of knowing certainly that there is a God.
THOUGH God has given us no innate ideas of himself; though he has stamped no original characters on our minds, wherein we may read his being; yet having furnished us with those faculties our minds are endowed with, he hath not left himself without witness: since we have sense, perception, and reason, and cannot want a clear proof of him, as long as we carry OURSELVES about us. Nor can we justly complain of our ignorance in this great point; since he has so plentifully provided us with the means to discover and know him; so far as is necessary to the end of our being, and the great concernment of our happiness. But, though this be the most obvious truth that reason discovers, and though its evidence be (if I mistake not) equal to mathematical certainty: yet it requires thought and attention; and the mind must apply itself to a regular deduction of it from some part of our intuitive knowledge, or else we shall be as uncertain and ignorant of this as of other propositions, which are in themselves capable of clear demonstration. To show, therefore, that we are capable of KNOWING, i.e. BEING CERTAIN that there is a God, and HOW WE MAY COME BY this certainty, I think we need go no further than OURSELVES, and that undoubted knowledge we have of our own existence.
2. For Man knows that he himself exists.
I think it is beyond question, that man has a clear idea of his own being; he knows certainly he exists, and that he is something. He that can doubt whether he be anything or no, I speak not to; no more than I would argue with pure nothing, or endeavour to convince nonentity that it were something. If any one pretends to be so sceptical as to deny his own existence, (for really to doubt of it is manifestly impossible,) let him for me enjoy his beloved happiness of being nothing, until hunger or some other pain convince him of the contrary. This, then, I think I may take for a truth, which every one's certain knowledge assures him of, beyond the liberty of doubting, viz. that he is SOMETHING THAT ACTUALLY EXISTS.
3. He knows also that Nothing cannot produce a Being; therefore Something must have existed from Eternity.
In the next place, man knows, by an intuitive certainty, that bare NOTHING CAN NO MORE PRODUCE ANY REAL BEING, THAN IT

CAN BE EQUAL TO TWO RIGHT ANGLES. If a man knows not that nonentity, or the absence of all being, cannot be equal to two right angles, it is impossible he should know any demonstration in Euclid. If, therefore, we know there is some real being, and that nonentity cannot produce any real being, it is an evident demonstration, that FROM ETERNITY THERE HAS BEEN SOMETHING; since what was not from eternity had a beginning; and what had a beginning must be produced by something else.

4. And that eternal Being must be most powerful.

Next, it is evident, that what had its being and beginning from another, must also have all that which is in and belongs to its being from another too. All the powers it has must be owing to and received from the same source. This eternal source, then, of all being must also be the source and original of all power; and so THIS ETERNAL BEING MUST BE ALSO THE MOST POWERFUL.

5. And most knowing.

Again, a man finds in HIMSELF perception and knowledge. We have then got one step further; and we are certain now that there is not only some being, but some knowing, intelligent being in the world. There was a time, then, when there was no knowing being, and when knowledge began to be; or else there has been also A KNOWING BEING FROM ETERNITY. If it be said, there was a time when no being had any knowledge, when that eternal being was void of all understanding; I reply, that then it was impossible there should ever have been any knowledge: it being as impossible that things wholly void of knowledge, and operating blindly, and without any perception, should produce a knowing being, as it is impossible that a triangle should make itself three angles bigger than two right ones. For it is as repugnant to the idea of senseless matter, that it should put into itself sense, perception, and knowledge, as it is repugnant to the idea of a triangle, that it should put into itself greater angles than two right ones.

6. And therefore God.

Thus, from the consideration of ourselves, and what we infallibly find in our own constitutions, our reason leads us to the knowledge of this certain and evident truth,—THAT THERE IS AN ETERNAL, MOST POWERFUL, AND MOST KNOWING BEING; which whether any one will please to call God, it matters not. The thing is evident; and from this idea duly considered, will easily be deduced all those other attributes, which we ought to ascribe to this eternal Being. [If, nevertheless, any one should be found so senselessly arrogant, as to suppose man alone knowing and wise, but yet the product of mere ignorance and chance; and that all the rest of the universe acted only by that blind haphazard; I shall leave with him that very rational and emphatical rebuke of Tully (1. ii. De Leg.), to be considered at his leisure: 'What can be more sillily arrogant and misbecoming, than for a man to think that he has a mind and understanding in him, but yet in all the universe beside there is no such thing? Or that those things, which with the utmost stretch of his reason he can scarce comprehend, should be moved and managed without any reason at all?' QUID EST ENIM VERIUS, QUAM NEMINEM ESSE OPORTERE TAM STULTE AROGANTEM, UT IN SE MENTEM ET RATIONEM PUTET INESSE IN COELO MUNDOQUE NON PUTET? AUT EA QUOE VIZ SUMMA INGENII RATIONE COMPREHENDAT, NULLA RATIONE MOVERI PUTET?]

From what has been said, it is plain to me we have a more certain knowledge of the existence of a God, than of anything: our senses have not immediately discovered to us. Nay, I presume I may say, that we more certainly know that there is a God, than that there is anything else without us. When I say we KNOW, I mean there is such a knowledge within our reach which we cannot miss, if we will but apply our minds to that, as we do to several other inquiries.

7. Our idea of a most perfect Being, not the sole Proof of a God.

How far the IDEA of a most perfect being, which a man, may frame in his mind, does or does not prove the EXISTENCE of a God, I will not here examine. For in the different make of men's tempers and application of their thoughts, some arguments prevail more on one, and some on another, for the confirmation of the same truth. But yet, I think, this I may say, that it is an ill way of establishing this truth, and silencing atheists, to lay the whole stress of so important a point as this upon that sole foundation: and take some men's having that idea of God in their minds, (for it is evident some men have none, and some worse than none, and the most very different,) for the only proof of a Deity; and out of an over fondness of that darling invention, cashier, or at least endeavour to invalidate all other arguments; and forbid us to hearken to those proofs, as being weak or fallacious, which our own existence, and the sensible parts of the universe offer so clearly and cogently to our thoughts, that I deem it impossible for a considering man to withstand them. For I judge it as certain and clear a truth as can anywhere be delivered, that 'the invisible things of God are clearly seen from the creation of the world, being understood by the things that are made, even his eternal power and Godhead.' Though our own being furnishes us, as I have shown, with an evident and incontestible proof of a Deity; and I believe nobody can avoid the cogency of it, who will but as carefully attend to it, as to any other demonstration of so many parts: yet this being so fundamental a truth, and of that consequence, that all religion and genuine morality depend thereon, I doubt not but I shall be forgiven by my reader if I go over some parts of this argument again, and enlarge a little more upon them.

8. Recapitulation Something from Eternity.

There is no truth more evident than that SOMETHING must be FROM ETERNITY. I never yet heard of any one so unreasonable, or that could suppose so manifest a contradiction, as a time wherein there was perfectly nothing. This being of all absurdities the greatest, to imagine that pure nothing, the perfect negation and absence of all beings, should ever produce any real existence.

It being, then, unavoidable for all rational creatures to conclude, that SOMETHING has existed from eternity; let us next see WHAT KIND OF THING that must be.

9. Two Sorts of Beings, cogitative and incogitative.

There are but two sorts of beings in the world that man knows or conceives. First, such as are purely material, without sense, perception, or thought, as the clippings of our beards, and parings of our nails.

Secondly, sensible, thinking, perceiving beings, such as we find ourselves to be. Which, if you please, we will hereafter call COGITATIVE and INCOGITATIVE beings; which to our present purpose, if for nothing else, are perhaps better terms than material and immaterial.

10. Incogitative Being cannot produce a Cogitative Being.

If, then, there must be something eternal, let us see what sort of being it must be. And to that it is very obvious to reason, that it must necessarily be a cogitative being. For it is as impossible to conceive that ever bare incogitative matter should produce a thinking intelligent being, as that nothing should of itself produce matter. Let us suppose any parcel of matter eternal, great or small, we shall find it, in itself, able to produce nothing. For example: let us suppose the matter of the next pebble we meet with eternal, closely united, and the parts firmly at rest together; if there were no other being in the world, must it not eternally remain so, a dead inactive lump? Is it possible to conceive it can add motion to itself, being purely matter, or produce anything? Matter, then, by its own strength, cannot produce in itself so much as motion: the motion it has must also be from eternity, or else be produced, and added to matter by some other being more powerful than matter; matter, as is evident, having not power to produce motion in itself. But let us suppose motion eternal too: yet matter, INCOGITATIVE matter and motion, whatever changes it might produce of figure and bulk, could never produce thought: knowledge will still be as far beyond the power of motion and matter to produce, as matter is beyond the power of nothing or nonentity to produce. And I appeal to every one's own thoughts, whether he cannot as easily conceive matter produced by NOTHING, as thought to be produced by pure matter, when, before, there was no such thing as thought or an intelligent being existing? Divide matter into as many parts as you will, (which we are apt to imagine a sort of spiritualizing, or making a thinking thing of it,) vary the figure and motion of it as much as you please—a globe, cube, cone, prism, cylinder, &c., whose diameters are but 100,000th part of a GRY, will operate no otherwise upon other bodies of proportionable bulk, than those of an inch or foot diameter; and you may as rationally expect to produce sense, thought, and knowledge, by putting together, in a certain figure and motion, gross particles of matter, as by those that are the very minutest that do anywhere exist. They knock, impel, and resist one another, just as the greater do; and that is all they can do. So that, if we will suppose NOTHING first or eternal, matter can never begin to be: if we suppose bare matter without motion, eternal, motion can never begin to be: if we suppose only matter and motion first, or eternal, thought can never begin to be. [For it is impossible to conceive that matter, either with or without motion, could have, originally, in and from itself, sense, perception, and knowledge; as is evident from hence, that then sense, perception, and knowledge, must be a property eternally inseparable from matter and every particle of it. Not to add, that, though our general or specific conception of matter makes us speak of it as one thing, yet really all matter is not one individual thing, neither is there any such thing existing as ONE material being, or ONE single body that we know or can conceive. And therefore, if matter were the eternal first cogitative being, there would not be one eternal, infinite, cogitative being, but an infinite number of eternal, finite, cogitative beings, independent one of another, of limited force, and distinct thoughts, which could never produce that order, harmony, and beauty which are to be found in nature. Since, therefore, whatsoever is the first eternal being must necessarily be cogitative; and] whatsoever is first of all things must necessarily contain in it, and actually have, at least, all the perfections that can ever after exist; nor can it ever give to another any perfection that it hath not either actually in itself, or, at least, in a higher degree; [it necessarily follows, that the first eternal being cannot be matter.]

11. Therefore, there has been an Eternal Wisdom.

If, therefore, it be evident, that something necessarily must exist from eternity, it is also as evident, that that something must necessarily be a cogitative being: for it is as impossible that incogitative matter should produce a cogitative being, as that nothing, or the negation of all being, should produce a positive being or matter.

12. The Attributes of the Eternal Cogitative Being.

Though this discovery of the NECESSARY EXISTANCE OF A ETERNAL MIND does sufficiently lead us into the knowledge of God; since it will hence follow, that all other knowing beings that have a beginning must depend on him, and have in other ways of knowledge or extent of power than what He gives them; and therefore, if he made those, he made all the less excellent pieces of this universe,—all inanimate beings whereby his omniscience, power, and providence will be established, and all his other attributes necessarily follow yet, to clear up this a little further, we will see what doubt can be raised against it.

13. Whether the Eternal Mind may be also material or no.

FIRST, Perhaps it will be said, that, though it be as clear as demonstration can make it, that there must be an eternal Being, and that Being must also be knowing: yet it does not follow but that thinking Being may also be MATERIAL. Let it be so, it equally still follows that there is a God. For there be an eternal, omniscient, omnipotent Being, it is certain that there is a God, whether you imagine that Being to be material or no. But herein, I suppose, lies the danger and deceit of that supposition:—there being no way to avoid the demonstration, that there is an eternal knowing Being, men devoted to matter, would willingly have it granted, that that knowing Being is material; and then, letting slide out of their minds, or the discourse, the demonstration whereby an eternal KNOWING Being was proved necessarily to exist, would argue all to be matter, and so deny a God, that is, an eternal cogitative Being: whereby they are so far from establishing, that they destroy their own hypothesis. For, if there can be, in their opinion, eternal matter, without any eternal cogitative Being, they manifestly separate matter and thinking, and suppose no necessary connexion of the one with the other, and so establish the necessity of an eternal Spirit, but not of matter; since it has been proved already, that an eternal cogitative Being is unavoidably to be granted. Now, if thinking and matter may be separated, the eternal existence of matter will not follow from the eternal existence of a cogitative Being, and they suppose it to no purpose.

14. Not material: First, because each Particle of Matter is not cogitative. But now let us see how they can satisfy themselves, or others, that this eternal thinking Being is material.

I. I would ask them, whether they imagine that all matter, EVERY PARTICLE OF MATTER, thinks? This, I suppose, they will scarce say; since then there would be as many eternal thinking beings as there are particles of matter, and so an infinity of gods. And yet, if they will not allow matter as matter, that is, every particle of matter, to be as well cogitative as extended, they will have as hard a task to make out to their own reasons a cogitative being out of incogitative particles, as an extended being out of unextended parts, if I may so speak.

15. II. Secondly, Because one Particle alone of Matter cannot be cogitative. If all matter does not think, I next ask, Whether it be ONLY ONE ATOM that does so? This has as many absurdities as the other; for then this atom of matter must be alone eternal or not. If this alone be eternal, then this alone, by its powerful thought or will, made all the rest of matter. And so we have the creation of matter by a powerful thought, which is that the materialists stick at; for if they suppose one single thinking atom to have produced all the rest of matter, they cannot ascribe that pre-eminency to it upon any other account than that of its thinking, the only supposed difference. But allow it to be by some other way which is above our conception, it must still be creation; and these men must give up their great maxim, EX NIHILO NIL FIT. If it be said, that all the rest of matter is equally eternal as that thinking atom, it will be to say anything at pleasure, though ever so absurd. For to suppose all matter eternal, and yet one small particle in knowledge and power infinitely above all the rest, is without any the least appearance of reason to frame an hypothesis. Every particle of matter, as matter, is capable of all the same figures and motions of any other; and I challenge any one, in his thoughts, to add anything else to one above another.

16. III. Thirdly, Because a System of incogitative Matter cannot be cogitative.

If then neither one peculiar atom alone can be this eternal thinking being; nor all matter, as matter, i. e. every particle of matter, can be it; it only remains, that it is some certain SYSTEM of matter, duly put together, that is this thinking eternal Being. This is that which, I imagine, is that notion which men are aptest to have of God; who would have him a material being, as most readily suggested to them by the ordinary conceit they have of themselves and other men, which they take to be material thinking beings. But this imagination, however more natural, is no less absurd than the other; for to suppose the eternal thinking Being to be nothing else but a composition of particles of matter, each whereof is incogitative, is to ascribe all the wisdom and knowledge of that eternal Being only to the juxta-position of parts; than which nothing can be more absurd. For unthinking particles of matter, however put together, can have nothing thereby added to them, but a new relation of position, which it is impossible should give thought and knowledge to them.

17. And whether this corporeal System is in Motion or at Rest.

But further: this corporeal system either has all its parts at rest, or it is a certain motion of the parts wherein its thinking consists. If it be perfectly at rest, it is but one lump, and so can have no privileges above one atom.

If it be the motion of its parts on which its thinking depends, all the thoughts there must be unavoidably accidental and limited; since all the particles that by motion cause thought, being each of them in itself without any thought, cannot regulate its own motions, much less be regulated by the thought of the whole; since that thought is not the cause of motion, (for then it must be antecedent to it, and so without it,) but the consequence of it; whereby freedom, power, choice, and all rational and wise thinking or acting, will be quite taken away: so that such a thinking being will be no better nor wiser than pure blind matter; since to resolve all into the accidental unguided motions of blind matter, or into thought depending on unguided motions of blind matter, is the same thing: not to mention the narrowness of such thoughts and knowledge that must depend on the motion of such parts. But there needs no enumeration of any more absurdities and impossibilities in this hypothesis (however full of them it be) than that before mentioned; since, let this thinking system be all or a part of the matter of the universe, it is impossible that any one particle should either know its own, or the motion of any other particle, or the whole know the motion of every particle; and so regulate its own thoughts or motions, or indeed have any thought resulting from such motion.

18. Matter not co-eternal with an Eternal Mind.

SECONDLY, Others would have Matter to be eternal, notwithstanding that they allow an eternal, cogitative, immaterial Being. This, though it take not away the being of a God, yet, since it denies one and the first great piece of his workmanship, the creation, let us consider it a little. Matter must be allowed eternal: Why? because you cannot conceive how it can be made out of nothing: why do you not also think yourself eternal? You will answer, perhaps, Because, about twenty or forty years since, you began to be. But if I ask you, what that YOU is, which began then to be, you can scarce tell me. The matter whereof you are made began not then to be: for if it did, then it is not eternal: but it began to be put together in such a fashion and frame as makes up your body; but yet that frame of particles is not you, it makes not that thinking thing you are; (for I have now to do with one who allows an eternal, immaterial, thinking Being, but would have unthinking Matter eternal too;) therefore, when did that thinking thing begin to be? If it did never begin to be, then have you always been a thinking thing from eternity; the absurdity whereof I need not confute, till I meet with one who is so void of understanding as to own it. If, therefore, you can allow a thinking thing to be made out of nothing, (as all things that are not eternal must be,) why also can you not allow it possible for a material being to be made out of nothing by an equal power, but that you have the experience of the one in view, and not of the other? Though, when well considered, creation [of a spirit will be found to require no less power than the creation of matter. Nay, possibly, if we would emancipate ourselves from vulgar notions, and raise our thoughts, as far as they would reach, to a closer contemplation of things, we might be able to aim at some dim and seeming conception how MATTER might at first be made, and begin to exist, by the power of that eternal first Being: but to give beginning and being to a SPIRIT would be found a more inconceivable effect of omnipotent power. But this being what would perhaps lead us too far from the notions on which the philosophy now in the world is built, it would not be pardonable to deviate so far from them; or to inquire, so far as grammar itself would authorize, if the common settled opinion opposes it: especially in this place, where the received doctrine serves well enough to our present purpose, and leaves this past doubt, that] the creation or beginning of any one [SUBSTANCE] out of nothing being once admitted, the creation of all other but the Creator himself, may, with the same ease, be supposed.

19. Objection: Creation out of nothing.

But you will say, Is it not impossible to admit of the making anything out of nothing, SINCE WE CANNOT POSSIBLY CONCEIVE IT? I answer, No. Because it is not reasonable to deny the power of an infinite being, because we cannot comprehend its operations. We do not deny other effects upon this ground, because we cannot possibly conceive the manner of their production. We cannot conceive how anything but impulse of body can move body; and yet that is not a reason sufficient to make us deny it possible, against the constant experience we have of it in ourselves, in all our voluntary motions; which are produced in us only by the free action or thought of our own minds, and are not, nor can be, the effects of the impulse or determination of the motion of blind matter in or upon our own bodies; for then it could not be in our power or choice to alter it. For example: my right hand writes, whilst my left hand is still: What causes rest in one, and motion in the other? Nothing but my will,—a thought of my mind; my thought only changing, the right hand rests, and the left hand moves. This is matter of fact, which cannot be denied: explain this and make it intelligible, and then the next step will be to understand creation. [For the giving a new determination to the motion of the animal spirits (which some make use of to explain voluntary motion) clears not the difficulty one jot. To alter the determination of motion, being in this case no easier nor less, than to give motion itself: since the new determination given to the animal spirits must be either immediately by thought, or by some other body put in their way by thought which was not in their way before, and so must owe ITS motion to thought: either of which leaves VOLUNTARY motion as unintelligible as it was before.] In the meantime, it is an over-valuing ourselves to reduce all to the narrow measure of our capacities; and to conclude all things impossible to be done, whose manner of doing exceeds our comprehension. This is to make our comprehension infinite, or God finite, when what He can do is limited to what we can conceive of it. If you do not understand the operations of your own finite mind, that thinking thing within you, do not deem it strange that you cannot comprehend the operations of that eternal infinite Mind, who made and governs all things, and whom the heaven of heavens cannot contain.

CHAPTER XI.

OF OUR KNOWLEDGE OF THE EXISTENCE OF OTHER THINGS.

1. Knowledge of the existence of other Finite Beings is to be had only by actual Sensation.

The knowledge of our own being we have by intuition. The existence of a God, reason clearly makes known to us, as has been shown.

The knowledge of the existence of ANY OTHER THING we can have only by SENSATION: for there being no necessary connexion of real existence with any IDEA a man hath in his memory; nor of any other existence but that of God with the existence of any particular man: no particular man can know the existence of any other being, but only when, by actual operating upon him, it makes itself perceived by him. For, the having the idea of anything in our mind, no more proves the existence of that thing, than the picture of a man evidences his being in the world, or the visions of a dream make thereby a true history.

2. Instance: Whiteness of this Paper.

It is therefore the ACTUAL RECEIVING of ideas from without that gives us notice of the existence of other things, and makes us know, that something doth exist at that time without us, which causes that idea in us; though perhaps we neither know nor consider how it does it. For it takes not from the certainty of our senses, and the ideas we receive by them, that we know not the manner wherein they are produced: v.g. whilst I write this, I have, by the paper affecting my eyes, that idea produced in my mind, which, whatever object causes, I call WHITE; by which I know that that quality or accident (i.e. whose appearance before my eyes always causes that idea) doth really exist, and hath a being without me. And of this, the greatest assurance I can possibly have, and to which my faculties can attain, is the testimony of my eyes, which are the proper and sole judges of this thing; whose testimony I have reason to rely on as so certain, that I can no more doubt, whilst I write this, that I see white and black, and that something really exists that causes that sensation in me, than that I write or move my hand; which is a certainty as great as human nature is capable of, concerning the existence of anything, but a man's self alone, and of God.

3. This notice by our Senses, though not so certain as Demonstration, yet may be called Knowledge, and proves the Existence of Things without us. The notice we have by our senses of the existing of things without us, though it be not altogether so certain as our intuitive knowledge, or the deductions of our reason employed about the clear abstract ideas of our own minds; yet it is an assurance that deserves the name of KNOWLEDGE. If we persuade ourselves that our faculties act and inform us right concerning the existence of those objects that affect them, it cannot pass for an ill-grounded confidence: for I think nobody can, in earnest, be so sceptical as to be uncertain of the existence of those things which he sees and feels. At least, he that can doubt so far, (whatever he may have with his own thoughts,) will never have any controversy with me; since he can never be sure I say anything contrary to his own opinion. As to myself, I think God has given me assurance enough of the existence of things without me: since, by their different application, I can produce in myself both pleasure and pain, which is one great concernment of my present state. This is certain: the confidence that our faculties do not herein deceive us, is the greatest assurance we are capable of concerning the existence of material beings. For we cannot act anything but by our faculties; nor talk of knowledge itself, but by the help of those faculties which are fitted to apprehend even what knowledge is.

But besides the assurance we have from our senses themselves, that they do not err in the information they give us of the existence of things without us, when they are affected by them, we are further confirmed in this assurance by other concurrent reasons:—

4. I. Confirmed by concurrent reasons:—First, Because we cannot have ideas of Sensation but by the Inlet of the Senses.

It is plain those perceptions are produced in us by exterior causes affecting our senses: because those that want the ORGANS of any sense, never can have the ideas belonging to that sense produced in their minds. This is too evident to be doubted: and therefore we cannot but be assured that they come in by the organs of that sense, and no other way. The organs themselves, it is plain, do not produce them: for then the eyes of a man in the dark would produce colours, and his nose smell roses in the winter: but we see nobody gets the relish of a pineapple, till he goes to the Indies, where it is, and tastes it.

5. II. Secondly, Because we find that an Idea from actual Sensation, and another from memory, are very distinct Perceptions.

Because sometimes I find that I CANNOT AVOID THE HAVING THOSE IDEAS PRODUCED IN MY MIND. For though, when my eyes are shut, or windows fast, I can at pleasure recal to my mind the ideas of light, or the sun, which former sensations had lodged in my memory; so I can at pleasure lay by THAT idea, and take into my view that of the smell of a rose, or taste of sugar. But, if I turn my eyes at noon towards the sun, I cannot avoid the ideas which the light or sun then produces in me. So that there is a manifest difference between the ideas laid up in my memory, (over which, if they were there only, I should have constantly the same power to dispose of them, and lay them by at pleasure,) and those which force themselves upon me, and I cannot avoid having. And therefore it must needs be some exterior cause, and the brisk acting of some objects without me, whose efficacy I cannot resist, that produces those ideas in my mind, whether I will or no. Besides, there is nobody who doth not perceive the difference in himself between contemplating the sun, as he hath the idea of it in his memory, and actually looking upon it: of which two, his perception is so distinct, that few of his ideas are more distinguishable one from another. And therefore he hath certain knowledge that they are not BOTH memory, or the actions of his mind, and fancies only within him; but that actual seeing hath a cause without.

6. III. Thirdly, Because Pleasure or Pain, which accompanies actual Sensation, accompanies not the returning of those Ideas without the external Objects.

Add to this, that many of those ideas are PRODUCED IN US WITH PAIN, which afterwards we remember without the least offence. Thus, the pain of heat or cold, when the idea of it is revived in our minds, gives us no disturbance; which, when felt, was very troublesome; and is again, when actually repeated: which is occasioned by the disorder the external object causes in our bodies when applied to them: and we remember the pains of hunger, thirst, or the headache, without any pain at all; which would either never disturb us, or else constantly do it, as often as we thought of it, were there nothing more but ideas floating in our minds, and appearances entertaining our fancies, without the real existence of things affecting us from abroad. The same may be said of PLEASURE, accompanying several actual sensations. And though mathematical demonstration depends not upon sense, yet the examining them by diagrams gives great credit to the evidence of our sight, and seems to give it a certainty approaching to that of demonstration itself. For, it would be very strange, that a man should allow it for an undeniable truth, that two angles of a figure, which he measures by lines and angles of a diagram, should be bigger one than the other, and yet doubt of the existence of those lines and angles, which by looking on he makes use of to measure that by.

7. IV. Fourthly, Because our Senses assist one another's Testimony of the Existence of outward Things, and enable us to predict.

Our SENSES in many cases BEAR WITNESS TO THE TRUTH OF EACH OTHER'S REPORT, concerning the existence of sensible things without us. He that SEES a fire, may, if he doubt whether it be anything more than a bare fancy, FEEL it too; and be convinced, by putting his hand in it. Which certainly could never be put into such exquisite pain by a bare idea or phantom, unless that the pain be a fancy too: which yet he cannot, when the burn is well, by raising the idea of it, bring upon himself again.

Thus I see, whilst I write this, I can change the appearance of the paper; and by designing the letters, tell BEFOREHAND what new idea it shall exhibit the very next moment, by barely drawing my pen over it: which will neither appear (let me fancy as much as I will) if my hands stand still; or though I move my pen, if my eyes be shut: nor, when those characters are once made on the paper, can I choose afterwards but see them as they are; that is, have the ideas of such letters as I have made. Whence it is manifest, that they are not barely the sport and play of my own imagination, when I find that the characters that were made at the pleasure of my own thoughts, do not obey them; nor yet cease to be, whenever I shall fancy it, but continue to affect my senses constantly and regularly, according to the figures I made them. To which if we will add, that the sight of those shall from another man, draw such sounds as I beforehand design they shall stand for, there will be little reason left to doubt that those words I write do really exist without me, when they cause a long series of regular sounds to affect my ears, which could not be the effect of my imagination, nor could my memory retain them in that order.

8. This Certainty is as great as our Condition needs.

But yet, if after all this any one will be so sceptical as to distrust his senses, and to affirm that all we see and hear, feel and taste, think and do, during our whole being, is but the series and deluding appearances of a long dream, whereof there is no reality; and therefore will question the existence of all things, or our knowledge of anything: I must desire him to consider, that, if all be a dream, then he doth but dream that he makes the question, and so it is not much matter that a waking man should answer him. But yet, if he pleases, he may dream that I make him this answer, That the certainty of things existing in RERUM NATURA when we have the testimony of our senses for it is not only as great as our frame can attain to, but as our condition needs. For, our faculties being suited not to the full extent of being, nor to a perfect, clear, comprehensive knowledge of things free from all doubt and scruple; but to the preservation of us, in whom they are; and accommodated to the use of life: they serve to our purpose well enough, if they will but give us certain notice of those things, which are convenient or inconvenient to us. For he that sees a candle burning, and hath experimented the force of its flame by putting his finger in it, will little doubt that this is something existing without him, which does him harm, and puts him to great pain: which is assurance enough, when no man requires greater certainty to govern his actions by than what is as certain as his actions themselves. And if our dreamer pleases to try whether the glowing heat of a glass furnace be barely a wandering imagination in a drowsy man's fancy, by putting his hand into it, he may perhaps be wakened into a certainty greater than he could wish, that it is something more than bare imagination. So that this evidence is as great as we can desire, being as certain to us as our pleasure or pain, i.e. happiness or misery; beyond which we have no concernment, either of knowing or being. Such an assurance of the existence of things without us is sufficient to direct us in the attaining the good and avoiding the evil which is caused by them, which is the important concernment we have of being made acquainted with them.

9. But reaches no further than actual Sensation.

In fine, then, when our senses do actually convey into our understandings any idea, we cannot but be satisfied that there doth something AT THAT TIME really exist without us, which doth affect our senses, and by them give notice of itself to our apprehensive faculties, and actually produce that idea which we then perceive: and we cannot so far distrust their testimony, as to doubt that such COLLECTIONS of simple ideas as we have observed by our senses to be united together, do really exist together. But this knowledge extends as far as the present testimony of our senses, employed about particular objects that do then affect them, and no further. For if I saw such a collection of simple ideas as is wont to be called MAN, existing together one minute since, and am now alone, I cannot be certain that the same man exists now, since there is no NECESSARY CONNEXION of his existence a minute since with his existence now: by a thousand ways he may cease to be, since I had the testimony of my senses for his existence. And if I cannot be certain that the man I saw last to-day is now in being, I can less be certain that he is so who hath been longer removed from my senses, and I have not seen since yesterday, or since the last year: and much less can I be certain of the existence of men that I never saw. And, therefore, though it be highly probable that millions of men do now exist, yet, whilst I am alone, writing this, I have not that certainty of it which we strictly call knowledge; though the great likelihood of it puts me past doubt, and it be reasonable for me to do several things upon the confidence that there are men (and men also of my acquaintance, with whom I have to do) now in the world: but this is but probability, not knowledge.

10. Folly to expect Demonstration in everything.

Whereby yet we may observe how foolish and vain a thing it is for a man of a narrow knowledge, who having reason given him to judge of the different evidence and probability of things, and to be swayed accordingly; how vain, I say, it is to expect demonstration and certainty in things not capable of it; and refuse assent to very rational propositions, and act contrary to very plain and clear truths, because they cannot be made out so evident, as to surmount every the least (I will not say reason, but) pretence of doubting. He that, in the ordinary affairs of life, would admit of nothing but direct plain demonstration, would be sure of nothing in this world, but of perishing quickly. The wholesomeness of his meat or drink would not give him reason to venture on it: and I would fain know what it is he could do upon such grounds as are capable of no doubt, no objection.

11. Past Existence of other things is known by Memory.

As WHEN OUR SENSES ARE ACTUALLY EMPLOYED ABOUT ANY OBJECT, we do know that it does exist; so BY OUR MEMORY we may be assured, that heretofore things that affected our senses have existed. And thus we have knowledge of the past existence of several things, whereof our senses having informed us, our memories still retain the ideas; and of this we are past all doubt, so long as we remember well. But this knowledge also reaches no further than our senses have formerly assured us. Thus, seeing water at this instant, it is an unquestionable truth to me that water doth exist: and remembering that I saw it yesterday, it will also be always true, and as long as my memory retains it always an undoubted proposition to me, that water did exist the 10th of July, 1688; as it will also be equally true that a certain number of very fine colours did exist, which at the same time I saw upon a bubble of that water: but, being now quite out of sight both of the water and bubbles too, it is no more certainly known to me that the water doth now exist, than that the bubbles or colours therein do so: it being no more necessary that water should exist to-day, because it existed yesterday, than that the colours or bubbles exist to-day, because they existed yesterday, though it be exceedingly much more probable; because water hath been observed to continue long in existence, but bubbles, and the colours on them, quickly cease to be.

12. The Existence of other finite Spirits not knowable, and rests on Faith. What ideas we have of spirits, and how we come by them, I have already shown. But though we have those ideas in our minds, and know we have them there, the having the ideas of spirits does not make us know that any such things do exist without us, or that there are any finite spirits, or any other spiritual beings, but the Eternal God. We have ground from revelation, and several other reasons, to believe with assurance that there are such creatures: but our senses not being able to discover them, we want the means of knowing their particular existences. For we can no more know that there are finite spirits really existing, by the idea we have of such beings in our minds, than by the ideas any one has of fairies or centaurs, he can come to know that things answering those ideas do really exist.

And therefore concerning the existence of finite spirits, as well as several other things, we must content ourselves with the evidence of faith; but universal, certain propositions concerning this matter are beyond our reach. For however true it may be, v.g., that all the intelligent spirits that God ever created do still exist, yet it can never make a part of our certain knowledge. These and the like propositions we may assent to, as highly probable, but are not, I fear, in this state capable of knowing. We are not, then, to put others upon demonstrating, nor ourselves upon search of universal certainty in all those matters; wherein we are not capable of any other knowledge, but what our senses give us in this or that particular.

13. Only particular Propositions concerning concrete Existances are knowable. By which it appears that there are two sorts of propositions:—(1) There is one sort of propositions concerning the existence of anything answerable to such an idea: as having the idea of an elephant, phoenix, motion, or an angel, in my mind, the first and natural inquiry is, Whether such a thing does anywhere exist? And this knowledge is only of particulars. No existence of anything without us, but only of God, can certainly be known further than our senses inform us, (2) There is another sort of propositions, wherein is expressed the agreement or disagreement of OUR ABSTRACT IDEAS, and their dependence on one another. Such propositions may be universal and certain. So, having the idea of God and myself, of fear and obedience, I cannot but be sure that God is to be feared and obeyed by me: and this proposition will be certain, concerning man in general, if I have

made an abstract idea of such a species, whereof I am one particular. But yet this proposition, how certain soever, that 'men ought to fear and obey God' proves not to me the EXISTENCE of MEN in the world; but will be true of all such creatures, whenever they do exist: which certainty of such general propositions depends on the agreement or disagreement to be discovered in those abstract ideas.

14. And all general Propositions that are known to be true concern abstract Ideas.

In the former case, our knowledge is the consequence of the existence of things, producing ideas in our minds by our senses: in the latter, knowledge is the consequence of the ideas (be they what they will) that are in our minds, producing there general certain propositions. Many of these are called AETERNAE VERITATES, and all of them indeed are so; not from being written, all or any of them, in the minds of all men; or that they were any of them propositions in any one's mind, till he, having got the abstract ideas, joined or separated them by affirmation or negation. But wheresoever we can suppose such a creature as man is, endowed with such faculties, and thereby furnished with such ideas as we have, we must conclude, he must needs, when he applies his thoughts to the consideration of his ideas, know the truth of certain propositions that will arise from the agreement or disagreement which he will perceive in his own ideas. Such propositions are therefore called ETERNAL TRUTHS, not because they are eternal propositions actually formed, and antecedent to the understanding that at any time makes them; nor because they are imprinted on the mind from any patterns that are anywhere out of the mind, and existed before: but because, being once made about abstract ideas, so as to be true, they will, whenever they can be supposed to be made again at any time, past or come, by a mind having those ideas, always actually be true. For names being supposed to stand perpetually for the same ideas, and the same ideas having immutably the same habitudes one to another, propositions concerning any abstract ideas that are once true must needs be ETERNAL VERITIES.

CHAPTER XII. OF THE IMPROVEMENT OF OUR KNOWLEDGE

1. Knowledge is not got from Maxims.

IT having been the common received opinion amongst men of letters, that MAXIMS were the foundation of all knowledge; and that the sciences were each of them built upon certain PRAECOGNITA, from whence the understanding was to take its rise, and by which it was to conduct itself in its inquiries into the matters belonging to that science, the beaten road of the Schools has been, to lay down in the beginning one or more GENERAL PROPOSITIONS, as foundations whereon to build the knowledge that was to be had of that subject. These doctrines, thus laid down for foundations of any science, were called PRINCIPLES, as the beginnings from which we must set out, and look no further backwards in our inquiries, as we have already observed.

2. (The Occasion of that Opinion.)

One thing which might probably give an occasion to this way of proceeding in other sciences, was (as I suppose) the good success it seemed to have in MATHEMATICS, wherein men, being observed to attain a great certainty of knowledge, these sciences came by pre-eminence to be called [word in Greek], and [word in Greek], learning, or things learned, thoroughly learned, as having of all others the greatest certainty, clearness, and evidence in them.

3. But from comparing clear and distinct Ideas.

But if any one will consider, he will (I guess) find, that the great advancement and certainty of real knowledge which men arrived to in these sciences, was not owing to the influence of these principles, nor derived from any peculiar advantage they received from two or three general maxims, laid down in the beginning; but from the clear, distinct, complete ideas their thoughts were employed about, and the relation of equality and excess so clear between some of them, that they had an intuitive knowledge, and by THAT a way to discover it in others; and this without the help of those maxims. For I ask, Is it not possible for a young lad to know that his whole body is bigger than his little finger, but by virtue of this axiom, that THE WHOLE IS BIGGER THAN A PART; nor be assured of it, till he has learned that maxim? Or cannot a country wench know that, having received a shilling from one that owes her three, and a shilling also from another that owes her three, the remaining debts in each of their hands are equal? Cannot she know this, I say, unless she fetch the certainty of it from this maxim, that IF YOU TAKE EQUALS FROM EQUALS, THE REMAINDER WILL BE EQUALS, a maxim which possibly she never heard or thought of? I desire any one to consider, from what has been elsewhere said, which is known first and clearest by most people, the particular instance, or the general rule; and which it is that gives life and birth to the other. These general rules are but the comparing our more general and abstract ideas, which are the workmanship of the mind, made, and names given to them for the easier dispatch in its reasonings, and drawing into comprehensive terms and short rules its various and multiplied observations. But knowledge began in the mind, and was founded on particulars; though afterwards, perhaps, no notice was taken thereof: it being natural for the mind (forward still to enlarge its knowledge) most attentively to lay up those general notions, and make the proper use of them, which is to disburden the memory of the cumbersome load of particulars. For I desire it may be considered, what more certainty there is to a child, or any one, that his body, little finger, and all, is bigger than his little finger alone, after you have given to his body the name WHOLE, and to his little finger the name PART, than he could have had before; or what new knowledge concerning his body can these two relative terms give him, which he could not have without them? Could he not know that his body was bigger than his little finger, if his language were yet so imperfect that he had no such relative terms as whole and part? I ask, further, when he has got these names, how is he more certain that his body is a whole, and his little finger a part, than he was or might be certain before he learnt those terms, that his body was bigger than his little finger? Any one may as reasonably doubt or deny that his little finger is a part of his body, as that it is less than his body. And he that can doubt whether it be less, will as certainly doubt whether it be a part. So that the maxim, the whole is bigger than a part, can never be made use of to prove the little finger less than the body, but when it is useless, by being brought to convince one of a truth which he knows already. For he that does not certainly know that any parcel of matter, with another parcel of matter joined to it, is bigger than either of them alone, will never be able to know it by the help of these two relative terms, whole and part, make of them what maxim you please.

4. Dangerous to build upon precarious Principles.

But be it in the mathematics as it will, whether it be clearer, that, taking an inch from a black line of two inches, and an inch from a red line of two inches, the remaining parts of the two lines will be equal, or that IF YOU

TAKE EQUALS FROM EQUALS, THE REMAINDER WILL BE EQUALS: which, I say, of these two is the clearer and first known, I leave to any one to determine, it not being material to my present occasion. That which I have here to do, is to inquire, whether, if it be the readiest way to knowledge to begin with general maxims, and build upon them, it be yet a safe way to take the PRINCIPLES which are laid down in any other science as unquestionable truths; and so receive them without examination, and adhere to them, without suffering them to be doubted of, because mathematicians have been so happy, or so fair, to use none but self-evident and undeniable. If this be so, I know not what may not pass for truth in morality, what may not be introduced and proved in natural philosophy.

Let that principle of some of the old philosophers, That all is Matter, and that there is nothing else, be received for certain and indubitable, and it will be easy to be seen by the writings of some that have revived it again in our days, what consequences it will lead us into. Let any one, with Polemo, take the world; or with the Stoics, the aether, or the sun; or with Anaximenes, the air, to be God; and what a divinity, religion, and worship must we needs have! Nothing can be so dangerous as PRINCIPLES thus TAKEN UP WITHOUT QUESTIONING OR EXAMINATION; especially if they be such as concern morality, which influence men's lives, and give a bias to all their actions. Who might not justly expect another kind of life in Aristippus, who placed happiness in bodily pleasure; and in Antisthenes, who made virtue sufficient to felicity? And he who, with Plato, shall place beatitude in the knowledge of God, will have his thoughts raised to other contemplations than those who look not beyond this spot of earth, and those perishing things which are to be had in it. He that, with Archelaus, shall lay it down as a principle, that right and wrong, honest and dishonest, are defined only by laws, and not by nature, will have other measures of moral rectitude and gravity, than those who take it for granted that we are under obligations antecedent to all human constitutions.

5. To do so is no certain Way to Truth.

If, therefore, those that pass for PRINCIPLES are NOT CERTAIN, (which we must have some way to know, that we may be able to distinguish them from those that are doubtful,) but are only made so to us by our blind assent, we are liable to be misled by them; and instead of being guided into truth, we shall, by principles, be only confirmed in mistake and error.

6. But to compare clear, complete Ideas, under steady Names.

But since the knowledge of the certainty of principles, as well as of all other truths, depends only upon the perception we have of the agreement or disagreement of our ideas, the way to improve our knowledge is not, I am sure, blindly, and with an implicit faith, to receive and swallow principles; but is, I think, to get and fix in our minds clear, distinct, and complete ideas, as far as they are to be had, and annex to them proper and constant names. And thus, perhaps, without any other principles, but BARELY CONSIDERING THOSE PERFECT IDEAS, and by COMPARING THEM ONE WITH ANOTHER; finding their agreement and disagreement, and their several relations and habitudes; we shall get more true and clear knowledge by the conduct of this one rule, than by taking up principles, and thereby putting our minds into the disposal of others.

7. The true Method of advancing Knowledge is by considering our abstract Ideas.

We must, therefore, if we will proceed as reason advises, adapt our methods of inquiry to THE NATURE OF THE IDEAS WE EXAMINE, and the truth we search after. General and certain truths are only founded in the habitudes and relations of ABSTRACT IDEAS. A sagacious and methodical application of our thoughts, for the finding out these relations, is the only way to discover all that can be put with truth and certainty concerning them into general propositions. By what steps we are to proceed in these, is to be learned in the schools of the mathematicians, who, from very plain and easy beginnings, by gentle degrees, and a continued chain of reasonings, proceed to the discovery and demonstration of truths that appear at first sight beyond human capacity. The art of finding proofs, and the admirable methods they have invented for the singling out and laying in order those intermediate ideas that demonstratively show the equality or inequality of unapplicable quantities, is that which has carried them so far, and produced such wonderful and unexpected discoveries: but whether something like this, in respect of other ideas, as well as those of magnitude, may not in time be found out, I will not determine. This, I think, I may say, that if other ideas that are the real as well as nominal essences of their species, were pursued in the way familiar to mathematicians, they would carry our thoughts further, and with greater evidence and clearness than possibly we are apt to imagine.

8. By which Morality also may be made clearer.

This gave me the confidence to advance that conjecture, which I suggest, (chap. iii.) viz. that MORALITY is capable of demonstration as well as mathematics. For the ideas that ethics are conversant about, being all real essences, and such as I imagine have a discoverable connexion and agreement one with another; so far as we can find their habitudes and relations, so far we shall be possessed of certain, real, and general truths; and I doubt not but, if a right method were taken, a great part of morality might be made out with that clearness, that could leave, to a considering man, no more reason to doubt, than he could have to doubt of the truth of propositions in mathematics, which have been demonstrated to him.

9. Our Knowledge of Substances is to be improved, not by contemplation of abstract ideas, but only by Experience.

In our search after the knowledge of SUBSTANCES, our want of ideas that are suitable to such a way of proceeding obliges us to a quite different method. We advance not here, as in the other, (where our abstract ideas are real as well as nominal essences,) by contemplating our ideas, and considering their relations and correspondences; that helps us very little for the reasons, that in another place we have at large set down. By which I think it is evident, that substances afford matter of very little GENERAL knowledge; and the bare contemplation of their abstract ideas will carry us but a very little way in the search of truth and certainty. What, then, are we to do for the improvement of our knowledge in substantial beings? Here we are to take a quite contrary course: the want of ideas of their real essences sends us from our own thoughts to the things themselves as they exist. EXPERIENCE HERE MUST TEACH ME WHAT REASON CANNOT: and it is by TRYING alone, that I can CERTAINLY KNOW, what other qualities co-exist with those of my complex idea, v.g. whether that yellow heavy, fusible body I call gold, be malleable, or no; which experience (which way ever it prove in that particular body I examine) makes me not certain, that it is so in all, or any other yellow, heavy, fusible bodies, but that which I have tried. Because it is no consequence one way or the other from my complex idea: the necessity or inconsistence of malleability hath no visible connexion with the combination of that colour, weight, and fusibility in any body. What I have said here of the nominal essence of gold, supposed to consist of a body of such a determinate colour, weight, and fusibility, will hold true, if malleableness, fixedness, and solubility in aqua regia be added to it. Our reasonings from these ideas will carry us but a little way in the certain discovery of the other properties in those masses of matter wherein all these are to be found. Because the OTHER properties of such bodies, depending not on these, but on that unknown real essence on which these also depend, we cannot by them discover the rest; we can go no further than the simple ideas of our nominal essence will carry us, which is very little beyond themselves; and so afford us but very sparingly any certain, universal, and useful truths. For, upon trial, having found that particular piece (and all others of that colour, weight, and fusibility, that I ever tried) malleable, that also makes now, perhaps, a part of my complex idea, part of my nominal essence of gold: whereby though I make my complex idea to which I affix the name gold, to consist of more simple ideas than before; yet still, it not containing the real essence of any species of bodies, it helps me not certainly to know (I say to know, perhaps it may be to conjecture) the other remaining properties of that body, further than they have a visible connexion with some or all of the simple ideas that make up my nominal essence. For example, I cannot be certain, from this complex idea, whether gold be fixed or no; because, as before, there is no NECESSARY connexion or inconsistence to be discovered betwixt a COMPLEX IDEA OF A BODY YELLOW, HEAVY, FUSIBLE, MALLEABLE; betwixt these, I say, and FIXEDNESS; so that I may certainly know, that in whatsoever body these are found, there fixedness is sure to be. Here, again, for assurance, I must apply myself to experience; as far as that reaches, I may have certain knowledge, but no further.

10. Experience may procure is Convenience, not Science.

I deny not but a man, accustomed to rational and regular experiments, shall be able to see further into the nature of bodies, and guess righter at their yet unknown properties, than one that is a stranger to them: but yet, as I have said, this is but judgment and opinion, not knowledge and certainty. This way of GETTING AND IMPROVING OUR KNOWLEDGE IN SUBSTANCES ONLY BY EXPERIENCE AND HISTORY, which is all that the weakness of our faculties in this state of mediocrity which we are in this world can attain to, makes me suspect that NATURAL PHILOSOPHY IS NOT CAPABLE IS BEING MADE A SCIENCE. We are able, I imagine, to reach very little general knowledge concerning the species of bodies, and their several properties. Experiments and historical observations we may have, from which we may draw advantages of ease and health, and thereby increase our stock of conveniences for this life; but beyond this I fear our talents reach not, nor are our faculties, as I guess, able to advance.

11. We are fitted for moral Science, but only for probable interpretations of external Nature.

From whence is it obvious to conclude, that, since our faculties are not fitted to penetrate into the internal fabric and real essences of bodies; but yet plainly discover to us the being of a God, and the knowledge of ourselves, enough to lead us into a full and clear discovery of our duty and great concernment; it will become us, as rational creatures, to employ those faculties we have about what they are most adapted to, and follow the direction of nature, where it seems to point us out the way. For it is rational to conclude, that our proper employment lies in those inquiries, and in that sort of knowledge which is most suited to our natural capacities, and carries in it our greatest interest, i.e. the condition of our eternal estate. Hence I think I may conclude, that MORALITY IS THE PROPER SCIENCE AND BUSINESS OF MANKIND IN GENERAL, (who are both concerned and fitted to search out their SUMMUM BONUM;) as several arts, conversant about several parts of nature, are the lot and private talent of particular men, for the common use of human life, and their own particular subsistence in this world. Of what consequence the discovery of one natural body and its properties may be to human life, the whole great continent of America is a convincing instance: whose ignorance in useful arts, and want of the greatest part of the conveniences of life, in a country that abounded with all sorts of natural plenty, I think may be attributed to their ignorance of what was to be found in a very ordinary, despicable stone, I mean the mineral of IRON. And whatever we think of our parts or improvements in this part of the world, where knowledge and plenty seem to vie with each other; yet to any one that will seriously reflect on it, I suppose it will appear past doubt, that, were the use of iron lost among us, we should in a few ages be unavoidably reduced to the wants and ignorance of the ancient savage Americans, whose natural endowments and provisions come no way short of those of the most flourishing and polite nations. So that he who first made known the use of that contemptible mineral, may be truly styled the father of arts, and author of plenty.

12. In the study of Nature we must beware of Hypotheses and wrong Principles.

I would not, therefore, be thought to disesteem or dissuade the study of NATURE. I readily agree the contemplation of his works gives us occasion to admire, revere, and glorify their Author: and, if rightly directed, may be of greater benefit to mankind than the monuments of exemplary charity that have at so great charge been raised by the founders of hospitals and almshouses. He that first invented printing, discovered the use of the compass, or made public the virtue and right use of KIN KINA, did more for the propagation of knowledge, for the supply and increase of useful commodities, and saved more from the grave than those who built colleges, workhouses, and hospitals. All that I would say is, that we should not be too forwardly possessed with the opinion or expectation of knowledge, where it is not to be had, or by ways that will not attain to it: that we should not take doubtful systems for complete sciences; nor unintelligible notions for scientifical demonstrations. In the knowledge of bodies, we must be content to glean what we can from particular experiments: since we cannot, from a discovery of their real essences, grasp at a time whole sheaves, and in bundles comprehend the nature and properties of whole species together. Where our inquiry is concerning co-existence, or repugnancy to co-exist, which by contemplation of our ideas we cannot discover; there experience, observation, and natural history, must give us, by our senses and by retail, an insight into corporeal substances. The knowledge of BODIES we must get by our senses, warily employed in taking notice of their qualities and operations on one another: and what we hope to know of SEPARATE SPIRITS in this world, we must, I think, expect only from revelation. He that shall consider how little general maxims, precarious principles, and hypotheses laid down at pleasure, have promoted true knowledge, or helped to satisfy the inquiries of rational men after real improvements; how little, I say, the setting out at that end has, for many ages together, advanced men's progress, towards the knowledge of natural philosophy, Will think we have reason to thank those who in this latter age have taken another course, and have trod out to us, though not an easier way to learned ignorance, yet a surer way to profitable knowledge.

13. The true Use of Hypotheses.

Not that we may not, to explain any phenomena of nature, make use of any probable hypothesis whatsoever: hypotheses, if they are well made, are at least great helps to the memory, and often direct us to new discoveries. But my meaning is, that we should not take up any one too hastily (which the mind, that would always penetrate into the causes of things, and have principles to rest on, is very apt to do) till we have very well examined particulars, and made several experiments, in that thing which we would explain by our hypothesis, and see whether it will agree to them all; whether our principles will carry us quite through, and not be as inconsistent with one phenomenon of nature, as they seem to accommodate and explain another. And at least that we take care that the name of PRINCIPLES deceive us not, nor impose on us, by making us receive that for an unquestionable truth, which is really at best but a very doubtful conjecture; such as are most (I had almost said all) of the hypotheses in natural philosophy.

14. Clear and distinct Ideas with settled Names, and the finding of those intermediate ideas which show their Agreement or Disagreement, are the Ways to enlarge our Knowledge.
But whether natural philosophy be capable of certainty or no, the ways to enlarge our knowledge, as far as we are capable, seems to me, in short, to be these two:—
First, The first is to get and settle in our minds [determined ideas of those things whereof we have general or specific names; at least, so many of them as we would consider and improve our knowledge in, or reason about.] [And if they be specific ideas of substances, we should endeavour also to make them as complete as we can, whereby I mean, that we should put together as many simple ideas as, being constantly observed to co-exist, may perfectly determine the species; and each of those simple ideas which are the ingredients of our complex ones, should be clear and distinct in our minds.] For it being evident that our knowledge cannot exceed our ideas; [as far as] they are either imperfect, confused, or obscure, we cannot expect to have certain, perfect, or clear knowledge. Secondly, The other is the art of finding out those intermediate ideas, which may show us the agreement or repugnancy of other ideas, which cannot be immediately compared.
15. Mathematics an instance of this.
That these two (and not the relying on maxims, and drawing consequences from some general propositions) are the right methods of improving our knowledge in the ideas of other modes besides those of quantity, the consideration of mathematical knowledge will easily inform us. Where first we shall find that he that has not a perfect and clear idea of those angles or figures of which he desires to know anything, is utterly thereby incapable of any knowledge about them. Suppose but a man not to have a perfect exact idea of a right angle, a scalenum, or trapezium, and there is nothing more certain than that he will in vain seek any demonstration about them. Further, it is evident, that it was not the influence of those maxims which are taken for principles in mathematics, that hath led the masters of that science into those wonderful discoveries they have made. Let a man of good parts know all the maxims generally made use of in mathematics ever so perfectly, and contemplate their extent and consequences as much as he pleases, he will, by their assistance, I suppose, scarce ever come to know that the square of the hypothenuse in a right-angled triangle is equal to the squares of the two other sides. The knowledge that 'the whole is equal to all its parts,' and 'if you take equals from equals, the remainder

will be equal,' &c., helped him not, I presume, to this demonstration: and a man may, I think, pore long enough on those axioms, without ever seeing one jot the more of mathematical truths. They have been discovered by the thoughts otherwise applied: the mind had other objects, other views before it, far different from those maxims, when it first got the knowledge of such truths in mathematics, which men, well enough acquainted with those received axioms, but ignorant of their method who first made these demonstrations, can never sufficiently admire. And who knows what methods to enlarge our knowledge in other parts of science may hereafter be invented, answering that of algebra in mathematics, which so readily finds out the ideas of quantities to measure others by; whose equality or proportion we could otherwise very hardly, or, perhaps, never come to know?

CHAPTER XIII.

SOME FURTHER CONSIDERATIONS CONCERNING OUR KNOWLEDGE.

1. Our Knowledge partly necessary partly voluntary.
Our knowledge, as in other things, so in this, has so great a conformity with our sight, that it is neither wholly necessary, nor wholly voluntary. If our knowledge were altogether necessary, all men's knowledge would not only be alike, but every man would know all that is knowable; and if it were wholly voluntary, some men so little regard or value it, that they would have extreme little, or none at all. Men that have senses cannot choose but receive some ideas by them; and if they have memory, they cannot but retain some of them; and if they have any distinguishing faculty, cannot but perceive the agreement or disagreement of some of them one with another; as he that has eyes, if he will open them by day, cannot but see some objects, and perceive a difference in them. But though a man with his eyes open in the light, cannot but see, yet there be certain objects which he may choose whether he will turn his eyes to; there may be in his reach a book containing pictures and discourses, capable to delight or instruct him, which yet he may never have the will to open, never take the pains to look into.
2. The application of our Faculties voluntary; but they being employed, we know as things are, not as we please.
There is also another thing in a man's power, and that is, though he turns his eyes sometimes towards an object, yet he may choose whether he will curiously survey it, and with an intent application endeavour to observe accurately all that is visible in it. But yet, what he does see, he cannot see otherwise than he does. It depends not on his will to see that black which appears yellow; nor to persuade himself, that what actually scalds him, feels cold. The earth will not appear painted with flowers, nor the fields covered with verdure, whenever he has a mind to it: in the cold winter, he cannot help seeing it white and hoary, if he will look abroad. Just thus is it with our understanding: all that is voluntary in our knowledge is, the employing or withholding any of our FACULTIES from this or that sort of objects, and a more or less accurate survey of them: but, THEY BEING EMPLOYED, OUR WILL HATH NO POWER TO DETERMINE THE KNOWLEDGE OF THE MIND ONE WAY OR ANOTHER; that is done

only by the objects themselves, as far as they are clearly discovered. And therefore, as far as men's senses are conversant about external objects, the mind cannot but receive those ideas which are presented by them, and be informed of the existence of things without: and so far as men's thoughts converse with their own determined ideas, they cannot but in some measure observe the agreement or disagreement that is to be found amongst some of them, which is so far knowledge: and if they have names for those ideas which they have thus considered, they must needs be assured of the truth of those propositions which express that agreement or disagreement they perceive in them, and be undoubtedly convinced of those truths. For what a man sees, he cannot but see; and what he perceives, he cannot but know that he perceives.

3. Instance in Numbers.

Thus he that has got the ideas of numbers, and hath taken the pains to compare one, two, and three, to six, cannot choose but know that they are equal: he that hath got the idea of a triangle, and found the ways to measure its angles and their magnitudes, is certain that its three angles are equal to two right ones; and can as little doubt of that, as of this truth, that, It is impossible for the same thing to be, and not to be.

4. Instance in Natural Religion.

He also that hath the idea of an intelligent, but frail and weak being, made by and depending on another, who is eternal, omnipotent, perfectly wise and good, will as certainly know that man is to honour, fear, and obey God, as that the sun shines when he sees it. For if he hath but the ideas of two such beings in his mind, and will turn his thoughts that way, and consider them, he will as certainly find that the inferior, finite, and dependent, is under an obligation to obey the supreme and infinite, as he is certain to find that three, four, and seven are less than fifteen; if he will consider and compute those numbers: nor can he be surer in a clear morning that the sun is risen; if he will but open his eyes, and turn them that way. But yet these truths, being ever so certain, ever so clear, he may be ignorant of either, or all of them, who will never take the pains to employ his faculties, as he should, to inform himself about them.

CHAPTER XIV. OF JUDGMENT.

1. Our Knowledge being short, we want something else.
The understanding faculties being given to man, not barely for speculation, but also for the conduct of his life, man would be at a great loss if he had nothing to direct him but what has the certainty of true knowledge. For that being very short and scanty, as we have seen, he would be often utterly in the dark, and in most of the actions of his life, perfectly at a stand, had he nothing to guide him in the absence of clear and certain knowledge. He that will not eat till he has demonstration that it will nourish him; he that will not stir till he infallibly knows the business he goes about will succeed, will have little else to do but to sit still and perish.

2. What Use to be made of this twilight State.
Therefore, as God has set some things in broad daylight; as he has given us some certain knowledge, though limited to a few things in comparison, probably as a taste of what intellectual creatures are capable of to excite in us a desire and endeavour after a better state: so, in the greatest part of our concernments, he has afforded us only the twilight, as I may so say, of probability; suitable, I presume, to that state of mediocrity and probationership he has been pleased to place us in here; wherein, to check our over-confidence and presumption, we might, by every day's experience, be made sensible of our short-sightedness and liableness to error; the sense whereof might be a constant admonition to us, to spend the days of this our pilgrimage with industry and care, in the search and following of that way which might lead us to a state of greater perfection. It being highly rational to think, even were revelation silent in the case, that, as men employ those talents God has given them here, they shall accordingly receive their rewards at the close of the day, when their sun shall set, and night shall put an end to their labours.

3. Judgement or assent to Probability, supplies our want of Knowledge.
The faculty which God has given man to supply the want of clear and certain knowledge, in cases where that cannot be had, is JUDGEMENT: whereby the mind takes its ideas to agree or disagree; or, which is the same, any proposition to be true or false, without perceiving a demonstrative evidence in the proofs. The mind sometimes exercises this judgment out of necessity, where demonstrative proofs and certain knowledge are not to be had; and sometimes out of laziness, unskilfulness, or haste, even where demonstrative and certain proofs are to be had. Men often stay not warily to examine the agreement or disagreement of two ideas, which they are

desirous or concerned to know; but, either incapable of such attention as is requisite in a long train of gradations, or impatient of delay, lightly cast their eyes on, or wholly pass by the proofs; and so, without making out the demonstration, determine of the agreement or disagreement of two ideas, as it were by a view of them as they are at a distance, and take it to be the one or the other, as seems most likely to them upon such a loose survey. This faculty of the mind, when it is exercised immediately about things, is called JUDGEMENT; when about truths delivered in words, is most commonly called ASSENT or DISSENT: which being the most usual way, wherein the mind has occasion to employ this faculty, I shall, under these terms, treat of it, as feast liable in our language to equivocation.

4. Judgement is the presuming Things to be so, without perceiving it.

Thus the mind has two faculties conversant (about truth and falsehood):—

First, KNOWLEDGE, whereby it certainly PERCEIVES, and is undoubtedly satisfied of the agreement or disagreement of any ideas.

Secondly, JUDGEMENT, which is the putting ideas together, or separating them from one another in the mind, when their certain agreement or disagreement is not perceived, but PRESUMED to be so; which is, as the word imports, taken to be so before it certainly appears. And if it so unites or separates them as in reality things are, it is right judgement.

CHAPTER XV. OF PROBABILITY.

1. Probability is the appearance of Agreement upon fallible Proofs.
As DEMONSTRATION is the showing the agreement or disagreement of two ideas, by the intervention of one or more proofs, which have a constant, immutable, and visible connexion one with another; so PROBABILITY is nothing but the appearance of such an agreement or disagreement, by the intervention of proofs, whose connexion is not constant and immutable, or at least is not perceived to be so, but is, or appears for the most part to be so, and is enough to induce the mind to judge the proposition to be true or false, rather than the contrary. For example: in the demonstration of it a man perceives the certain, immutable connexion there is of equality between the three angles of a triangle, and those intermediate ones which are made use of to show their equality to two right ones; and so, by an intuitive knowledge of the agreement or disagreement of the intermediate ideas in each step of the progress, the whole series is continued with an evidence, which clearly shows the agreement or disagreement of those three angles in equality to two right ones: and thus he has certain knowledge that it is so. But another man, who never took the pains to observe the demonstration, hearing a mathematician, a man of credit, affirm the three angles of a triangle to be equal to two right ones, assents to it, i.e. receives it for true: in which case the foundation of his assent is the probability of the thing; the proof being such as for the most part carries truth with it: the man on whose testimony he receives it, not being wont to affirm anything contrary to or besides his knowledge, especially in matters of this kind: so that that which causes his assent to this proposition, that the three angles of a triangle are equal to two right ones, that which makes him take these ideas to agree, without knowings them to do so, is the wonted veracity of the speaker in other cases, or his supposed veracity in this.
2. It is to supply our Want of Knowledge.
Our knowledge, as has been shown, being very narrow, and we not happy enough to find certain truth in everything which we have occasion to consider; most of the propositions we think, reason, discourse—nay, act upon, are such as we cannot have undoubted knowledge of their truth: yet some of them border so near upon certainty, that we make no act, according to the assent, as resolutely as if they were infallibly demonstrated, and that our knowledge of them was perfect and certain. But there being degrees herein, from the very neighbourhood of certainty and demonstration, quite

down to improbability and unlikeness, even to the confines of impossibility; and also degrees of assent from full assurance and confidence, quite down to conjecture, doubt, and distrust: I shall come now, (having, as I think, found out THE BOUNDS OF HUMAN KNOWLEDGE AND CERTAINTY,) in the next place, to consider THE SEVERAL DEGREES AND GROUNDS OF PROBABILITY, AND ASSENT OR FAITH.

3. Being that which makes us presume Things to be true, before we know them to be so.

Probability is likeliness to be true, the very notation of the word signifying such a proposition, for which there be arguments or proofs to make it pass, or be received for true. The entertainment the mind gives this sort of propositions is called BELIEF, ASSENT, or OPINION, which is the admitting or receiving any proposition for true, upon arguments or proofs that are found to persuade us to receive it as true, without certain knowledge that it is so. And herein lies the difference between PROBABILITY and CERTAINTY, FAITH, and KNOWLEDGE, that in all the parts of knowledge there is intuition; each immediate idea, each step has its visible and certain connexion: in belief, not so. That which makes me believe, is something extraneous to the thing I believe; something not evidently joined on both sides to, and so not manifestly showing the agreement or disagreement of those ideas that are under consideration.

4. The Grounds of Probability are two: Conformity with our own Experience, or the Testimony of others.

Probability then, being to supply the defect of our knowledge, and to guide us where that fails, is always conversant about propositions whereof we have no certainty, but only some inducements to receive them for true. The grounds of it are, in short, these two following:—

First, The conformity of anything with our own knowledge, observation, and experience.

Secondly, The testimony of others, vouching their observation and experience. In the testimony of others is to be considered: 1. The number. 2. The integrity. 3. The skill of the witnesses. 4. The design of the author, where it is a testimony out of a book cited. 5. The consistency of the parts, and circumstances of the relation. 6. Contrary testimonies.

5. In this, all the Arguments pro and con ought to be examined, before we come to a Judgment.

Probability wanting that intuitive evidence which, infallibly determines the understanding and produces certain knowledge, the mind, if it WILL

PROCEED RATIONALLY, ought to examine all the grounds of probability, and see how they make more or less for or against any proposition, before it assents to or dissents from it; and, upon a due balancing the whole, reject or receive it, with a more or less firm assent, proportionably to the preponderancy of the greater grounds of probability on one side or the other. For example:—

If I myself see a man walk on the ice, it is past probability; it is knowledge. But if another tells me he saw a man in England, in the midst of a sharp winter, walk upon water hardened with cold, this has so great conformity with what is usually observed to happen, that I am disposed by the natures of the thing itself to assent to it; unless some manifest suspicion attend the relation of that matter of fact. But if the same thing be told to one born between the tropics, who never saw nor heard of any such thing before, there the whole probability relies on testimony: and as the relators are more in number, and of more credit, and have no interest to speak contrary to the truth, so that matter of fact is like to find more or less belief. Though to a man whose experience has always been quite contrary, and who has never heard of anything like it, the most untainted credit of a witness will scarce be able to find belief. As it happened to a Dutch ambassador, who entertaining the king of Siam with the particularities of Holland, which he was inquisitive after, amongst other things told him, that the water in his country would sometimes, in cold weather, be so hard, that men walked upon it, and that it would bear an elephant, if he were there. To which the king replied, HITHERTO *I* HAVE BELIEVED THE STRANGE THINGS YOU HAVE TOLD ME, BECAUSE *I* LOOK UPON YOU AS A SOBER FAIR MAN, BUT NOW *I* AM SURE YOU LIE.

6. Probable arguments capable of great Variety.

Upon these grounds depends the probability of any proposition: and as the conformity of our knowledge, as the certainty of observations, as the frequency and constancy of experience, and the number and credibility of testimonies do more or less agree or disagree with it, so is any proposition in itself more or less probable. There is another, I confess, which, though by itself it be no true ground of probability, yet is often made use of for one, by which men most commonly regulate their assent, and upon which they pin their faith more than anything else, and that is, THE OPINION OF OTHERS; though there cannot be a more dangerous thing to rely on, nor more likely to mislead one; since there is much more falsehood and error among men, than truth and knowledge. And if the opinions and persuasions of others, whom we know and think well of, be a ground of assent, men have reason to be Heathens in Japan, Mahometans in Turkey, Papists in Spain, Protestants in England, and Lutherans in Sweden. But of this wrong ground of assent I shall have occasion to speak more at large in another place.

CHAPTER XVI. OF THE DEGREES OF ASSENT.

1. Our Assent ought to be regulated by the Grounds of Probability.
The grounds of probability we have laid down in the foregoing chapter: as they are the foundations on which our ASSENT is built, so are they also the measure whereby its several degrees are, or ought to be regulated: only we are to take notice, that, whatever grounds of probability there may be, they yet operate no further on the mind which searches after truth, and endeavours to judge right, than they appear; at least, in the first judgment or search that the mind makes. I confess, in the opinions men have, and firmly stick to in the world, their assent is not always from an actual view of the reasons that at first prevailed with them: it being in many cases almost impossible, and in most, very hard, even for those who have very admirable memories, to retain all the proofs which, upon a due examination, made them embrace that side of the question. It suffices that they have once with care and fairness sifted the matter as far as they could; and that they have searched into all the particulars, that they could imagine to give any light to the question; and, with the best of their skill, cast up the account upon the whole evidence: and thus, having once found on which side the probability appeared to THEM, after as full and exact an inquiry as they can make, they lay up the conclusion in their memories, as a truth they have discovered; and for the future they remain satisfied with the testimony of their memories, that this is the opinion that, by the proofs they have once seen of it, deserves such a degree of their assent as they afford it.

2. These can not always be actually in View; and then we must content ourselves with the remembrance that we once saw ground for such a Degree of Assent.
This is all that the greatest part of men are capable of doing, in regulating their opinions and judgments; unless a man will exact of them, either to retain distinctly in their memories all the proofs concerning any probable truth, and that too, in the same order, and regular deduction of consequences in which they have formerly placed or seen them; which sometimes is enough to fill a large volume on one single question: or else they must require a man, for every opinion that he embraces, every day to examine the proofs: both which are impossible. It is unavoidable, therefore, that the memory be relied on in the case, and that men be persuaded of several opinions, whereof the proofs are not actually in their thoughts; nay, which perhaps they are not able actually to recall. Without

this, the greatest part of men must be either very sceptics; or change every moment, and yield themselves up to whoever, having lately studied the question, offers them arguments, which, for want of memory, they are not able presently to answer.

3. The ill consequence of this, if our former Judgments were not rightly made.

I cannot but own, that men's sticking to their past judgment, and adhering firmly to conclusions formerly made, is often the cause of great obstinacy in error and mistake. But the fault is not that they rely on their memories for what they have before well judged, but because they judged before they had well examined. May we not find a great number (not to say the greatest part) of men that think they have formed right judgments of several matters; and that for no other reason, but because they never thought otherwise? that themselves to have judged right, only because they never questioned, never examined, their own opinions? Which is indeed to think they judged right, because they never judged at all. And yet these, of all men, hold their opinions with the greatest stiffness; those being generally the most fierce and firm in their tenets, who have least examined them. What we once KNOW, we are certain is so: and we may be secure, that there are no latent proofs undiscovered, which may overturn our knowledge, or bring it in doubt. But, in matters of PROBABILITY, it is not in every case we can be sure that we have all the particulars before us, that any way concern the question; and that there is no evidence behind, and yet unseen, which may cast the probability on the other side, and outweigh all that at present seems to preponderate with us. Who almost is there that hath the leisure, patience, and means to collect together all the proofs concerning most of the opinions he has, so as safely to conclude that he hath a clear and full view; and that there is no more to be alleged for his better information? And yet we are forced to determine ourselves on the one side or other. The conduct of our lives, and the management of our great concerns, will not bear delay: for those depend, for the most part, on the determination of our judgment in points wherein we are not capable of certain and demonstrative knowledge, and wherein it is necessary for us to embrace the one side or the other.

4. The right Use of it, mutual Charity and Forbearance, in a necessary diversity of opinions.

Since, therefore, it is unavoidable to the greatest part of men, if not all, to have several OPINIONS, without certain and indubitable proofs of their truth; and it carries too great an imputation of ignorance, lightness, or folly for men to quit and renounce their former tenets presently upon the offer of an argument which they cannot immediately answer, and show the insufficiency of: it would, methinks, become all men to maintain peace, and the common offices of humanity, and friendship, in the diversity of opinions; since we cannot reasonably expect that any one should readily and obsequiously quit his own opinion, and embrace ours, with a blind resignation to an authority which the understanding of man acknowledges not. For however it may often mistake, it can own no other guide but reason, nor blindly submit to the will and dictates of another. If he you would bring over to your sentiments be one that examines before he assents, you must give him leave at his leisure to go over the account again, and, recalling what is out of his mind, examine all the particulars, to see on which side the advantage lies: and if he will not think our arguments of weight enough to engage him anew in so much pains, it is but what we often do ourselves in the like case; and we should take it amiss if others should prescribe to us what points we should study. And if he be one who takes his opinions upon trust, how can we imagine that he should renounce those tenets which time and custom have so settled in his mind, that he thinks them self-evident, and of an unquestionably certainty; or which he takes to be impressions he has received from God himself, or from men sent by him? How can we expect, I say, that opinions thus settled should be given up to the arguments or authority of a stranger or adversary, especially if there be any suspicion of interest or design, as there never fails to be, where men find themselves ill-trusted? We should do well to commiserate our mutual ignorance, and endeavour to remove it in all the gentle and fair ways of information; and not instantly treat others ill, as obstinate and perverse, because they will not renounce their own, and receive our opinions, or at least those we would force upon them, when it is more than probable that we are no less obstinate in not embracing some of theirs. For where is the man that has incontestable evidence of the truth of all that he holds, or of the falsehood of all he condemns; or can say that he has examined to the bottom all his own, or other men's opinions? The necessity of believing without knowledge, nay often upon very slight grounds, in this fleeting state of action and blindness we are in, should make us more busy and careful to inform ourselves than constrain others. At least, those who have not thoroughly examined to the bottom all their own tenets, must confess they are unfit to prescribe to others; and are unreasonable in imposing that as truth on other men's belief, which they themselves have not searched into, nor weighed the arguments of probability, on which they should receive or reject it. Those who have fairly and truly examined, and are thereby got past doubt in all the doctrines they profess and govern themselves by, would have a juster pretence to require others to follow them: but these are so few in number, and find so little reason to be magisterial in their opinions, that nothing insolent and imperious is to be expected from them: and there is reason to think, that, if men were better instructed themselves, they would be less imposing on others.

5. Probability is either of sensible Matter of Fact, capable of human testimony, or of what is beyond the evidence of our senses.

But to return to the grounds of assent, and the several degrees of it, we are to take notice, that the propositions we receive upon inducements of PROBABILITY are of TWO SORTS: either concerning some particular existance, or, as it is usually termed, matter of fact, which, falling under observation, is capable of human testimony; or else concerning things, which being beyond the discovery of our senses, are not capable of any such testimony.

6. Concerning the FIRST of these, viz. PARTICULAR MATTER OF FACT.

I. The concurrent Experience of ALL other Men with ours, produces Assurance approaching to Knowledge.

Where any particular thing, consonant to the constant observation of ourselves and others in the like case, comes attested by the concurrent reports of all that mention it, we receive it as easily, and build as firmly upon it, as if it were certain knowledge; and we reason and act thereupon with as little doubt as if it were perfect demonstration. Thus, if all Englishmen, who have occasion to mention it, should affirm that it froze in England the last winter, or that there were swallows seen there in the summer, I think a man could almost as little doubt of it as that seven and four are eleven. The first, therefore, and HIGHEST DEGREE OF PROBABILITY, is, when the general consent of all men, in all ages, as far as it can be known, concurs with a man's constant and never-failing experience in like cases, to confirm the truth of any particular matter of fact attested by fair witnesses: such are all the stated constitutions and properties of bodies, and the regular proceedings of causes and effects in the ordinary course of nature. This we call an argument from the nature of things themselves. For what our own and other men's CONSTANT OBSERVATION has found always to be after the same manner, that we with reason conclude to be the effect of steady and regular causes; though they come not within the reach of our knowledge. Thus, That fire warmed a man, made lead fluid, and changed the colour or consistency in wood or charcoal; that iron sunk in water, and swam in quicksilver: these and the like propositions about particular facts, being agreeable to our constant experience, as often as we have to do with these matters; and being generally spoke of (when mentioned by others) as things found constantly to be so, and therefore not so much as controverted by anybody—we are put past doubt that a relation affirming any such thing to have been, or any predication that it will happen again in the same manner, is very true. These PROBABILITIES rise so near to CERTAINTY, that they govern our thoughts as absolutely, and influence all our actions as fully, as the most evident demonstration; and in what concerns us we make little or no difference between them and certain knowledge. Our belief, thus grounded, rises to ASSURANCE.

7. II. Unquestionable Testimony, and our own Experience that a thing is for the most part so, produce Confidence.

The NEXT DEGREE OF PROBABILITY is, when I find by my own experience, and the agreement of all others that mention it, a thing to be for the most part so, and that the particular instance of it is attested by many and undoubted witnesses: v.g. history giving us such an account of men in all ages, and my own experience, as far as I had an opportunity to observe, confirming it, that most men prefer their private advantage to the public: if all historians that write of Tiberius, say that Tiberius did so, it is extremely probable. And in this case, our assent has a sufficient foundation to raise itself to a degree which we may call CONFIDENCE.

8. III. Fair Testimony, and the Nature of the Thing indifferent, produce unavoidable Assent.

In things that happen indifferently, as that a bird should fly this or that way; that it should thunder on a man's right or left hand, &c., when any particular matter of fact is vouched by the concurrent testimony of unsuspected witnesses, there our assent is also UNAVOIDABLE. Thus: that there is such a city in Italy as Rome: that about one thousand seven hundred years ago, there lived in it a man, called Julius Caesar; that he was a general, and that he won a battle against another, called Pompey. This, though in the nature of the thing there be nothing for nor against it, yet being related by historians of credit, and contradicted by no one writer, a man cannot avoid believing it, and can as little doubt of it as he does of the being and actions of his own acquaintance, whereof he himself is a witness.

9. Experience and Testimonies clashing, infinitely vary the Degrees of Probability.

Thus far the matter goes easy enough. Probability upon such grounds carries so much evidence with it, that it naturally determines the judgment, and leaves us as little liberty to believe or disbelieve, as a demonstration does, whether we will know, or be ignorant. The difficulty is, when testimonies contradict common experience, and the reports of history and witnesses clash with the ordinary course of nature, or with one another; there it is, where diligence, attention, and exactness are required, to form a right judgment, and to proportion the assent to the different evidence and probability of the thing: which rises and falls, according as those two foundations of credibility, viz. COMMON OBSERVATION IN LIKE CASES, and PARTICULAR TESTIMONIES IN THAT PARTICULAR INSTANCE, favour or contradict it. These are liable to so great variety of contrary observations, circumstances, reports, different qualifications, tempers, designs, oversights, &c., of the reporters, that it is impossible to reduce to precise rules the various degrees wherein men give their assent. This only may be said in general, That as the arguments and proofs PRO and CON, upon due examination, nicely weighing every particular circumstance, shall to any one appear, upon the whole matter, in a greater or less degree to preponderate on either side; so they are fitted to produce in the mind such different entertainments, as we call BELIEF, CONJECTURE, GUESS, DOUBT, WAVERING, DISTRUST, DISBELIEF, &c.

10. Traditional Testimonies, the further removed the less their Proof becomes.

This is what concerns assent in matters wherein testimony is made use of: concerning which, I think, it may not be amiss to take notice of a rule observed in the law of England; which is, That though the attested copy of a record be good proof, yet the copy of a copy, ever so well attested, and by ever so credible witnesses, will not be admitted as a proof in judicature. This is so generally approved as reasonable, and suited to the wisdom and caution to be used in our inquiry after material truths, that I never yet heard of any one that blamed it. This practice, if it be allowable in the decisions of right and wrong, carries this observation along with it, viz. THAT ANY TESTIMONY, THE FURTHER OFF IT IS FROM THE ORIGINAL TRUTH, THE LESS FORCE AND PROOF IT HAS. The being and existence of the thing itself, is what I call the original truth. A credible man vouching his knowledge of it is a good proof; but if another equally credible do witness it from his report, the testimony is weaker: and a third that attests the hearsay of an hearsay is yet less considerable. So that in traditional truths, each remove weakens the force of the proof: and the more hands the tradition has successively passed through, the less strength and evidence does it receive from them. This I thought necessary to be taken notice of: because I find amongst some men the quite contrary commonly practised, who look on opinions to gain force by growing older; and what a thousand years since would not, to a rational man contemporary with the first voucher, have appeared at all probable, is now urged as certain beyond all question, only because several have since, from him, said it one after another. Upon this ground propositions, evidently false or doubtful enough in their first beginning, come, by an inverted rule of probability, to pass for authentic truths; and those which found or deserved little credit from the mouths of their first authors, are thought to grow venerable by age, are urged as undeniable.

11. Yet History is of great Use.

I would not be thought here to lessen the credit and use of HISTORY: it is all the light we have in many cases, and we receive from it a great part of the useful truths we have, with a convincing evidence. I think nothing more valuable than the records of antiquity: I wish we had more of them, and more uncorrupted. But this truth itself forces me to say, That no probability can rise higher than its first original. What has no other evidence than the single testimony of one only witness must stand or fall by his only testimony, whether good, bad, or indifferent; and though cited afterwards by hundreds of others, one after another, is so far from receiving any strength thereby, that it is only the weaker. Passion, interest, inadvertency, mistake of his meaning, and a thousand odd reasons, or capricios, men's minds are acted by, (impossible to be discovered,) may make one man quote another man's words or meaning wrong. He that has but ever so little examined the citations of writers, cannot doubt how little credit the quotations deserve, where the originals are wanting; and consequently how much less quotations of quotations can be relied on. This is certain, that what in one age was affirmed upon slight grounds, can never after come to be more valid in future ages by being often repeated. But the further still it is from the original, the less valid it is, and has always less force in the mouth or writing of him that last made use of it than in his from whom he received it.

12. Secondly, In things which Sense cannot discover, Analogy is the great Rule of Probability.

[SECONDLY], The probabilities we have hitherto mentioned are only such as concern matter of fact, and such things as are capable of observation and testimony. There remains that other sort, concerning which men entertain opinions with variety of assent, though THE THINGS BE SUCH, THAT FALLING NOT UNDER THE REACH OF OUR SENSES, THEY ARE NOT CAPABLE OF TESTIMONY. Such are, 1. The existence, nature and operations of finite immaterial beings without us; as spirits, angels, devils, &c. Or the existence of material beings which, either for their smallness in themselves or remoteness from us, our senses cannot take notice of—as, whether there be any plants, animals, and intelligent inhabitants in the planets, and other mansions of the vast universe. 2. Concerning the manner of operation in most parts of the works of nature: wherein, though we see the sensible effects, yet their causes are unknown, and we perceive not the ways and manner how they are produced. We see animals are generated, nourished, and move; the loadstone draws iron; and the parts of a candle, successively melting, turn into flame, and give us both light and heat. These and the like effects we see and know: but the causes that operate, and the manner they are produced in, we can only guess and probably conjecture. For these and the like, coming not within the scrutiny of human senses, cannot be examined by them, or be attested by anybody; and therefore can appear more or less probable, only as they more or less agree to truths that are established in our minds, and as they hold proportion to other parts of our knowledge and observation. ANALOGY in these matters is the only help we have, and it is from that alone we draw all our grounds of probability. Thus, observing that the bare rubbing of two bodies violently one upon another, produces heat, and very often fire itself, we have reason to think, that what we call HEAT and FIRE consists in a violent agitation of the imperceptible minute parts of the burning matter. Observing likewise that the different refractions of pellucid bodies produce in our eyes the different appearances of several colours; and also, that the different ranging and laying the superficial parts of several bodies, as of velvet, watered silk, &c., does the like, we think it probable that the COLOUR and shining of bodies is in them nothing but the different arrangement and refraction of their minute and insensible parts. Thus, finding in all parts of the creation, that fall under human observation, that there is A GRADUAL CONNEXION OF ONE WITH ANOTHER, WITHOUT ANY GREAT OR DISCERNIBLE GAPS BETWEEN, IN ALL THAT GREAT VARIETY OF THINGS WE SEE IN THE WORLD, which are so closely linked together, that, in the several ranks of beings, it is not easy to discover the bounds betwixt them; we have reason to be persuaded that, BY SUCH GENTLE STEPS, things ascend upwards in degrees of perfection. It is a hard matter to say where sensible and rational begin, and where insensible and irrational end: and who is there quick-sighted enough to determine precisely which is the lowest species of living things, and which the first of those which have no life? Things, as far as we can observe, lessen and augment, as the quantity does in a regular cone; where, though there be a manifest odds betwixt the bigness of the diameter at a remote distance, yet the difference between the upper and under, where they touch one another, is hardly discernible. The difference is exceeding great between some men and some animals: but if we will compare the understanding and abilities of some men and some brutes, we shall find so little difference, that it will be hard to say, that that of the man is either clearer or larger. Observing, I say, such gradual and gentle descents downwards in those parts of the creation that are beneath man, the rule of analogy may make it probable, that it is so also in things above us and our observation; and that there are several ranks of intelligent beings, excelling us in several degrees of perfection, ascending upwards towards the infinite perfection of the Creator, by gentle steps and differences, that are every one at no great distance from the next to it. This sort of probability, which is the best conduct of rational experiments, and the rise of hypothesis, has also its use and influence; and a wary reasoning from analogy leads us often into the discovery of truths and useful productions, which would otherwise lie concealed.

13. One Case where contrary Experience lessens not the Testimony.

Though the common experience and the ordinary course of things have justly a mighty influence on the minds of men, to make them give or refuse credit to anything proposed to their belief; yet there is one case, wherein the strangeness of the fact lessens not the assent to a fair testimony given of it. For where such supernatural events are suitable to ends aimed at by Him who has the power to change the course of nature, there, UNDER SUCH CIRCUMSTANCES, that may be the fitter to procure belief, by how much the more they are beyond or contrary to ordinary observation. This is the proper case of MIRACLES, which, well attested, do not only find credit themselves, but give it also to other truths, which need such confirmation.

14. The bare Testimony of Divine Revelation is the highest Certainty.

Besides those we have hitherto mentioned, there is one sort of propositions that challenge the highest degree of our assent, upon bare testimony, whether the thing proposed agree or disagree with common experience, and the ordinary course of things, or no. The reason whereof is, because the testimony is of such an one as cannot deceive nor be deceived: and that is of God himself. This carries with it an assurance beyond doubt, evidence beyond exception. This is called by a peculiar name, REVELATION, and our assent to it, FAITH, which [as absolutely determines our minds, and as perfectly excludes all wavering,] as our knowledge itself; and we may as well doubt of our own being, as we can whether any revelation from God be true. So that faith is a settled and sure principle of assent and assurance, and leaves no manner of room for doubt or hesitation. ONLY WE MUST BE SURE THAT IT BE A DIVINE REVELATION, AND THAT WE UNDERSTAND IT RIGHT: else we shall expose ourselves to all the extravagancy of enthusiasm, and all the error of wrong principles, if we have faith and assurance in what is not DIVINE revelation. And therefore, in those cases, our assent can be rationally no higher than the evidence of its being a revelation, and that this is the meaning of the expressions it is delivered in. If the evidence of its being a revelation, or that this is its true sense, be only on probable proofs, our assent can reach no higher than an assurance or diffidence, arising from the more or less apparent probability of the proofs. But of FAITH, and the precedency it ought to have before other arguments of persuasion, I shall speak more hereafter; where I treat of it as it is ordinarily placed, in contradistinction to reason; though in truth it be nothing else but AN ASSENT FOUNDED ON THE HIGHEST REASON.

CHAPTER XVII. OF REASON

1. Various Significations of the word Reason.
THE word REASON in the English language has different significations: sometimes it is taken for true and clear principles: sometimes for clear and fair deductions from those principles: and sometimes for the cause, and particularly the final cause. But the consideration I shall have of it here is in a signification different from all these; and that is, as it stands for a faculty in man, that faculty whereby man is supposed to be distinguished from beasts, and wherein it is evident he much surpasses them.
2. Wherein Reasoning consists.
If general knowledge, as has been shown, consists in a perception of the agreement or disagreement of our own ideas, and the knowledge of the existence of all things without us (except only of a God, whose existence every man may certainly know and demonstrate to himself from his own existence), be had only by our senses, what room is there for the exercise of any other faculty, but OUTWARD SENSE and INWARD PERCEPTION? What need is there of REASON? Very much: both for the enlargement of our knowledge, and regulating our assent. For it hath to do both in knowledge and opinion, and is necessary and assisting to all our other intellectual faculties, and indeed contains two of them, viz. SAGACITY and ILLATION. By the one, it finds out; and by the other, it so orders the intermediate ideas as to discover what connexion there is in each link of the chain, whereby the extremes are held together; and thereby, as it were, to draw into view the truth sought for, which is that which we call ILLATION or INFERENCE, and consists in nothing but the perception of the connexion there is between the ideas, in each step of the deduction; whereby the mind comes to see, either the certain agreement or disagreement of any two ideas, as in demonstration, in which it arrives at KNOWLEDGE; or their probable connexion, on which it gives or withholds its assent, as in OPINION. Sense and intuition reach but a very little way. The greatest part of our knowledge depends upon deductions and intermediate ideas: and in those cases where we are fain to substitute assent instead of knowledge, and take propositions for true, without being certain they are so, we have need to find out, examine, and compare the grounds of their probability. In both these cases, the faculty which finds out the means, and rightly applies them, to discover certainty in the one, and probability in the other, is that which we call REASON. For, as reason perceives the necessary and indubitable connexion of all the ideas or proofs

one to another, in each step of any demonstration that produces knowledge; so it likewise perceives the probable connexion of all the ideas or proofs one to another, in every step of a discourse, to which it will think assent due. This is the lowest degree of that which can be truly called reason. For where the mind does not perceive this probable connexion, where it does not discern whether there be any such connexion or no; there men's opinions are not the product of judgment, or the consequence of reason, but the effects of chance and hazard, of a mind floating at all adventures, without choice and without direction.

3. Reason in its four degrees.

So that we may in REASON consider these FOUR DEGREES: the first and highest is the discovering and finding out of truths; the second, the regular and methodical disposition of them, and laying them in a clear and fit order, to make their connexion and force be plainly and easily perceived; the third is the perceiving their connexion; and the fourth, a making a right conclusion. These several degrees may be observed in any mathematical demonstration; it being one thing to perceive the connexion of each part, as the demonstration is made by another; another to perceive the dependence of the conclusion on all the parts; a third, to make out a demonstration clearly and neatly one's self; and something different from all these, to have first found out these intermediate ideas or proofs by which it is made.

4. Whether Syllogism is the great Instrument of Reason.

There is one thing more which I shall desire to be considered concerning reason; and that is, whether SYLLOGISM, as is generally thought, be the proper instrument of it, and the usefullest way of exercising this faculty. The causes I have to doubt are these:—

First Cause to doubt this.

FIRST, Because syllogism serves our reason but in one only of the forementioned parts of it; and that is, to show the CONNEXION OF THE PROOFS in any one instance, and no more; but in this it is of no great use, since the mind can perceive such connexion, where it really is, as easily, nay, perhaps better, without it.

Men can reason well who cannot make a Syllogism.

If we will observe the actings of our own minds, we shall find that we reason best and clearest, when we only observe the connexion of the proof, without reducing our thoughts to any rule of syllogism. And therefore we may take notice, that there are many men that reason exceeding clear and rightly, who know not how to make a syllogism. He that will look into many parts of Asia and America, will find men reason there perhaps as acutely as himself, who yet never heard of a syllogism, nor can reduce any one argument to those forms: [and I believe scarce any one makes syllogisms in reasoning within himself.] Indeed syllogism is made use of, on occasion, to discover a fallacy hid in a rhetorical flourish, or cunningly wrapt up in a smooth period; and, stripping an absurdity of the cover of wit and good language, show it in its naked deformity. But the mind is not taught to reason by these rules; it has a native faculty to perceive the coherence or incoherence of its ideas, and can range them right without any such perplexing repetitions. Tell a country gentlewoman that the wind is south-west, and the weather lowering, and like to rain, and she will easily understand it is not safe for her to go abroad thin clad in such a day, after a fever: she clearly sees the probable connexion of all these, viz. south-west wind, and clouds, rain, wetting, taking cold, relapse, and danger of death, without tying them together in those artificial and cumbersome fetters of several syllogisms, that clog and hinder the mind, which proceeds from one part to another quicker and clearer without them: and the probability which she easily perceives in things thus in their native state would be quite lost, if this argument were managed learnedly, and proposed in MODE and FIGURE. For it very often confounds the connexion; and, I think, every one will perceive in mathematical demonstrations, that the knowledge gained thereby comes shortest and clearest without syllogism.

Secondly, Because though syllogism serves to show the force or fallacy of an argument, made use of in the usual way of discoursing, BY SUPPLYING THE ABSENT PROPOSITION, and so, setting it before the view in a clear light; yet it no less engages the mind in the perplexity of obscure, equivocal, and fallacious terms, wherewith this artificial way of reasoning always abounds: it being adapted more to the attaining of victory in dispute than the discovery and confirmation of truth in fair enquiries.

5. Syllogism helps little in Demonstration, less in Probability.

But however it be in knowledge, I think I may truly say, it is OF FAR LESS, OR NO USE AT ALL IN PROBABILITIES. For the assent there being to be determined by the preponderancy, after due weighing of all the proofs, with all circumstances on both sides, nothing is so unfit to assist the mind in that as syllogism; which running away with one assumed probability, or one topical argument, pursues that till it has led the mind quite out of sight of the thing under consideration; and, forcing it upon some remote difficulty, holds it fast there; entangled perhaps, and, as it were, manacled, in the chain of syllogisms, without allowing it the liberty, much less affording it the helps, requisite to show on which side, all things considered, is the greater probability.

6. Serves not to increase our Knowledge, but to fence with the Knowledge we suppose we have.

But let it help us (as perhaps may be said) in convincing men of their errors and mistakes: (and yet I would fain see the man that was forced out of his opinion by dint of syllogism,) yet still it fails our reason in that part, which, if not its highest perfection, is yet certainly its hardest task, and that which we most need its help in; and that is THE FINDING OUT OF PROOFS, AND MAKING NEW DISCOVERIES. The rules of syllogism serve not to furnish the mind with those intermediate ideas that may show the connexion of remote ones. This way of reasoning discovers no new proofs, but is the art of marshalling and ranging the old ones we have already. The forty-seventh proposition of the first book of Euclid is very true; but the discovery of it, I think, not owing to any rules of common logic. A man knows first and then he is able to prove syllogistically. So that syllogism comes after knowledge, and then a man has little or no need of it. But it is chiefly by the finding out those ideas that show the connexion of distant ones, that our stock of knowledge is increased, and that useful arts and sciences are advanced. Syllogism, at best, is but the art of fencing with the little knowledge we have, without making any addition to it. And if a man should employ his reason all this way, he will not do much otherwise than he who, having got some iron out of the bowels of the earth, should have it beaten up all into swords, and put it into his servants' hands to fence with and bang one another. Had the King of Spain employed the hands of his people, and his Spanish iron so, he had brought to light but little of that treasure that lay so long hid in the dark entrails of America. And I am apt to think that he who shall employ all the force of his reason only in brandishing of syllogisms, will discover very little of that mass of knowledge which lies yet concealed in the secret recesses of nature; and which, I am apt to think, native rustic reason (as it formerly has done) is likelier to open a way to, and add to the common stock of mankind, rather than any scholastic proceeding by the strict rules of MODE and FIGURE.

7. Other Helps to reason than Syllogism should be sought.

I doubt not, nevertheless, but there are ways to be found to assist our reason in this most useful part; and this the judicious Hooker encourages me to say, who in his Eccl. Pol. 1. i. Section 6, speaks thus: 'If there might be added the right helps of true art and learning, (which helps, I must plainly confess, this age of the world, carrying the name of a learned age, doth neither much know nor generally regard,) there would undoubtedly be almost as much difference in maturity of judgment between men therewith inured, and that which men now are, as between men that are now, and innocents.' I do not pretend to have found or discovered here any of those 'right helps of art,' this great man of deep thought mentions: but that is plain, that syllogism, and the logic now in use, which were as well known in his days, can be none of those he means. It is sufficient for me, if by a Discourse, perhaps something out of the way, I am sure, as to me, wholly new and unborrowed, I shall have given occasion to others to cast about for new discoveries, and to seek in their own thoughts for those right helps of art, which will scarce be found, I fear, by those who servilely confine themselves to the rules and dictates of others. For beaten tracks lead this sort of cattle, (as an observing Roman calls them,) whose thoughts reach only to imitation, NON QUO EUNDUM EST, SED QUO ITUR. But I can be bold to say, that this age is adorned with some men of that strength of judgment and largeness of comprehension, that, if they would employ their thoughts on this subject, could open new and undiscovered ways to the advancement of knowledge.

8. We can reason about Particulars; and the immediate object of all our reasonings is nothing but particular ideas.

Having here had occasion to speak of syllogism in general, and the use of it in reasoning, and the improvement of our knowledge, it is fit, before I leave this subject, to take notice of one manifest mistake in the rules of syllogism: viz. that no syllogistical reasoning can be right and conclusive, but what has at least one GENERAL proposition in it. As if we could not reason, and have knowledge about particulars: whereas, in truth, the matter rightly considered, the immediate object of all our reasoning and knowledge, is nothing but particulars. Every man's reasoning and knowledge is only about the ideas existing in his own mind; which are truly, every one of them, particular existences: and our knowledge and reason about other things, is only as they correspond with those our particular ideas. So that the perception of the agreement or disagreement of our particular ideas, is the whole and utmost of all our knowledge. Universality is but accidental to it, and consists only in this, that the particular ideas about which it is are such as more than one particular, thing can correspond with and be represented by. But the perception of the agreement or disagreement of our particular ideas, and consequently our knowledge, is equally clear and certain, whether either, or both, or neither of those ideas, be capable of representing more real beings than one, or no.

9. Our Reason often fails us.

REASON, though it penetrates into the depths of the sea and earth, elevates our thoughts as high as the stars, and leads us through the vast spaces and large rooms of this mighty fabric, yet it comes far short of the real extent of even corporeal being. And there are many instances wherein it fails us: as,

First, In cases when we have no Ideas.

I. It perfectly fails us, where our ideas fail. It neither does nor can extend itself further than they do. And therefore, wherever we have no ideas, our reasoning stops, and we are at an end of our reckoning: and if at any time we reason about words which do not stand for any ideas, it is only about those sounds, and nothing else.

10. Secondly, Because our Ideas are often obscure or imperfect.

II. Our reason is often puzzled and at a loss, because of the obscurity, confusion, or imperfection of the ideas it is employed about; and there we are involved in difficulties and contradictions. Thus, not having any perfect idea of the LEAST EXTENSION OF MATTER, nor of INFINITY, we are at a loss about the divisibility of matter; but having perfect, clear, and distinct ideas of NUMBER, our reason meets with none of those inextricable difficulties in numbers, nor finds itself involved in any contradictions about them. Thus, we having but imperfect ideas of the operations of our minds, and of the beginning of motion, or thought how the mind produces either of them in us, and much imperfecter yet of the operation of God, run into great difficulties about FREE CREATED AGENTS, which reason cannot well extricate itself out of.

11. III. Thirdly, Because we perceive not intermediate Ideas to show conclusions.

Our reason is often at a stand, because it perceives not those ideas, which could serve to show the certain or probable agreement or disagreement of any other two ideas: and in this some men's faculties far outgo others. Till algebra, that great instrument and instance of human sagacity, was discovered, men with amazement looked on several of the demonstrations of ancient mathematicians, and could scarce forbear to think the finding several of those proofs to be something more than human.

12. IV. Fourthly, Because we often proceed upon wrong Principles.

The mind, by proceeding upon false principles, is often engaged in absurdities and difficulties, brought into straits and contradictions, without knowing how to free itself: and in that case it is in vain to implore the help of reason, unless it be to discover the falsehood and reject the influence of those wrong principles. Reason is so far from clearing the difficulties which the building upon false foundations brings a man into, that if he will pursue it, it entangles him the more, and engages him deeper in perplexities.

13. V. Fifthly, Because we often employ doubtful Terms.

As obscure and imperfect ideas often involve our reason, so, upon the same ground, do dubious words and uncertain signs, often, in discourses and arguings, when not warily attended to, puzzle men's reason, and bring them to a nonplus. But these two latter are our fault, and not the fault of reason. But yet the consequences of them are nevertheless obvious; and the perplexities or errors they fill men's minds with are everywhere observable.

14. Our highest Degree of Knowledge is intuitive, without Reasoning.

Some of the ideas that are in the mind, are so there, that they can be by themselves immediately compared one with another: and in these the mind is able to perceive that they agree or disagree as clearly as that it has them. Thus the mind perceives, that an arch of a circle is less than the whole circle, as clearly as it does the idea of a circle: and this, therefore, as has been said, I call INTUITIVE KNOWLEDGE; which is certain, beyond all doubt, and needs no probation, nor can have any; this being the highest of all human certainty. In this consists the evidence of all those MAXIMS which nobody has any doubt about, but every man (does not, as is said, only assent to, but) KNOWS to be true, as soon as ever they are proposed to his understanding. In the discovery of and assent to these truths, there is no use of the discursive faculty, NO NEED OF REASONING, but they are known by a superior and higher degree of evidence. And such, if I may guess at things unknown, I am apt to think that angels have now, and the spirits of just men made perfect shall have, in a future state, of thousands of things which now either wholly escape our apprehensions, or which our short-sighted reason having got some faint glimpse of, we, in the dark, grope after.

15. The next is got by Reasoning.

But though we have, here and there, a little of this clear light, some sparks of bright knowledge, yet the greatest part of our ideas are such, that we cannot discern their agreement or disagreement by an immediate comparing them. And in all these we have NEED OF REASONING, and must, by discourse and inference, make our discoveries. Now of these there are two sorts, which I shall take the liberty to mention here again:—

First, through Reasonings that are Demonstrative.

First, Those whose agreement or disagreement, though it cannot be seen by an immediate putting them together, yet may be examined by the intervention of other ideas which can be compared with them. In this case, when the agreement or disagreement of the intermediate idea, on both sides, with those which we would compare, is PLAINLY DISCERNED: there it amounts to DEMONSTRATION whereby knowledge is produced, which, though it be certain, yet it is not so easy, nor altogether so clear as intuitive knowledge. Because in that there is barely one simple intuition, wherein there is no room for any the least mistake or doubt: the truth is seen all perfectly at once. In demonstration, it is true, there is intuition too, but not altogether at once; for there must be a remembrance of the intuition of the agreement of the medium, or intermediate idea, with that we compared it with before, when we compare it with the other: and where there be many mediums, there the danger of the mistake is the greater. For each agreement or disagreement of the ideas must be observed and seen in each step of the whole train, and retained in the memory, just as it is; and the mind must be sure that no part of what is necessary to make up the demonstration is omitted or overlooked. This makes some demonstrations long and perplexed, and too hard for those who have not strength of parts distinctly to perceive, and exactly carry so many particulars orderly in their heads. And even those who are able to master such intricate speculations, are fain sometimes to go over them again, and there is need of more than one review before they can arrive at certainty. But yet where the mind clearly retains the intuition it had of the agreement of any idea with another, and that with a third, and that with a fourth, &c., there the agreement of the first and the fourth is a demonstration, and produces certain knowledge; which may be called RATIONAL KNOWLEDGE, as the other is intuitive.

16. Secondly, to supply the narrowness of Demonstrative and Intuitive Knowledge we have nothing but Judgment upon probable reasoning.

Secondly, There are other ideas, whose agreement or disagreement can no otherwise be judged of but by the intervention of others which have not a certain agreement with the extremes, but an USUAL or LIKELY one: and in these is that the JUDGMENT is properly exercised; which is the acquiescing of the mind, that any ideas do agree, by comparing them with such probable mediums. This, though it never amounts to knowledge, no, not to that which is the lowest degree of it; yet sometimes the intermediate ideas tie the extremes so firmly together, and the probability is so clear and strong, that ASSENT as necessarily follows it, as KNOWLEDGE does demonstration. The great excellency and use of the judgment is to observe right, and take a true estimate of the force and weight of each probability; and then casting them up all right together, choose that side which has the overbalance.

17. Intuition, Demonstration, Judgment.

INTUITIVE KNOWLEDGE is the perception of the CERTAIN agreement or disagreement of two ideas immediately compared together.

RATIONAL KNOWLEDGE is the perception of the CERTAIN agreement or disagreement of any two ideas, by the intervention of one or more other ideas.

JUDGMENT is the thinking or taking two ideas to agree or disagree, by the intervention of one or more ideas, whose certain agreement or disagreement with them it does not perceive, but hath observed to be FREQUENT and USUAL.

18. Consequences of Words, and Consequences of Ideas.

Though the deducing one proposition from another, or making inferences in WORDS, be a great part of reason, and that which it is usually employed about; yet the principal act of ratiocination is THE FINDING THE AGREEMENT OR DISAGREEMENT OF TWO IDEAS ONE WITH ANOTHER, BY THE INTERVENTION OF A THIRD. As a man, by a yard, finds two houses to be of the same length, which could not be brought together to measure their equality by juxta-position. Words have their consequences, as the signs of such ideas: and things agree or disagree, as really they are; but we observe it only by our ideas.

19. Four sorts of Arguments.

Before we quit this subject, it may be worth our while a little to reflect on FOUR SORTS OF ARGUMENTS, that men, in their reasonings with others, do ordinarily make use of to prevail on their assent; or at least so to awe them as to silence their opposition.

First, Argumentum ad verecundiam.

I. The first is, to allege the opinions of men, whose parts, learning, eminency, power, or some other cause has gained a name, and settled their reputation in the common esteem with some kind of authority. When men are established in any kind of dignity, it is thought a breach of modesty for others to derogate any way from it, and question the authority of men who are in possession of it. This is apt to be censured, as carrying with it too much pride, when a man does not readily yield to the determination of approved authors, which is wont to be received with respect and submission by others: and it is looked upon as insolence, for a man to set up and adhere to his own opinion against the current stream of antiquity; or to put it in the balance against that of some learned doctor, or otherwise approved writer. Whoever backs his tenets with such authorities, thinks he ought thereby to carry the cause, and is ready to style it impudence in any one who shall stand out against them. This I think may be called ARGUMENTUM AD VERECUNDIAM.

20. Secondly, Argumentum ad Ignorantiam.

II. Secondly, Another way that men ordinarily use to drive others, and force them to submit their judgments, and receive the opinion in debate, is to require the adversary to admit what they allege as a proof, or to assign a better. And this I call ARGUMENTUM AD IGNORANTIAM.

21. Thirdly, Argumentum ad hominem.

III. Thirdly, A third way is to press a man with consequences drawn from his own principles or concessions. This is already known under the name of ARGUMENTUM AD HOMINEM.

22. Fourthly, Argumentum ad justicium. The Fourth alone advances us in knowledge and judgment.

IV. The fourth is the using of proofs drawn from any of the foundations of knowledge or probability. This I call ARGUMENTUM AD JUSTICIUM. This alone, of all the four, brings true instruction with it, and advances us in our way to knowledge. For, 1. It argues not another man's opinion to be right, because I, out of respect, or any other consideration but that of conviction, will not contradict him. 2. It proves not another man to be in the right way, nor that I ought to take the same with him, because I know not a better. 3. Nor does it follow that another man is in the right way, because he has shown me that I am in the wrong. I may be modest, and therefore not oppose another man's persuasion: I may be ignorant, and not be able to produce a better: I may be in an error, and another may show me that I am so. This may dispose me, perhaps, for the reception of truth, but helps me not to it: that must come from proofs and arguments, and light arising from the nature of things themselves, and not from my shamefacedness, ignorance, or error.

23. Above, contrary, and according to Reason.

By what has been before said of reason, we may be able to make some guess at the distinction of things, into those that are according to, above, and contrary to reason. 1. ACCORDING TO REASON are such propositions whose truth we can discover by examining and tracing those ideas we have from sensation and reflection; and by natural deduction find to be true or probable. 2. ABOVE REASON are such propositions whose truth or probability we cannot by reason derive from those principles. 3. CONTRARY TO REASON are such propositions as are inconsistent with or irreconcilable to our clear and distinct ideas. Thus the existence of one God is according to reason; the existence of more than one God, contrary to reason; the resurrection of the dead, above reason. ABOVE REASON also may be taken in a double sense, viz. either as signifying above probability, or above certainty: and in that large sense also, CONTRARY TO REASON, is, I suppose, sometimes taken.

24. Reason and Faith not opposite, for Faith must be regulated by Reason. There is another use of the word REASON, wherein it is OPPOSED TO FAITH: which, though it be in itself a very improper way of speaking, yet common use has so authorized it, that it would be folly either to oppose or hope to remedy it. Only I think it may not be amiss to take notice, that, however faith be opposed to reason, faith is nothing but a firm assent of the mind: which, if it be regulated, as is our duty, cannot be afforded to anything but upon good reason; and so cannot be opposite to it. He that believes without having any reason for believing, may be in love with his own fancies; but neither seeks truth as he ought, nor pays the obedience due to his Maker, who would have him use those discerning faculties he has given him, to keep him out of mistake and error. He that does not this to the best of his power, however he sometimes lights on truth, is in the right but by chance; and I know not whether the luckiness of the accident will excuse the irregularity of his proceeding. This at least is certain, that he must be accountable for whatever mistakes he runs into: whereas he that makes use of the light and faculties God has given him, and seeks sincerely to discover truth by those helps and abilities he has, may have this satisfaction in doing his duty as a rational creature, that, though he should miss truth, he will not miss the reward of it. For he governs his assent right, and places it as he should, who, in any case or matter whatsoever, believes or disbelieves according as reason directs him. He that doth otherwise, transgresses against his own light, and misuses those faculties which were given him to no other end, but to search and follow the clearer evidence and greater probability. But since reason and faith are by some men opposed, we will so consider them in the following chapter.

CHAPTER XVIII.

OF FAITH AND REASON, AND THEIR DISTINCT PROVINCES.

1. Necessary to know their boundaries.

It has been above shown, 1. That we are of necessity ignorant, and want knowledge of all sorts, where we want ideas. 2. That we are ignorant, and want rational knowledge, where we want proofs. 3. That we want certain knowledge and certainty, as far as we want clear and determined specific ideas. 4. That we want probability to direct our assent in matters where we have neither knowledge of our own nor testimony of other men to bottom our reason upon. From these things thus premised, I think we may come to lay down THE MEASURES AND BOUNDARIES BETWEEN FAITH AND REASON: the want whereof may possibly have been the cause, if not of great disorders, yet at least of great disputes, and perhaps mistakes in the world. For till it be resolved how far we are to be guided by reason, and how far by faith, we shall in vain dispute, and endeavour to convince one another in matters of religion.

2. Faith and Reason, what, as contradistingushed.

I find every sect, as far as reason will help them, make use of it gladly: and where it fails them, they cry out, It is matter of faith, and above reason. And I do not see how they can argue with any one, or ever convince a gainsayer who makes use of the same plea, without setting down strict boundaries between faith and reason; which ought to be the first point established in all questions where faith has anything to do.

REASON, therefore, here, as contradistinguished to FAITH, I take to be the discovery of the certainty or probability of such propositions or truths, which the mind arrives at by deduction made from such ideas, which it has got by the use of its natural faculties; viz. by sensation or reflection.

FAITH, on the other side, is the assent to any proposition, not thus made out by the deductions of reason, but upon the credit of the proposer, as coming from God, in some extraordinary way of communication. This way of discovering truths to men, we call REVELATION.

3. First, No new simple Idea can be conveyed by traditional Revelation.

FIRST, Then I say, that NO MAN INSPIRED BY GOD CAN BY ANY REVELATION COMMUNICATE TO OTHERS ANY NEW SIMPLE IDEAS WHICH THEY HAD NOT BEFORE FROM SENSATION OR

REFLECTION. For, whatsoever impressions he himself may have from the immediate hand of God, this revelation, if it be of new simple ideas, cannot be conveyed to another, either by words or any other signs. Because words, by their immediate operation on us, cause no other ideas but of their natural sounds: and it is by the custom of using them for signs, that they excite and revive in our minds latent ideas; but yet only such ideas as were there before. For words, seen or heard, recal to our thoughts those ideas only which to us they have been wont to be signs of, but cannot introduce any perfectly new, and formerly unknown simple ideas. The same holds in all other signs; which cannot signify to us things of which we have before never had any idea at all.

Thus whatever things were discovered to St. Paul, when he was rapt up into the third heaven; whatever new ideas his mind there received, all the description he can make to others of that place, is only this, That there are such things, 'as eye hath not seen, nor ear heard, nor hath it entered into the heart of man to conceive.' And supposing God should discover to any one, supernaturally, a species of creatures inhabiting, for example, Jupiter or Saturn, (for that it is possible there may be such, nobody can deny,) which had six senses; and imprint on his mind the ideas conveyed to theirs by that sixth sense: he could no more, by words, produce in the minds of other men those ideas imprinted by that sixth sense, than one of us could convey the idea of any colour, by the sound of words, into a man who, having the other four senses perfect, had always totally wanted the fifth, of seeing. For our simple ideas, then, which are the foundation, and sole matter of all our notions and knowledge, we must depend wholly on our reason, I mean our natural faculties; and can by no means receive them, or any of them, from traditional revelation. I say, TRADITIONAL REVELATION, in distinction to ORIGINAL REVELATION. By the one, I mean that first impression which is made immediately by God on the mind of any man, to which we cannot set any bounds; and by the other, those impressions delivered over to others in words, and the ordinary ways of conveying our conceptions one to another.

4. Secondly, Traditional Revelation may make us know Propositions knowable also by Reason, but not with the same Certainty that Reason doth.

SECONDLY, I say that THE SAME TRUTHS MAY BE DISCOVERED, AND CONVEYED DOWN FROM REVELATION, WHICH ARE DISCERNABLE TO US BY REASON, AND BY THOSE IDEAS WE NATURALLY MAY HAVE. So God might, by revelation, discover the truth of any proposition in Euclid; as well as men, by the natural use of their faculties, come to make the discovery themselves. In all things of this kind there is little need or use of revelation, God having furnished us with natural and surer means to arrive at the knowledge of them. For whatsoever truth we come to the clear discovery of, from the knowledge and contemplation of our own ideas, will always be certainer to us than those which are conveyed to us by TRADITIONAL REVELATION. For the knowledge we have that this revelation came at first from God, can never be so sure as the knowledge we have from the clear and distinct perception of the agreement or disagreement of our own ideas: v.g. if it were revealed some ages since, that the three angles of a triangle were equal to two right ones, I might assent to the truth of that proposition, upon the credit of the tradition, that it was revealed: but that would never amount to so great a certainty as the knowledge of it, upon the comparing and measuring my own ideas of two right angles, and the three angles of a triangle. The like holds in matter of fact knowable by our senses; v.g. the history of the deluge is conveyed to us by writings which had their original from revelation: and yet nobody, I think, will say he has as certain and clear a knowledge of the flood as Noah, that saw it; or that he himself would have had, had he then been alive and seen it. For he has no greater an assurance than that of his senses, that it is writ in the book supposed writ by Moses inspired: but he has not so great an assurance that Moses wrote that book as if he had seen Moses write it. So that the assurance of its being a revelation is less still than the assurance of his senses.

5. Even Original Revelation cannot be admitted against the clear Evidence of Reason.

In propositions, then, whose certainty is built upon the clear perception of the agreement or disagreement of our ideas, attained either by immediate intuition, as in self-evident propositions, or by evident deductions of reason in demonstrations we need not the assistance of revelation, as necessary to gain our assent, and introduce them into our minds. Because the natural ways of knowledge could settle them there, or had done it already; which is the greatest assurance we can possibly have of anything, unless where God immediately reveals it to us: and there too our assurance can be no greater than our knowledge is, that it IS a revelation from God. But yet nothing, I think, can, under that title, shake or overrule plain knowledge; or rationally prevail with any man to admit it for true, in a direct contradiction to the clear evidence of his own understanding. For, since no evidence of our faculties, by which we receive such revelations, can exceed, if equal, the certainty of our intuitive knowledge, we can never receive for a truth anything that is directly contrary to our clear and distinct knowledge; v.g. the ideas of one body and one place do so clearly agree, and the mind has so evident a perception of their agreement, that we can never assent to a proposition that affirms the same body to be in two distant places at once, however it should pretend to the authority of a divine revelation: since the evidence, first, that we deceive not ourselves, in ascribing it to God; secondly, that we understand it right; can never be so great as the evidence of our own intuitive knowledge, whereby we discern it impossible for the same body to be in two places at once. And therefore NO PROPOSITION CAN BE RECEIVED FOR DIVINE REVELATION, OR OBTAIN THE ASSENT DUE TO ALL SUCH, IF IT BE CONTRADICTORY TO OUR CLEAR INTUITIVE KNOWLEDGE. Because this would be to subvert the principles and foundations of all knowledge, evidence, and assent whatsoever: and there would be left no difference between truth and falsehood, no measures of credible and incredible in the world, if doubtful propositions shall take place before self-evident; and what we certainly know give way to what we may possibly be mistaken in. In propositions therefore contrary to the clear perception of the agreement or disagreement of any of our ideas, it will be in vain to urge them as matters of faith. They cannot move our assent under that or any other title whatsoever. For faith can never convince us of anything that contradicts our knowledge. Because, though faith be founded on the testimony of God (who cannot lie) revealing any proposition to us: yet we cannot have an assurance of the truth of its being a divine revelation greater than our own knowledge. Since the whole strength of the certainty depends upon our knowledge that God revealed it; which, in this case, where the proposition supposed revealed contradicts our knowledge or reason, will always have this objection hanging to it, viz. that we cannot tell how to conceive that to come from God, the bountiful Author of our being, which, if received for true, must overturn all the principles and foundations of knowledge he has given us; render all our faculties useless; wholly destroy the most excellent part of his workmanship, our understandings; and put a man in a condition wherein he will have less light, less conduct than the beast that perisheth. For if the mind of man can never have a clearer (and perhaps not so clear) evidence of anything to be a divine revelation, as it has of the principles of its own reason, it can never have a ground to quit the clear evidence of its reason, to give a place to a proposition, whose revelation has not a greater evidence than those principles have.

6. Traditional Revelation much less.

Thus far a man has use of reason, and ought to hearken to it, even in immediate and original revelation, where it is supposed to be made to himself. But to all those who pretend not to immediate revelation, but are required to pay obedience, and to receive the truths revealed to others, which, by the tradition of writings, or word of mouth, are conveyed down to them, reason has a great deal more to do, and is that only which can induce us to receive them. For matter of faith being only divine revelation, and nothing else, faith, as we use the word, (called commonly DIVINE FAITH), has to do with no propositions, but those which are supposed to be divinely revealed. So that I do not see how those who make revelation alone the sole object of faith can say, That it is a matter of faith, and not of reason, to believe that such or such a proposition, to be found in such or such a book, is of divine inspiration; unless it be revealed that that proposition, or all in that book, was communicated by divine inspiration. Without such a revelation, the believing, or not believing, that proposition, or book, to be of divine authority, can never be matter of faith, but matter of reason; and such as I must come to an assent to only by the use of my reason, which can never require or enable me to believe that which is contrary to itself: it being impossible for reason ever to procure any assent to that which to itself appears unreasonable.

In all things, therefore, where we have clear evidence from our ideas, and those principles of knowledge I have above mentioned, reason is the proper judge; and revelation, though it may, in consenting with it, confirm its dictates, yet cannot in such cases invalidate its decrees: nor can we be obliged, where we have the clear and evident sentence of reason, to quit it for the contrary opinion, under a pretence that it is matter of faith: which can have no authority against the plain and clear dictates of reason.

7. Thirdly, things above Reason are, when revealed, the proper matter of faith.

But, THIRDLY, There being many things wherein we have very imperfect notions, or none at all; and other things, of whose past, present, or future existence, by the natural use of our faculties, we can have no knowledge at all; these, as being beyond the discovery of our natural faculties, and ABOVE REASON, are, when revealed, THE PROPER MATTER OF FAITH. Thus, that part of the angels rebelled against God, and thereby lost their first happy state: and that the dead shall rise, and live again: these and the like, being beyond the discovery of reason, are purely matters of faith, with which reason has directly nothing to do.

8. Or not contrary to Reason, if revealed, are Matter of Faith; and must carry it against probable conjectures of Reason.

But since God, in giving us the light of reason, has not thereby tied up his own hands from affording us, when he thinks fit, the light of revelation in any of those matters wherein our natural faculties are able to give a probable determination; REVELATION, where God has been pleased to give it, MUST CARRY IT AGAINST THE PROBABLE CONJECTURES OF REASON. Because the mind not being certain of the truth of that it does not evidently know, but only yielding to the probability that appears in it, is bound to give up its assent to such a testimony which, it is satisfied, comes from one who cannot err, and will not deceive. But yet, it still belongs to reason to judge of the truth of its being a revelation, and of the signification of the words wherein it is delivered. Indeed, if anything shall be thought revelation which is contrary to the plain principles of reason, and the evident knowledge the mind has of its own clear and distinct ideas; there reason must be hearkened to, as to a matter within its province. Since a man can never have so certain a knowledge, that a proposition which contradicts the clear principles and evidence of his own knowledge was divinely revealed, or that he understands the words rightly wherein it is delivered, as he has that the contrary is true, and so is bound to consider and judge of it as a matter of reason, and not swallow it, without examination, as a matter of faith.

9. Revelation in Matters where Reason cannot judge, or but probably, ought to be hearkened to.

First, Whatever proposition is revealed, of whose truth our mind, by its natural faculties and notions, cannot judge, that is purely matter of faith, and above reason.

Secondly, All propositions whereof the mind, by the use of its natural faculties, can come to determine and judge, from naturally acquired ideas, are matter of reason; with this difference still, that, in those concerning which it has but an uncertain evidence, and so is persuaded of their truth only upon probable grounds, which still admit a possibility of the contrary to be true, without doing violence to the certain evidence of its own knowledge, and overturning the principles of all reason; in such probable propositions, I say, an evident revelation ought to determine our assent, even against probability. For where the principles of reason have not evidenced a proposition to be certainly true or false, there clear revelation, as another principle of truth and ground of assent, may determine; and so it may be matter of faith, and be also above reason. Because reason, in that particular matter, being able to reach no higher than probability, faith gave the determination where reason came short; and revelation discovered on which side the truth lay.

10. In Matters where Reason can afford certain Knowledge, that is to be hearkened to.

Thus far the dominion of faith reaches, and that without any violence or hindrance to reason; which is not injured or disturbed, but assisted and improved by new discoveries of truth, coming from the eternal fountain of all knowledge. Whatever God hath revealed is certainly true: no doubt can be made of it. This is the proper object of faith: but whether it be a DIVINE revelation or no, reason must judge; which can never permit the mind to reject a greater evidence to embrace what is less evident, nor allow it to entertain probability in opposition to knowledge and certainty. There can be no evidence that any traditional revelation is of divine original, in the words we receive it, and in the sense we understand it, so clear and so certain as that of the principles of reason: and therefore NOTHING THAT IS CONTRARY TO, AND INCONSISTENT WITH, THE CLEAR AND SELF-EVIDENT DICTATES OF REASON, HAS A RIGHT TO BE URGED OR ASSENTED TO AS A MATTER OF FAITH, WHEREIN REASON HATH NOTHING TO DO. Whatsoever is divine revelation, ought to overrule all our opinions, prejudices, and interest, and hath a right to be received with full assent. Such a submission as this, of our reason to faith, takes not away the landmarks of knowledge: this shakes not the foundations of reason, but leaves us that use of our faculties for which they were given us.

11. If the Boundaries be not set between Faith and Reason, no Enthusiasm or Extravagancy in Religion can be contradicted.

If the provinces of faith and reason are not kept distinct by these boundaries, there will, in matters of religion, be no room for reason at all; and those extravagant opinions and ceremonies that are to be found in the several religions of the world will not deserve to be blamed. For, to this crying up of faith in OPPOSITION to reason, we may, I think, in good measure ascribe those absurdities that fill almost all the religions which possess and divide mankind. For men having been principled with an opinion, that they must not consult reason in the things of religion, however apparently contradictory to common sense and the very principles of all their knowledge, have let loose their fancies and natural superstition; and have been by them led into so strange opinions, and extravagant practices in religion, that a considerate man cannot but stand amazed, at their follies, and judge them so far from being acceptable to the great and wise God, that he cannot avoid thinking them ridiculous and offensive to a sober good man. So that, in effect, religion, which should most distinguish us from beasts, and ought most peculiarly to elevate us, as rational creatures, above brutes, is that wherein men often appear most irrational, and more senseless than beasts themselves. CREDO, QUIA IMPOSSIBILE EST: I believe, because it is impossible, might, in a good man, pass for a sally of zeal; but would prove a very ill rule for men to choose their opinions or religion by.

CHAPTER XIX. [not in early editions]

CHAPTER XX.

OF WRONG ASSENT, OR ERROR.

1. Causes of Error, or how men come to give assent contrary to probability. KNOWLEDGE being to be had only of visible and certain truth, ERROR is not a fault of our knowledge, but a mistake of our judgment giving assent to that which is not true.

But if assent be grounded on likelihood, if the proper object and motive of our assent be probability, and that probability consists in what is laid down in the foregoing chapters, it will be demanded HOW MEN COME TO GIVE THEIR ASSENTS CONTRARY TO PROBABILITY. For there is nothing more common than contrariety of opinions; nothing more obvious than that one man wholly disbelieves what another only doubts of, and a third steadfastly believes and firmly adheres to.

The reasons whereof, though they may be very various, yet, I suppose may all be reduced to these four:

I. WANT OF PROOFS.

II. WANT OF ABILITY TO USE THEM.

III. WANT OF WILL TO SEE THEM.

IV. WRONG MEASURES OF PROBABILITY.

2. First cause of Error, Want of Proofs. FIRST, By WANT OF PROOFS, I do not mean only the want of those proofs which are nowhere extant, and so are nowhere to be had; but the want even of those proofs which are in being, or might be procured. And thus men want proofs, who have not the convenience or opportunity to make experiments and observations themselves, tending to the proof of any proposition; nor likewise the convenience to inquire into and collect the testimonies of others: and in this state are the greatest part of mankind, who are given up to labour, and enslaved to the necessity of their mean condition, whose lives are worn out only in the provisions for living. These

men's opportunities of knowledge and inquiry are commonly as narrow as their fortunes; and their understandings are but little instructed, when all their whole time and pains is laid out to still the croaking of their own bellies, or the cries of their children. It is not to be expected that a man who drudges on all his life in a laborious trade, should be more knowing in the variety of things done in the world than a packhorse, who is driven constantly forwards and backwards in a narrow lane and dirty road, only to market, should be skilled in the geography of the country. Nor is it at all more possible, that he who wants leisure, books, and languages, and the opportunity of conversing with variety of men, should be in a condition to collect those testimonies and observations which are in being, and are necessary to make out many, nay most, of the propositions that, in the societies of men, are judged of the greatest moment; or to find out grounds of assurance so great as the belief of the points he would build on them is thought necessary. So that a great part of mankind are, by the natural and unalterable state of things in this world, and the constitution of human affairs, unavoidably given over to invincible ignorance of those proofs on which others build, and which are necessary to establish those opinions: the greatest part of men, having much to do to get the means of living, are not in a condition to look after those of learned and laborious inquiries.

3. Objection, What shall become of those who want Proofs? Answered.

What shall we say, then? Are the greatest part of mankind, by the necessity of their condition, subjected to unavoidable ignorance, in those things which are of greatest importance to them? (for of those it is obvious to inquire.) Have the bulk of mankind no other guide but accident and blind chance to conduct them to their happiness or misery? Are the current opinions, and licensed guides of every country sufficient evidence and security to every man to venture his great concernments on; nay, his everlasting happiness or misery? Or can those be the certain and infallible oracles and standards of truth, which teach one thing in Christendom and another in Turkey? Or shall a poor countryman be eternally happy, for having the chance to be born in Italy; or a day-labourer be unavoidably lost, because he had the ill-luck to be born in England? How ready some men may be to say some of these things, I will not here examine: but this I am sure, that men must allow one or other of these to be true, (let them choose which they please,) or else grant that God has furnished men with faculties sufficient to direct them in the way they should take, if they will but seriously employ them that way, when their ordinary vocations allow them the leisure. No man is so wholly taken up with the attendance on the means of living, as to have no spare time at all to think of his soul, and inform himself in matters of religion. Were men as intent upon this as they are on things of lower concernment, there are none so enslaved to the necessities of life who might not find many vacancies that might be husbanded to this advantage of their knowledge.

4. People hindered from Inquiry.

Besides those whose improvements and informations are straitened by the narrowness of their fortunes, there are others whose largeness of fortune would plentifully enough supply books, and other requisites for clearing of doubts, and discovering of truth: but they are cooped in close, by the laws of their countries, and the strict guards of those whose interest it is to keep them ignorant, lest, knowing more, they should believe the less in them. These are as far, nay further, from the liberty and opportunities of a fair inquiry, than these poor and wretched labourers we before spoke of: and however they may seem high and great, are confined to narrowness of thought, and enslaved in that which should be the freest part of man, their understandings. This is generally the case of all those who live in places where care is taken to propagate truth without knowledge; where men are forced, at a venture, to be of the religion of the country; and must therefore swallow down opinions, as silly people do empiric's pills, without knowing what they are made of, or how they will work, and having nothing to do but believe that they will do the cure: but in this are much more miserable than they, in that they are not at liberty to refuse swallowing what perhaps they had rather let alone; or to choose the physician, to whose conduct they would trust themselves.

5. Second Cause of Error, Want of skill to use Proofs.

SECONDLY, Those who WANT SKILL TO USE THOSE EVIDENCES THEY HAVE OF PROBABILITIES; who cannot carry a train of consequences in their heads; nor weigh exactly the preponderancy of contrary proofs and testimonies, making every circumstance its due allowance; may be easily misled to assent to positions that are not probable. There are some men of one, some but of two syllogisms, and no more; and others that can but advance one step further. These cannot always discern that side on which the strongest proofs lie; cannot constantly follow that which in itself is the more probable opinion. Now that there is such a difference between men, in respect of their understandings, I think nobody, who has had any conversation with his neighbours, will question: though he never was at Westminster-Hall or the Exchange on the one hand, nor at Alms-houses or Bedlam on the other.

Which great difference in men's intellectuals, whether it rises from any defect in the organs of the body, particularly adapted to thinking; or in the dulness or untractableness of those faculties for want of use; or, as some think, in the natural differences of men's souls themselves; or some, or all of these together; it matters not here to examine: only this is evident, that there is a difference of degrees in men's understandings, apprehensions, and reasonings, to so great a latitude, that one may, without doing injury to mankind, affirm, that there is a greater distance between some men and others in this respect, than between some men and some beasts. But how this comes about is a speculation, though of great consequence, yet not necessary to our present purpose.

6. Third cause of Error, Want of Will to use them.

THIRDLY, There are another sort of people that want proofs, not because they are out of their reach, but BECAUSE THEY WILL NOT USE THEM: who, though they have riches and leisure enough, and want neither parts nor learning, may yet, through their hot pursuit of pleasure, or business, or else out of laziness or fear that the doctrines whose truth they would inquire into would not suit well with their opinions, lives or designs, may never come to the knowledge of, nor give their assent to, those possibilities which lie so much within their view, that, to be convinced of them, they need but turn their eyes that way. We know some men will not read a letter which is supposed to bring ill news; and many men forbear to cast up their accounts, or so much as think upon their estates, who have reason to fear their affairs are in no very good posture. How men, whose plentiful fortunes allow them leisure to improve their understandings, can satisfy themselves with a lazy ignorance, I cannot tell: but methinks they have a low opinion of their souls, who lay out all their incomes in provisions for the body, and employ none of it to procure the means and helps of knowledge; who take great care to appear always in a neat and splendid outside, and would think themselves miserable in coarse clothes, or a patched coat, and yet contentedly suffer their minds to appear abroad in a piebald livery of coarse patches and borrowed shreds, such as it has pleased chance, or their country tailor (I mean the common opinion of those they have conversed with) to clothe them in. I will not here mention how unreasonable this is for men that ever think of a future state, and their concernment in it, which no rational man can avoid to do sometimes: nor shall I take notice what a shame and confusion it is to the greatest contemners of knowledge, to be found ignorant in things they are concerned to know. But this at least is worth the consideration of those who call themselves gentlemen, That, however they may think credit, respect, power, and authority the concomitants of their birth and fortune, yet they will find all these still carried away from them by men of lower condition, who surpass them in knowledge. They who are blind will always be led by those that see, or else fall into the ditch: and he is certainly the most subjected, the most enslaved, who is so in his understanding. In the foregoing instances some of the causes have been shown of wrong assent, and how it comes to pass, that probable doctrines are not always received with an assent proportionable to the reasons which are to be had for their probability: but hitherto we have considered only such probabilities whose proofs do exist, but do not appear to him who embraces the error.

7. Fourth cause of Error, Wrong Measures of Probability: which are—
FOURTHLY, There remains yet the last sort, who, even where the real probabilities appear, and are plainly laid before them, do not admit of the conviction, nor yield unto manifest reasons, but do either suspend their assent, or give it to the less probable opinion. And to this danger are those exposed who have taken up WRONG MEASURES OF PROBABILITY, which are:

I. PROPOSITIONS THAT ARE IN THEMSELVES CERTAIN AND EVIDENT, BUT DOUBTFUL AND FALSE, TAKEN UP FOR PRINCIPLES.

II. RECEIVED HYPOTHESES.

III. PREDOMINANT PASSIONS OR INCLINATIONS.

IV. AUTHORITY.

8. I. Doubtful Propositions taken for Principles.
The first and firmest ground of probability is the conformity anything has to our own knowledge; especially that part of our knowledge which we have embraced, and continue to look on as PRINCIPLES. These have so great an influence upon our opinions, that it is usually by them we judge of truth, and measure probability; to that degree, that what is inconsistent with our principles, is so far from passing for probable with us, that it will not be allowed possible. The reverence borne to these principles is so great, and their authority so paramount to all other, that the testimony, not only of other men, but the evidence of our own senses are often rejected, when

they offer to vouch anything contrary to these established rules. How much the doctrine of INNATE PRINCIPLES, and that principles are not to be proved or questioned, has contributed to this, I will not here examine. This I readily grant, that one truth cannot contradict another: but withal I take leave also to say, that every one ought very carefully to beware what he admits for a principle, to examine it strictly, and see whether he certainly knows it to be true of itself, by its own evidence, or whether he does only with assurance believe it to be so, upon the authority of others. For he hath a strong bias put into his understanding, which will unavoidably misguide his assent, who hath imbibed WRONG PRINCIPLES, and has blindly given himself up to the authority of any opinion in itself not evidently true.

9. Instilled in childhood.

There is nothing more ordinary than children's receiving into their minds propositions (especially about matters of religion) from their parents, nurses, or those about them: which being insinuated into their unwary as well as unbiassed understandings, and fastened by degrees, are at last (equally whether true or false) riveted there by long custom and education, beyond all possibility of being pulled out again. For men, when they are grown up, reflecting upon their opinions, and finding those of this sort to be as ancient in their minds as their very memories, not having observed their early insinuation, nor by what means they got them, they are apt to reverence them as sacred things, and not to suffer them to be profaned, touched, or questioned: they look on them as the Urim and Thummim set up in their minds immediately by God himself, to be the great and unerring deciders of truth and falsehood, and the judges to which they are to appeal in all manner of controversies.

10. Of irresistible efficacy.

This opinion of his principles (let them be what they will) being once established in any one's mind, it is easy to be imagined what reception any proposition shall find, how clearly soever proved, that shall invalidate their authority, or at all thwart with these internal oracles; whereas the grossest absurdities and improbabilities, being but agreeable to such principles, go down glibly, and are easily digested. The great obstinacy that is to be found in men firmly believing quite contrary opinions, though many times equally absurd, in the various religions of mankind, are as evident a proof as they are an unavoidable consequence of this way of reasoning from received traditional principles. So that men will disbelieve their own eyes, renounce the evidence of their senses, and give their own experience the lie, rather than admit of anything disagreeing with these sacred tenets. Take an intelligent Romanist that, from the first dawning of any notions in his understanding, hath had this principle constantly inculcated, viz. that he must believe as the church (i.e. those of his communion) believes, or that the pope is infallible, and this he never so much as heard questioned, till at forty or fifty years old he met with one of other principles: how is he prepared easily to swallow, not only against all probability, but even the clear evidence of his senses, the doctrine of TRANSUBSTANTIATION? This principle has such an influence on his mind, that he will believe that to be flesh which he sees to be bread. And what way will you take to convince a man of any improbable opinion he holds, who, with some philosophers, hath laid down this as a foundation of reasoning, That he must believe his reason (for so men improperly call arguments drawn from their principles) against his senses? Let an enthusiast be principled that he or his teacher is inspired, and acted by an immediate communication of the Divine Spirit, and you in vain bring the evidence of clear reasons against his doctrine. Whoever, therefore, have imbibed wrong principles, are not, in things inconsistent with these principles, to be moved by the most apparent and convincing probabilities, till they are so candid and ingenuous to themselves, as to be persuaded to examine even those very principles, which many never suffer themselves to do.

11. Received Hypotheses.

Next to these are men whose understandings are cast into a mould, and fashioned just to the size of a received HYPOTHESIS. The difference between these and the former, is, that they will admit of matter of fact, and agree with dissenters in that; but differ only in assigning of reasons and explaining the manner of operation. These are not at that open defiance with their senses, with the former: they can endure to hearken to their information a little more patiently; but will by no means admit of their reports in the explanation of things; nor be prevailed on by probabilities, which would convince them that things are not brought about just after the same manner that they have decreed within themselves that they are. Would it not be an insufferable thing for a learned professor, and that which his scarlet would blush at, to have his authority of forty years standing, wrought out of hard rock, Greek and Latin, with no small expense of time and candle, and confirmed by general tradition and a reverend beard, in an instant overturned by an upstart novelist? Can any one expect that he should be made to confess, that what he taught his scholars thirty years ago was all error and mistake; and that he sold them hard words and ignorance at a very dear rate. What probabilities, I say, are sufficient to prevail in such a case? And who ever, by the most cogent arguments, will be prevailed with to disrobe himself at once of all his old opinions, and pretences to knowledge and learning, which with hard study he hath all this time been labouring for; and turn himself out stark naked, in quest afresh of new notions? All the arguments that can be used will be as little able to prevail, as the wind did with the traveller to part with his cloak, which he held only the faster. To this of wrong hypothesis may be reduced the errors that may be occasioned by a true hypothesis, or right principles, but not rightly understood. There is nothing more familiar than this. The instances of men contending for different opinions, which they all derive from the infallible truth of the Scripture, are an undeniable proof of it. All that call themselves Christians, allow the text that says,[word in Greek], to carry in it the obligation to a very weighty duty. But yet how very erroneous will one of their practices be, who, understanding nothing but the French, take this rule with one translation to be, REPENTEZ-VOUS, repent; or with the other, FATIEZ PENITENCE, do penance.

12. III. Predominant Passions.

Probabilities which cross men's appetites and prevailing passions run the same fate. Let ever so much probability hang on one side of a covetous man's reasoning, and money on the other; it is easy to foresee which will outweigh. Earthly minds, like mud walls, resist the strongest batteries: and though, perhaps, sometimes the force of a clear argument may make some impression, yet they nevertheless stand firm, and keep out the enemy, truth, that would captivate or disturb them. Tell a man passionately in love, that he is jilted; bring a score of witnesses of the falsehood of his mistress, it is ten to one but three kind words of hers shall invalidate all their testimonies. QUOD VOLUMUS, FACILE CREDIMUS; what suits our wishes, is forwardly believed, is, I suppose, what every one hath more than once experimented: and though men cannot always openly gainsay or resist the force of manifest probabilities that make against them, yet yield they not to the argument. Not but that it is the nature of the understanding constantly to close with the more probable side; but yet a man hath a power to suspend and restrain its inquiries, and not permit a full and satisfactory examination, as far as the matter in question is capable, and will bear it to be made. Until that be done, there will be always these two ways left of evading the most apparent probabilities:

13. Two Means of evading Probabilities: 1. Supposed Fallacy latent in the words employed.

First, That the arguments being (as for the most part they are) brought in words, THERE MAY BE A FALLACY LATENT IN THEM: and the consequences being, perhaps, many in train, they may be some of them incoherent. There are very few discourses so short, clear, and consistent, to which most men may not, with satisfaction enough to themselves, raise this doubt; and from whose conviction they may not, without reproach of disingenuity or unreasonableness, set themselves free with the old reply, Non persuadebis, etiamsi persuaseris; though I cannot answer, I will not yield.

14. Supposed unknown Arguments for the contrary.

Secondly, Manifest probabilities maybe evaded, and the assent withheld, upon this suggestion, That I know not yet all that may be said on the contrary side. And therefore, though I be beaten, it is not necessary I should yield, not knowing what forces there are in reserve behind. This is a refuge against conviction so open and so wide, that it is hard to determine when a man is quite out of the verge of it.

15. What Probabilities naturally determine the Assent.

But yet there is some end of it; and a man having carefully inquired into all the grounds of probability and unlikeliness; done his utmost to inform himself in all particulars fairly, and cast up the sum total on both sides; may, in most cases, come to acknowledge, upon the whole matter, on which side the probability rests: wherein some proofs in matter of reason, being suppositions upon universal experience, are so cogent and clear, and some testimonies in matter of fact so universal, that he cannot refuse his assent. So that I think we may conclude, that, in propositions, where though the proofs in view are of most moment, yet there are sufficient grounds to suspect that there is either fallacy in words, or certain proofs as considerable to be produced on the contrary side; there assent, suspense, or dissent, are often voluntary actions. But where the proofs are such as make it highly probable, and there is not sufficient ground to suspect that there is either fallacy of words (which sober and serious consideration may discover) nor equally valid proofs yet undiscovered, latent on the other side (which also the nature of the thing may, in some cases, make plain to a considerate man;) there, I think, a man who has weighed them can scarce refuse his assent to the side on which the greater probability appears. Whether it be probable that a promiscuous jumble of printing letters should often fall into a method and order, which should stamp on paper a coherent discourse; or that a blind fortuitous concourse of atoms, not guided by an understanding agent, should frequently constitute the bodies of any species of animals: in these and the like cases, I think, nobody that considers them can be one jot at a stand which side to take, nor at all waver in his assent. Lastly, when there can be no supposition (the thing in its own nature indifferent, and wholly depending upon the testimony of witnesses) that there is as fair testimony against, as for the matter of fact attested; which by inquiry is to be learned, v.g. whether there was one thousand seven hundred years ago such a man at Rome as Julius Caesar: in all such cases, I say, I think it is not in any rational man's power to refuse his assent; but that it necessarily follows, and closes with such probabilities. In other less clear cases, I think it is in man's power to suspend his assent; and perhaps content himself with the proofs he has, if they favour the opinion that suits with his inclination or interest, and so stop from further search. But that a man should afford his assent to that side on which the less probability appears to him, seems to me utterly impracticable, and as impossible as it is to believe the same thing probable and improbable at the same time.

16. Where it is in our Power to suspend our Judgment.

As knowledge is no more arbitrary than perception; so, I think, assent is no more in our power than knowledge. When the agreement of any two ideas appears to our minds, whether immediately or by the assistance of reason, I can no more refuse to perceive, no more avoid knowing it, than I can avoid seeing those objects which I turn my eyes to, and look on in daylight; and what upon full examination I find the most probable, I cannot deny my assent to. But, though we cannot hinder our knowledge, where the agreement is once perceived; nor our assent, where the probability manifestly appears upon due consideration of all the measures of it: yet we can hinder both KNOWLEDGE and ASSENT, BY STOPPING OUR INQUIRY, and not employing our faculties in the search of any truth. If it were not so, ignorance, error, or infidelity, could not in any case be a fault. Thus, in some cases we can prevent or suspend our assent: but can a man versed in modern or ancient history doubt whether there is such a place as Rome, or whether there was such a man as Julius Caesar? Indeed, there are millions of truths that a man is not, or may not think himself concerned to know; as whether our king Richard the Third was crooked or no; or whether Roger Bacon was a mathematician or a magician. In these and such like cases, where the assent one way or other is of no importance to the interest of any one; no action, no concernment of his following or depending thereon, there it is not strange that the mind should give itself up to the common opinion, or render itself to the first comer. These and the like opinions are of so little weight and moment, that, like motes in the sun, their tendencies are very rarely taken notice of. They are there, as it were, by chance, and the mind lets them float at liberty. But where the mind judges that the proposition has concernment in it: where the assent or not assenting is thought to draw consequences of moment after it, and good and evil to depend on choosing or refusing the right side, and the mind sets itself seriously to inquire and examine the probability: there I think it is not in our choice to take which side we please, if manifest odds appear on either. The greater probability, I think, in that case will determine the assent: and a man can no more avoid assenting, or taking it to be true, where he perceives the greater probability, than he can avoid knowing it to be true, where he perceives the agreement or disagreement of any two ideas.

If this be so, the foundation of error will lie in wrong measures of probability; as the foundation of vice in wrong measures of good.

17. IV. Authority

The fourth and last wrong measure of probability I shall take notice of, and which keeps in ignorance or error more people than all the other together, is that which I have mentioned in the foregoing chapter: I mean the giving up our assent to the common received opinions, either of our friends or party, neighbourhood or country. How many men have no other ground for their tenets, than the supposed honesty, or learning, or number of those of the same profession? As if honest or bookish men could not err; or truth were to be established by the vote of the multitude: yet this with most men serves the turn. The tenet has had the attestation of reverend antiquity; it comes to me with the passport of former ages, and therefore I am secure in the reception I give it: other men have been and are of the same opinion, (for that is all is said,) and therefore it is reasonable for me to embrace it. A man may more justifiably throw up cross and pile for his opinions, than take them up by such measures. All men are liable to error, and most men are in many points, by passion or interest, under temptation to it. If we could but see the secret motives that influenced the men of name and learning in the world, and the leaders of parties, we should not always find that it was the embracing of truth for its own sake, that made them espouse the doctrines they owned and maintained. This at least is certain, there is not an opinion so absurd, which a man may not receive upon this ground. There is no error to be named, which has not had its professors: and a man shall never want crooked paths to walk in, if he thinks that he is in the right way, wherever he has the footsteps of others to follow. 18. Not so many men in Errors as is commonly supposed.

But, notwithstanding the great noise is made in the world about errors and opinions, I must do mankind that right as to say, THERE ARE NOT SO MANY MEN IN ERRORS AND WRONG OPINIONS AS IS COMMONLY SUPPOSED. Not that I think they embrace the truth; but indeed, because concerning those doctrines they keep such a stir about, they have no thought, no opinion at all. For if any one should a little catechise the greatest part of the partizans of most of the sects in the world, he would not find, concerning those matters they are so zealous for, that they have any opinions of their own: much less would he have reason to think that they took them upon the examination of arguments and appearance of probability. They are resolved to stick to a party that education or interest has engaged them in; and there, like the common soldiers of an army, show their courage and warmth as their leaders direct, without ever examining, or so much as knowing, the cause they contend for. If a man's life shows that he has no serious regard for religion; for what reason should we think that he beats his head about the opinions of his church, and troubles himself to examine the grounds of this or that doctrine? It is enough for him to obey his leaders, to have his hand and his tongue ready for the support of the common cause, and thereby approve himself to those who can give him credit, preferment, or protection in that society. Thus men become professors of, and combatants for, those opinions they were never convinced of nor proselytes to; no, nor ever had so much as floating in their heads: and though one cannot say there are fewer improbable or erroneous opinions in the world than there are, yet this is certain; there are fewer that actually assent to them, and mistake them for truths, than is imagined.

CHAPTER XXI.

OF THE DIVISION OF THE SCIENCES.

1. Science may be divided into three sorts.

All that can fall within the compass of human understanding, being either, FIRST, the nature of things, as they are in themselves, their relations, and their manner of operation: or, SECONDLY, that which man himself ought to do, as a rational and voluntary agent, for the attainment of any end, especially happiness: or, THIRDLY, the ways and means whereby the knowledge of both the one and the other of these is attained and communicated; I think science may be divided properly into these three sorts:—

2. First, Physica.

FIRST, The knowledge of things, as they are in their own proper beings, then constitution, properties, and operations; whereby I mean not only matter and body, but spirits also, which have their proper natures, constitutions, and operations, as well as bodies. This, in a little more enlarged sense of the word, I call [word in Greek: physika], or NATURAL PHILOSOPHY. The end of this is bare speculative truth: and whatsoever can afford the mind of man any such, falls under this branch, whether it be God himself, angels, spirits, bodies; or any of their affections, as number, and figure, &c.

3. Secondly, Practica.

SECONDLY, [word in Greek: praktika], The skill of right applying our own powers and actions, for the attainment of things good and useful. The most considerable under this head is ETHICS, which is the seeking out those rules and measures of human actions, which lead to happiness, and the means to practise them. The end of this is not bare speculation and the knowledge of truth; but right, and a conduct suitable to it.

4. Thirdly, [word in Greek: Semeiotika]

THIRDLY, the third branch may be called [word in Greek: Semeiotika], or THE DOCTRINE OF SIGNS; the most usual whereof being words, it is aptly enough termed also [word in Greek: Logika], LOGIC: the business whereof is to consider the nature of signs, the mind makes use of for the understanding of things, or conveying its knowledge to others. For, since the things the mind contemplates are none of them, besides itself, present to the understanding, it is necessary that something else, as a sign or representation of the thing it considers, should be present to it: and these are IDEAS. And because the scene of ideas that makes one man's thoughts cannot be laid open to the immediate view of another, nor laid up anywhere but in the memory, a no very sure repository: therefore to communicate our thoughts to one another, as well as record them for our own use, signs of our ideas are also necessary: those which men have found most convenient, and therefore generally make use of, are ARTICULATE SOUNDS. The consideration, then, of IDEAS and WORDS as the great instruments of knowledge, makes no despicable part of their contemplation who would take a view of human knowledge in the whole extent of it. And perhaps if they were distinctly weighed, and duly considered, they would afford us another sort of logic and critic, than what we have been hitherto acquainted with.

5. This is the first and most general Division of the Objects of our Understanding.

This seems to me the first and most general, as well as natural division of the objects of our understanding. For a man can employ his thoughts about nothing, but either, the contemplation of THINGS themselves, for the discovery of truth; or about the things in his own power, which are his own ACTIONS, for the attainment of his own ends; or the SIGNS the mind makes use of both in the one and the other, and the right ordering of them, for its clearer information. All which three, viz. THINGS, as they are in themselves knowable; ACTIONS as they depend on us, in order to happiness; and the right use of SIGNS in order to knowledge, being TOTO COELO different, they seemed to me to be the three great provinces of the intellectual world, wholly separate and distinct one from another.

The End